The Complete Idiot's Ami Pro R...
(Use this card to avoid reading anything mo...

Selecting Text with the M...

TO SELECT THIS . . .	DO THIS . . .
A word	Double-click on the word.
A sentence	Press **Ctrl** and click on the sentence.
A paragraph	Press **Ctrl** and double-click in the paragraph.
A column in a table	Click at the top of the column.
A row in a table	Click in front of the row.
A frame or other object	Click on it.
A frame or object underneath other objects	Press **Ctrl** and click on it.

Quick Review: How to Open, Save, and Close Documents

To start a new document:

Open the File menu and select New. Select a special style sheet, or press **Enter** to use the default.

To open an existing document:

Click on the **Open** button on the Default SmartIcons set or use the File Open command. Change drives/directories if needed, and then select a file from the list. Click on Preview to view a document before opening it. Click **OK** or press **Enter** to open the selected document.

To save an existing document:

Click on the **Save** button on the Default SmartIcons set or use the File Save command. If this is the first time you've saved the document, change drives/directories if needed, and then type a name for the file (up to eight characters). Enter a document description if you like. Click **OK** or press **Enter** to save the document.

To close a document once it's been saved:

Double-click on the **Control-menu box** (the box with the – in the upper left corner of the document window) or press **Ctrl+F4**.

Making Text Look Pretty with the Keyboard

TO CHANGE CHARACTERS TO:	PRESS THIS KEY COMBINATION:
Bold	Ctrl+B
Italic	Ctrl+I
Single Underline	Ctrl+U
Fast Format	Ctrl+T
Normal text	Ctrl+N
TO CHANGE PARAGRAPHS TO THIS:	**PRESS THIS KEY COMBINATION:**
Left-aligned text	Ctrl+L
Right-aligned text	Ctrl+R
Centered text	Ctrl+E
Justified text	Ctrl+J
Modify a paragraph style	Ctrl+A

alpha
books

I–con Do It Myself!

ICON		FUNCTION	ICON		FUNCTION
	Open	Opens an existing document.		Fast Format	Copies text formatting.
	Save	Saves the document you're working on.		Left Align	Left-aligns text.
	Print	Prints the current document.		Center	Centers text.
	Print Envelope	Prints an envelope to match your letter.		Ruler	Displays or hides the ruler.
	Full Page View	Toggles between Full Page and your current view.		Create Frame	Creates a frame.
	Undo	Undoes the last action or command.		Table	Creates a table.
	Cut	Removes text and stores it for placement elsewhere.		Spelling	Checks the current document for spelling errors.
	Copy	Copies text for placement elsewhere.		Thesaurus	Looks up an alternative to the selected word.
	Paste	Inserts stored text at current location.		Grammar	Checks the current document for grammatical errors.
	Bold	Adds **bold** attribute to text.		Draw	Creates a drawing.
	Italic	Adds *italic* attribute to text.		Chart	Creates a graph from table data.
	Underline	Adds <u>underline</u> attribute to text.		Next set	Displays the next SmartIcon set.

Status Quo: Using the Status Bar

Change to a different font with the Face button.

View the document path, date and time, or current position by clicking here.

Change SmartIcon sets by clicking here.

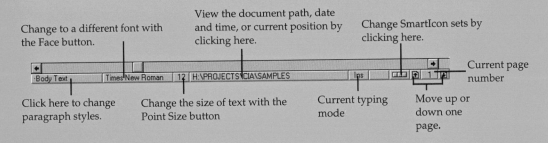

Current page number

Click here to change paragraph styles.

Change the size of text with the Point Size button

Current typing mode

Move up or down one page.

Bending the Rules: Using the Ruler

Drag to change all indents but the first line.

Pleasure's hard to measure when you use the ruler to change margins, indents, and to set tabs:

Drag to change the left indent for all lines.

Drag to change first line indent.

Click ruler to set tabs.

Drag to change right indent.

Drag to change left margin.

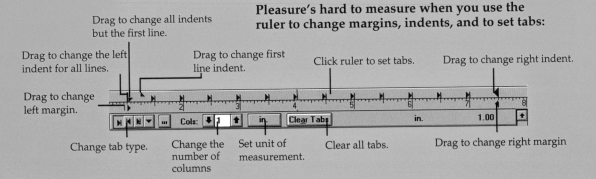

Change tab type.

Change the number of columns

Set unit of measurement.

Clear all tabs.

Drag to change right margin

The Complete

IDIOT'S

Guide to

AMI PRO™

by Jennifer Fulton

alpha
books

A Division of Prentice Hall Computer Publishing
201 W. 103rd Street, Indianapolis, Indiana 46290 USA

International Standard Book Number:1-56761-453-1
Library of Congress Catalog Card Number: 93-74019

96 95 94   8 7 6 5 4 3 2 1

Interpretation of the printing code: the rightmost number of the first series of numbers is the year of the book's printing; the rightmost number of the second series of numbers is the number of the book's printing. For example, a printing code of 94-1 shows that the first printing of the book occurred in 1994.

Screen reproductions in this book were created by means of the program Collage Plus from Inner Media, Inc., Hollis, NH.

Printed in the United States of America

Publisher
Marie Butler-Knight

Managing Editor
Elizabeth Keaffaber

Development Editor
Mary Cole Rack

Production Editor
Michelle Shaw

Copy Editor
Audra Gable

Cover Designer
Scott Cook

Designer
Amy Peppler-Adams, Roger Morgan

Illustrations
Steve Vanderbosch

Indexer
Craig Small

Production Team
*Gary Adair, Katy Bodenmiller, Brad Chinn, Kim Cofer, Meshell Dinn,
Mark Enochs, Stephanie Gregory, Jenny Kucera, Beth Rago, Marc Shecter,
Kris Simmons, Greg Simsic, Carol Stamile*

*Special thanks to C. Herbert Feltner for ensuring the technical accuracy of
this book.*

Contents at a Glance

Contents

Dedication

To my sister Noreen—Thanks for inspiring me to write in the first place.

Introduction

You're no idiot, but if Ami Pro makes you feel like one, you need a book that can help. What you don't need is a book that assumes you are (or want to become) an Ami Pro wizard. You don't need someone to tell you that Ami Pro is one of the most complex word processors around. (You've already learned that the hard way.) You're a busy person with a real life, and you're just trying to get a stupid letter, memo, or report written, spell-checked, and printed.

Why Do You Need This Book?

With so many computer books on the market, why do you need this one? Well, first off, this book won't assume that you know anything at all about how to use Ami Pro—or Windows itself, for that matter.

This book doesn't assume you want to (or have the time to) learn everything there is to know about Ami Pro. The most common tasks are broken down into easy-to-read chapters that you can finish in a short time. Simply open the book when you have a question or a problem, read what you need to, and get back to your life.

How Do I Use This Book?

For starters, don't actually *read* this book! (At least not the whole thing.) When you need a quick answer, use the Table of Contents or the Index to find the right section. Each section is self-contained, with exactly what you need to know to solve your problem or to answer your question.

If you're supposed to press a particular key, you'll know it because that key will appear in bold, as in:

Press **Enter** to continue.

Sometimes you'll be asked to press two keys at the same time. This is called a *key combination*. Key combinations appear in this book with a plus sign between them. The plus means that you should hold the first key down while you press the second key listed. For example:

Press **Alt+F** to open the File menu.

In this case, you should hold the **Alt** key down, and then press the letter **F**. Then something will happen. Alt is a pretty popular key; it's used with practically all the letters on the keyboard to do one thing or another (more on this later). The bold letter F that you see in the word File is there to remind you that you should press the letter F with the Alt key to open the File menu.

There are some special boxed notes in this book that will help you learn just what you need:

> ## By the Way . . .
> These boxes contain special hints from yours truly.

> ## Put It to Work
> These boxes provide safe ways to practice what you learn.

Easy-to-understand definitions for every computer term let you "speak like a geek."

Skip this background fodder unless you're truly interested.

These notes and tips show the easiest way to perform some task.

There's help when things go wrong!

Acknowledgments

Again, thanks to everyone at Alpha Books who helped make this book a reality. It's nice to be part of such a great team.

Trademarks

All terms mentioned in this book that are known to be trademarks or service marks are listed below. In addition, terms suspected of being trademarks or service marks have been appropriately capitalized. Alpha Books cannot attest to the accuracy of this information. Use of a term in this book should not be regarded as affecting the validity of any trademark or service mark.

Ami Pro is a trademark of Lotus Development Corporation.

Lotus 1-2-3 is a registered trademark of Lotus Development Corporation.

Part I
Dad Does Word Processing

My dad used to work at home a lot, and one day my brother Mike decided that Dad needed a computer, so he bought him one. After getting him started with a few basics ("Here's the keyboard, just type"), Mike left him alone. Later, Dad showed me a letter he'd printed: two paragraphs followed by four blank pages. Dad was very puzzled by this, so he asked, "Do you think it needs a new ribbon?" It was pretty apparent that Mike had left out some of the essentials.

That's the same problem with most computer books today; they assume you know something, and they end up leaving out the essentials. In this section, you'll learn all those things Mike should have told my dad about using a word processor (including the fact that you shouldn't lean the manual against the Enter key or you'll end up printing four blank pages at the end of your document).

Chapter 1

The Top Ten Things You Need to Know About Ami Pro

Just about everyone I know spent most of high school avoiding *actually reading books* by simply skimming the plot lines of novels and plays and such through a popular set of "notes" (sold in, of all places, the high school bookstore). Following in that fine tradition, here's a "Jennifer's Notes" version of the amazing facts you'll find within these pages. When you're done with this list, don't feel obligated to read any further—unless of course you're so caught up by my writing style that you just can't put this book down—or you have a 10-page report due to your boss tomorrow.

1. Ami Pro is a Windows program.

Because Ami Pro is a Windows program, you must know something about Windows in order to use it. If you're a stranger to Windows, read Chapter 3, and I'll introduce the two of you.

2. Don't press Enter at the end of each line of text—only at the end of a paragraph.

If you're accustomed to using a typewriter, you're also used to returning the carriage to the left margin at the end of every line. Word processors are different; when you press Enter, you create a new paragraph. So how do you get to the next line if you don't press Enter? Well, as you type, words *wrap* between the left and right margins automatically. If you add or delete text in a paragraph, the existing text adjusts itself to fit the margins. Chapter 6 explains the ins and outs of typing text.

3. Don't use the Spacebar to center text.

If you want your heading to be centered, don't use the Spacebar to move to the starting position. Instead, use *center alignment*, which centers any amount of text between the left and right margins. In Chapter 12, you'll learn how to set up centered, right-aligned, or left-aligned text.

4. Save your work often.

Even a momentary power outage can make a simply horrible day even worse. When you turn off your computer, everything you're working on is erased from the computer's memory—so *save, save, save* it first! Better yet, make Ami Pro save your documents at timed intervals, so you won't ever be caught with your computer down. In Chapter 9, you'll learn how to save your documents.

5. When you want to change the way text looks, select it!

Select the text you want, and then click on a button or use a menu command to change it. For example, you can select a heading by moving the mouse to the beginning of the text, pressing and holding the left mouse button, and moving the mouse to the end of the text to highlight it. Once the heading is highlighted (*selected*), you can choose commands to make the heading larger, bold, underlined, etc. In Chapter 6, you'll learn how to select text, and in Chapter 11, you'll learn how to make your text look the way you want it to.

6. You can perform most of your editing tasks faster and easier with a mouse than you can with the keyboard.

Just about any type of task (such as changing the look of text or saving or printing a document) can be done faster and easier with a mouse. With the SmartIcons, you click on a button to make changes or perform some task. You say you don't know how to use a mouse? Don't worry—you'll learn all about it in Chapter 3.

7. What you see is what you get— but it'll cost you.

The default viewing mode for Ami Pro is Layout mode. In *Layout mode*, you'll see pictures, graphs, and columns as they will appear when printed. But showing you all that stuff can slow down Ami Pro a bit; see Chapter 7 for other ways you can look at your document that won't slow down the program as much.

8. Just 'cause you're a beginner doesn't mean you have to start at the beginning.

If you know what type of document you want to create (like a memo or a simple letter), let an Ami Pro style sheet do the work for you. Just open a new document, select a style sheet, and let a mighty *macro* (a recorded set of instructions) perform the basic styling tasks: setting up your document with headings, page numbers, margins, and whatever's needed. With a style sheet and its faithful macro sidekick, all you have to do is enter some text, and your new document is practically finished! Click your heels three times and jump to Chapter 8 for more info.

9. Ami Pro lets you use all your Windows programs together.

Ami Pro can import part of a spreadsheet from any Windows program, such as Excel or Lotus for Windows. It can even create a link between your document and the imported item's native program, so that changes made to the imported item are reflected in your document automatically. Whew! In Chapter 21, you'll learn how to import data and pictures from other programs.

10. Ami Pro lets you create your own style.

The *style* of a paragraph controls how it should look—its margins, alignment (such as centered), indentations, and so on. For example, you can create a Heading style that makes your headings bold and centered. By changing one of the style's settings, you change all paragraphs of that style—in one simple step. For example, if you changed the Heading style to include underline, then all headings within your document would change to bold, centered, and underlined. In addition, Ami Pro comes with a collection of predesigned style sheets for you to choose from, or modify to fit your mood. Chapters 14 and 15 give you the lowdown on styles— how to create them and how to use them.

Chapter 2
A Kinder, Gentler Introduction to Word Processing

In This Chapter

- ☛ What is a word processor?
- ☛ Why learning to use a word processor is worth the time
- ☛ Things you can do with a word processor
- ☛ What is desktop publishing?

The Stone Age: Using a Typewriter to Record Thought

Back in the Stone Age of typewriters and correction fluid, Ogg groaned with frustration as he watched his boss fill his freshly typed pages with red lines, deletion marks, and new text. As a lonely pterodactyl cried for its mate, Ogg returned crestfallen to his desk and retyped the entire 10-page report. Poor Ogg—if only he'd had a *word processor*.

What Makes a Word Processor So Great?

A **word processor** lets you enter, edit, format, and print text. It can be used to type letters, reports, and envelopes, and to complete other tasks you would normally do on a typewriter.

Admittedly, learning to use a word processor takes a bit more time than learning to use a typewriter, but look at the advantages: no more correction fluid on your fingers, no more sticky letter keys to unjam, no more platen grease smearing the sides of an important paper. If he'd only had a word processor, Ogg could have made all of his boss' changes and been home in time for a hot bowl of woolly mammoth stew—but no! Instead of chucking his typewriter into the nearest tar pit (where it belonged), Ogg retyped the entire report. With a word processor, Ogg could have:

- ☛ Inserted text into existing paragraphs, and watched in amazement as other text automatically moved down—while staying within the margins.

- ☛ Deleted text with the same ease as he inserted new text—other text would just "self-adjust" between the margins.

- ☛ Checked the report for spelling errors before printing it.

- ☛ Centered his title easily, and added bold lettering to make it stand out.

- ☛ Added a big chart that made the report so nice-looking, his boss would get a promotion—and Ogg would get special parking privileges for his dinosaur.

- ☛ Printed an extra copy of the report for his own files, instead of spending half the Stone Age waiting at the copier.

- ☛ Reused the same report next month, by changing some figures and replacing the word "March" with "April" throughout the report.

Without a word processor, Ogg probably spent the rest of his life retyping the same report—but not you! Armed with your Ami Pro program and this nifty book, you'll soon learn how to do all these things and more. But first, let's look at a typical day with a word processor.

A Day in the Life of a Word Processor

As you create your document in Ami Pro, you'll follow a basic pattern:

1. **Open an existing document, or create a new one.** You start your work session by typing text into a new document, or by editing an existing one. You'll learn about working with documents in Chapter 8.

2. **Type in some text.** This part of the process is easy; just type! Okay, there are some things you should know before you start typing, and you'll learn them in this chapter and in Chapter 6.

3. **Read what you've written, and make changes.** *Edit* your text until it's right: copy or move text from one place to another; delete or insert text to clarify a point. You'll learn some easy editing techniques in Chapter 6.

4. **Add pizzazz.** Improve the way your document looks with *formatting*. You'll learn how to format text in Chapter 11. To save time while formatting, create a *style* you can reapply over and over with a few short keystrokes. Jump to Chapters 14 and 15 *before* you tackle that big report, and you'll save yourself a lot of hassles.

5. **Spell check your document.** Ami Pro has a *spell checker* that corrects your words if necessary. You can also use the *grammar checker* to look for errors in context. Of course, nothing can

Editing is the process of changing existing information within a document. Editing in a word processor usually involves spell-checking, grammar checking, and changing formatting until the document is judged to be complete.

Formatting is the process of changing the *look* of a character (by making it bold, underlined, and slightly bigger, for example) or a paragraph (by centering the paragraph between the margins, or by adding an automatic indentation for the first line, for example).

A **style** is a collection of specifications for formatting text. A style may include information for the font, size, attributes (bold, italic, etc.), margins, and spacing of a section of text. Applying a style to selected text automatically reformats it to meet the style's specifications.

replace the actual process of re-reading your text for sense, but these powerful tools help ensure that your documents look professional—or, if you spell like me, these tools can make your documents *understandable*. You'll learn more about them in Chapter 18.

6. **Save your document.** Once you're sure you have a document you like, you should save it. Actually, it's best to save a document *often* during the editing phase so you can't lose any changes. You'll learn how to save your document in Chapter 9.

7. **Print your document.** Nothing is better than holding the finished product in your own hands. You'll learn how to print your documents in Chapter 10.

Aunt Betty's Dilly Documents: A Recipe

Here's that step-by-step list again, in a shortened form; consider it a recipe for avoiding disasters. (Notice that I've added a few extra steps to remind you to save, save, save!)

Open a document or create a new one.

Type some text.

Save your document.

Re-read it and make changes.

Save your document.

Format text (make it bold, underlined, whatever suits you).

Save it for a rainy day!

Spell check it.

Save it again.

Read it one last time to catch the stuff that spell check doesn't. Run the grammar checker.

Save that puppy!

Okay, print!

Take the rest of the day off. You've earned it. Yes, you can tell your boss or your kids I said it was okay—I'm sure that will make a convincing argument. If not, drop this book on your toe and scream "Injury!" and then limp home for a well-deserved rest.

Oggs and Ends of Using a Word Processor

Even Ogg had a few things to learn before he could use a word processor. Here's the "sound-bite" version of your need-to-know news:

The thing you create with a word processor is called a document. "Document" is just a hoity-toity word for something like a memo, a letter, or a report. If you ever need help from a PC guru, make sure you throw it in (if you can do an English accent, it's even better): "Pardon me, but I think I'm having trouble with this *document.*"

The cursor marks the place where text will be inserted. The *cursor* is a blinking vertical line that acts like the tip of a pencil; anything you type appears at the cursor. You'll learn more about the cursor as we go on. To be real cool, call the cursor by its nickname: *insertion point.*

What you see isn't necessarily what you get. The right-hand edge of your screen may not be the right-hand margin of your document. Ami Pro provides several ways to view a document on-screen; in one mode, the text is large and comfortable to work with, but you may not see the right-hand margin of your document when you work in that mode. You'll learn more about viewing modes in Chapter 7.

A blue border marks the edges of a page. Just pass over the blue (or similarly solid-colored) border when you see it; it tells Ami Pro where one page ends and another begins. If you add text in the middle of a page, the excess text at the bottom of that page will flow onto the next page automatically.

Format text in italic, bold, or underline if you like.

Change views to see the text near the right margin.

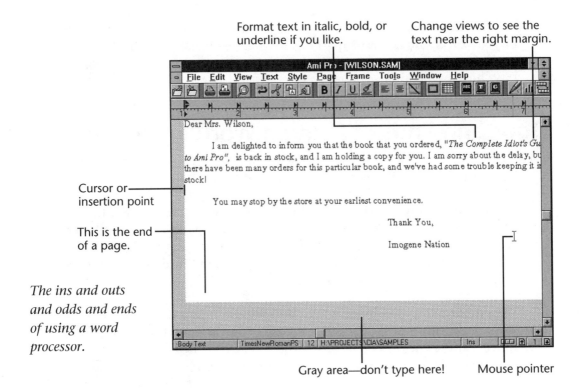

Cursor or insertion point

This is the end of a page.

The ins and outs and odds and ends of using a word processor.

Gray area—don't type here!

Mouse pointer

So What's All This Fuss About Desktop Publishing?

"High-end" (in other words, expensive) word processors, such as Ami Pro, give you a lot of bang for your buck by including tons of features you'll probably use only occasionally, if at all. It's not that the people at Lotus want to confuse you by including too much stuff in Ami Pro; it's just that when you need to do something special with a piece of paper, they want you to be able to do it with Ami Pro (so you don't go off and try some other product). One of the special things you may want to do someday is *desktop publishing*.

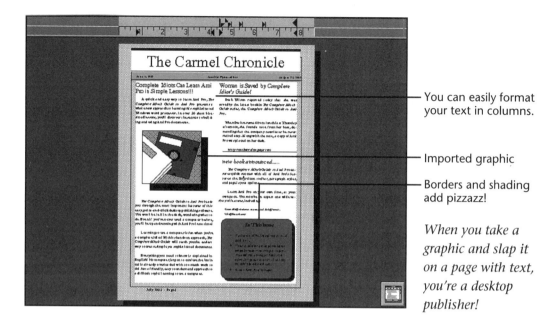

You can easily format your text in columns.

Imported graphic

Borders and shading add pizzazz!

When you take a graphic and slap it on a page with text, you're a desktop publisher!

You can do most of the more popular desktop publishing chores (typing text in columns, placing graphics anywhere on a page, or adding borders and shading to emphasize certain words) in Ami Pro. If you chose Ami Pro over other Windows word processors (such as Word for Windows or WordPerfect for Windows), you're in for some really good news: Ami Pro makes desktop publishing a snap. (True, the other word processors claim they're easy, but Ami Pro really is.)

With Ami Pro, you can do almost as many desktop publishing chores as the big guys—PageMaker and Ventura Publisher. So if you're looking to impress your boss with a flashy report for the big meeting, or if you've just been placed in charge of the parent/teacher newsletter at your local school, simply skip ahead to Chapter 20 for a lesson in creating newspaper-style columns, and Chapters 21, 22, and 23 for instructions on how to manipulate text and graphics in Ami Pro.

SPEAK LIKE A GEEK

Desktop publishing (DTP) is a process that allows you to combine text and graphics on the same page, and manipulate the text and the graphics on-screen. Desktop publishing programs are commonly used to create newsletters, brochures, flyers, résumés, and business cards.

The Least You Need to Know

It's a kinder, gentler world out there, thanks to word processors. Never again will you be faced with a dried-up bottle of white-out. And what's more, a word processor is so much faster than a typewriter when you need to:

- ☞ Insert and delete text from an existing document.

- ☞ Check for spelling and grammatical errors.

- ☞ Punch up your prose with bold, underlined, and italicized passages.

- ☞ Add pizzazz to your documents with charts and graphics.

- ☞ Print extra copies of your documents.

Chapter 3
For Those of Us Who Don't Do Windows

In This Chapter

- How to start Windows
- How to use a mouse
- The parts of a Windows window
- Moving windows around
- Closing windows
- Sizing a window so it's "just right"
- Exiting the Windows program

When I was first learning to use Windows, I felt overwhelmed. I'd never really used a mouse before, and all those boxes on my screen made me feel like a moving company. The only thought that kept me going was that (for the most part) I'd never have to see that ol' DOS prompt again. Also, I knew that once I learned how to use the mouse and manipulate windows, I'd know almost everything I needed to know to use *all* my Windows programs. So that's what you'll learn in this chapter—the basic stuff you'll use every day, in every Windows *program*—including Ami Pro.

The **monitor** is the television-like screen where the computer displays information.

The **DOS prompt** looks something like **C>** or **C:\>**; it appears on-screen to indicate that DOS is ready to accept a command, and where to type that command.

A set of instructions written in a special "machine language" that the computer understands is called a **program**. Typical programs are word processors, spreadsheets, databases, and games.

A Logical Place to Start

I am occasionally hit by bouts of logic, and during a recent episode, it occurred to me that before I show you how to use Windows, I should show you how to start it. It's relatively easy.

First, turn on your computer. Look for a switch on the front, back, or right-hand side of that big box thing. You may also have to turn on your *monitor* (it looks like a TV, but it gets lousy reception). When you turn on your computer, Windows may start all by itself. If it does, pass Go and skip on down to the next section.

If you get a menu listing Windows as one of the options, then using the keyboard press the number in front of the selection and press **Enter**. If instead you get a rather unassuming DOS prompt that resembles C> or C:\>, type **WIN** and press **Enter**.

Minimize button

Program Manager window

Active programs minimized to icons

Welcome to the wonderful world of Windows.

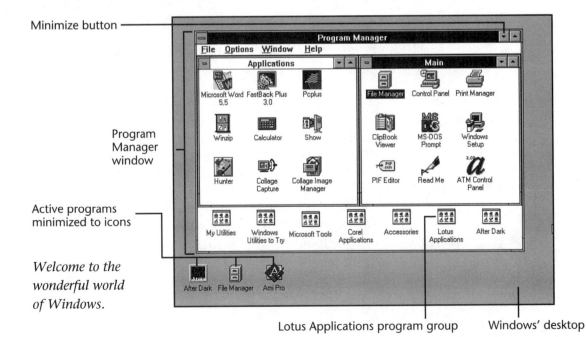

Lotus Applications program group   Windows' desktop

Don't panic if your screen doesn't look exactly like mine; that's the point of Windows—you can customize it to work the way you do. When you start Windows, the main program, Program Manager, is usually open and ready to go. *Program Manager* helps you switch between programs and customize the way they work with Windows.

Making Friends with a Mouse

Using Windows (and Windows programs like Ami Pro) without a mouse is like trying to pull something out of the oven without mitts. It can be done, but why take the chance of getting burned? So play it smart: get a *mouse!*

If you type **WIN** and your PC just sits there and does nothing, first make sure you've pressed the **Enter** key. If nothing happens, try this: type **CD\WINDOWS**, press **Enter**, type **WIN**, and press **Enter** again. If it still doesn't work, take two aspirin and see your PC guru in the morning. Tell her your Windows won't open.

The proper way to hold your furless friend.

To get to know your mouse quickly, here are some easy tips:

☛ Place the mouse in the middle of the *mouse pad*, with its cord extending away from you.

☛ Rest your hand on the mouse, with your palm at its base. Grip the mouse with your thumb and ring finger. When curled, your fingers should rest lightly on the buttons at the top of the mouse. Rest your index finger on the left mouse button and your middle finger on the right button. (If your mouse has a middle button, ignore it.)

☞ Move the little guy around. Don't be surprised if this feels a bit funny—remember what it felt like to drive a car for the first time? To me, it felt like the car would go completely out of control unless I held the wheel as tightly as I could. But you'll get used to your furless friend in no time.

☞ Practice moving the mouse on the mouse pad to make the on-screen pointer point to different boxes and windows. (I know what your mother always told you, but in this case, it is polite to point.) If you move the mouse slowly, the pointer will move slowly, and about the same distance. If you move the mouse quickly, the pointer steps on the gas and moves a greater distance on-screen.

☞ If you run out of mouse pad but you need to move further on the screen, just pick the critter up and place it back in the middle of the pad. When you lift the mouse, the pointer doesn't move; it's the roller on the bottom that moves it.

Right on the (Left) Button!

You can get Ami Pro to perform an action by *pointing* at something on-screen and either *clicking* or *double-clicking* with the left mouse button (unless you are specifically told to use the right). So to click on a button (a small picture representing some command), just move the mouse pointer over the picture, and press the left mouse button one time. You don't have to be terribly accurate; just get the mouse pointer into the right vicinity and click. Windows will figure out what you're trying to do.

Some actions require you *to drag* the mouse instead of clicking it. (No, we're not dragging it along the floor.) When you drag, you point at something, press the left mouse button, and hold it down. (Think of it as grabbing something with the pointer—once you "have it," don't let go.) Then, still holding the left mouse button down, move the mouse in any direction, and you'll end up dragging the object on-screen in the same direction. By dragging, you can move stuff around on your screen, such as words, paragraphs, and drawings (if you add any).

> **By the Way . . .**
>
> As a general rule of thumb, you click on things to highlight or choose them, double-click to activate or start them, and drag to select them and/or move them.

Now that you know how to use a mouse, you're ready to move on to something with a lot more buttons: the keyboard.

Playing with a Full Keyboard

Windows and Ami Pro were devised to work more easily with a mouse or trackball than with a keyboard. There are, however, some special *key combinations* that allow you to perform common tasks without a mouse.

TECHNO NERD TEACHES

If you use Windows on a portable computer, such as a laptop, you may be using a "dead mouse"—but don't set any rat traps just yet! You don't move this kind of mouse, which is why it's nicknamed a "dead mouse." (Its real name is *trackball*.) A trackball has its roller ball on top, and you move the mouse pointer by moving the roller ball with your thumb.

SPEAK LIKE A GEEK

To **click**, move the mouse pointer over an object or icon, and press and release the mouse button once.

To **double-click**, press and release the mouse button twice quickly.

To **drag** the mouse, first move the mouse pointer to the starting position. Press and hold the left mouse button, move the mouse to the ending position, and then release the mouse button.

Personally, I find that pressing multiple keys at the same time (such as Ctrl+Shift+End, a key combination that selects text) makes my hands ache, so I'm going to speak to you throughout this book as though you own a mouse. Windows without a mouse is about as pointless as lasagna without the pasta.

By the Way . . .

If you're allergic to mice—or if you are switching from a keyboard-intense word processor, such as WordPerfect—you may prefer using the keyboard over using a mouse. So in Chapter 4, I'll show you how to use the keyboard to select commands. But you should still make an effort to learn to use the mouse for moving and copying text; it's the fastest and easiest way!

If you've ever used a typewriter, you'll notice that the computer keyboard is similar, but different. Don't let all those keys intimidate you—the keyboard is easy to use when you learn the functions of the keys.

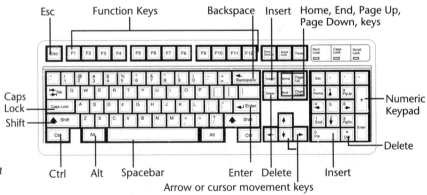

Has anybody seen my keys?

Here are the functions of some of the keys that are not so obvious:

Enter   In Ami Pro, you press the Enter key at the end of a *paragraph*, which is any grouping of words that should be treated as a unit—this includes not only normal paragraphs, but also single-line paragraphs (such as chapter titles, section headings, and captions for charts or other figures).

> ## By the Way . . .
> The Enter key is something that computer manufacturers like to hide by marking it with obscure symbols, such as a bent arrow pointing to the left, or by labeling it with a "meaningful" word like "Return."

Esc   Called the Escape key, Esc is used to cancel commands or to back out of an operation in Ami Pro.

Function keys   These keys are sometimes called the F keys because they all begin with an "F." You'll find them either at the top or on the left-hand side of the keyboard. Each program assigns its own special meanings to them. For example, in Ami Pro, F1 opens Help, and F4 creates a bulleted list.

Shift   The Shift key is used just as it is on a typewriter: to type capital letters and special characters (such as #$%?>). In some programs, you can use the Shift key with other keys to issue commands with the keyboard. For example, in Ami Pro, Shift+Delete removes (cuts) the selected text from its current location so you can move it somewhere else.

Alt and Ctrl   The Alt and Ctrl (Control) keys are used like the Shift key; press either of them with another key to issue commands with the keyboard. For example, in Ami Pro, Ctrl+B (when pressed together) bolds selected text, and Alt+F together opens (selects) the File menu.

Caps Lock   This locks in the capital letters. Unlike the "Shift Lock" on a typewriter, however, you will not get an exclamation point when you press the 1 key (*even with the Caps Lock on*). To get ! when the Caps Lock is on, you must still press the **Shift** key and **1** at the same time. The same is true of @, #, and other special characters.

Backspace   Press this key to erase the character to the left of the cursor. Use the Backspace key to erase all or part of a paragraph.

Arrow or cursor movement keys   Hmmm Kemosabe, the cursor go that-a-way. (These keys will make the cursor move in the direction of the arrow.)

SPEAK LIKE A GEEK

The **default** is the particular value or setting that a program uses automatically until you specify a different one. Some default values are built-in, and cannot be changed by the user (you).

Spacebar   Use the Spacebar to insert a space between words and at the end of sentences. Don't be a space cadet and use the Spacebar to move the cursor—you'll just end up inserting spaces you don't want. Use the arrow keys or the mouse instead.

Insert (Ins)   If Insert is on (which is the *default* in Ami Pro), text you type is inserted between characters, beginning at the current cursor position, and it pushes existing characters to the right. Press Insert to switch to Overtype mode, and what you type will replace existing characters.

Delete (Del)   Deletes the character to the right of the cursor.

Home, End, Page Up, Page Down keys   Home moves the cursor to the beginning of a line; End moves the cursor to the end of a line; Page Down displays the next screen of text; and Page Up displays the previous screen.

Windows You Don't Look Through

The basic component of Windows is (yes, you guessed it) *windows*. Windows are boxes on your screen that you can open, close, move, resize, and otherwise manipulate to your heart's content because in Windows, you have total control of what's displayed on your screen. Playing with windows is like rearranging the furniture in the living room without ever leaving the sofa—you'll hardly work up a sweat.

First, let's open a window so we have the same something to look at:

1. Point to the Lotus Applications program group icon. A *program group* is a special window that's used to group several applications together. For example, in the Lotus Applications program group, you find two program icons: Ami Pro 3 and Dialog Editor. A program group *icon* is simply a program group that's been minimized (reduced to a small symbol on the screen). So look for a miniature window-like thing with the words "Lotus Applications" written below it.

2. Double-click on the program group icon to open the program group. (If at first it doesn't work, try again. There's a rhythm to double-clicking, and most of us have to practice a few times to get the hang of it.) Now the program group window is open, and you can see the two Ami Pro icons: Derek, and his other brother Derek.

3. Maximize the Lotus Applications program group. Click on the **Maximize** button (that's the one pointing north—or up). The Lotus Applications program group will expand to fill the Program Manager window. It will not fill the entire screen unless the Program Manager itself is maximized; the little windows can't get any fatter than the big guy, Program Manager.

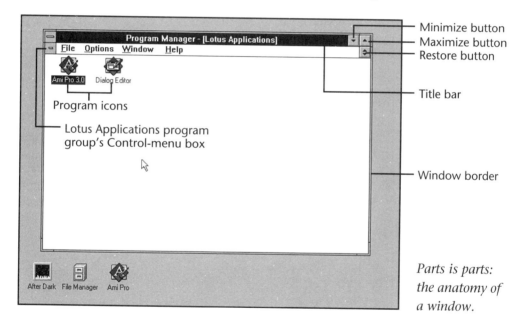

Parts is parts: the anatomy of a window.

Now that the window is open, let's look at its parts:

Title bar   This displays the title for the window.

Control-menu box   Every program group window has one. Click here to display a menu with commands for resizing, closing, and moving windows.

Minimize button   Click here to reduce the window to an icon at the bottom of your screen.

Maximize button   Click here to increase the window to fill your screen.

Restore button   Click here to restore the window to its previous size. "Restore" is a relative term. You'll learn later in this chapter how to change the size of a window, so remember when you start resizing windows, the Restore button returns a window to its immediately previous size—not the original size.

Playing with Windows

In Windows, you can run multiple programs at the same time. It's like those new TVs that have the "preview" square in the upper right-hand corner so you can watch two things at once (as if 100 channels isn't enough).

With Windows and its nifty "multitasking" capability, you can run a spreadsheet program (such as Lotus) and Ami Pro, and jump between the two whenever you want to. (You could also run a game (such as Solitaire) and Ami Pro, and switch between them whenever the boss comes in, or when you hear the kids come home from school. Each program you start has its own window that will take up all or part of the screen, depending on how you size it. By manipulating your windows, you can see several programs at one time, and fly between them with the greatest of ease.

By the Way . . .
Why is the capability to run multiple programs such a big deal? With two programs running at the same time, it's easy to exchange data from one to the other. For example, you could compute the department budget in a spreadsheet program, and then copy that data into the department report you're writing in Ami Pro.

Changing the size of a window is easy. For example, you can restore the Lotus Applications program group to the size it was before you maximized it. Just click on the **Restore** button (the double-headed arrow) to restore the window. Cool, eh?

You can maximize the window again by clicking on the **Maximize** button (the North-to-Alaska-pointing arrow). Go ahead and do that now.

If you click on the Restore button again, the window will be returned to its former petite self. Click on the **Restore** button and watch that weight come off!

You can minimize a window (reduce it to an icon at the bottom of the Program Manager window) by clicking on the Minimize button. Minimize the Lotus Applications program group now by clicking on the **Minimize** button (the South-to-the border-pointing arrow—it points down). You open a minimized window by double-clicking on the window's icon. Go ahead and double-click—it'll make you feel good!

Too Big or Too Small? Goldilocks Does Windows

If a window is too big when it's maximized, and too small when it's minimized, how do you resize a window so it's *just right?* Answer: you drag it!

Let's practice getting a window just the right size by playing with our Lotus Applications program group. To resize a window, move the pointer very slowly to the window's edge. (The mouse pointer will turn into a double-headed-which-way-do-I-go? arrow.) When it does, press the left mouse button and hold it down. While you're holding the mouse button down, drag the edge outward to make the window bigger, or inward to make it smaller. You'll see a ghostly image of the window edge as you drag. Continue to hold the mouse button down, and you can play with the window's size as long as you want. When you've got the window just right, release the mouse button.

> When you minimize a window, sometimes it plays hide-and seek behind other open windows. If you can't find the Lotus Applications program group after you minimize it, open the **Window** menu by clicking on it or by pressing **Alt+W**. When the menu is open, select the Lotus Applications program group from the list by clicking on it or by pressing its number.

If a window is maximized so that it fills your screen, you won't be able to resize it manually, because it won't have a border. (What a drag!) Instead, click on the **Restore** button to restore the window to its previous size, and then resize it manually if necessary.

A window cannot be bigger than the Program Manager window. If you look back at the last figure, you'll see that the Program Manager window does not fill my screen. (That gray background you see is the Windows *desktop*, and the Program Manager sits on top of it.) However, you can maximize your Program Manager window so it fills the screen; then any window that's maximized within it will also fill the screen. How do you do that? Just click the Program Manager's **Maximize** button, that's how!

If you see a message that says "This will close your Windows session," click on the word **Cancel**. You get this message when you close the Program Manager window, which tells Windows that you want to exit. (And you're not supposed to do that until the next section!)

Moving Day

Before I can start work, everything has to be in its proper place on my desk. I put my coffee cup to the left of my computer, and the mouse pad to the right; books and other reference items that I want to trip over throughout the day are placed on the floor.

When you work in Windows, you can move your windows around until you get everything in its proper place. To move a window, you drag it by its *title bar* (the band at the top of the window that shows the program's name).

Let's practice on our Lotus Applications program group. Point at the title bar at the top of the window. Then press the left mouse button and hold it down. Holding down the mouse button, drag the title bar around the screen (remember that you can't drag a program group off the Program Manager window). You'll see a ghostly image of the window as you drag. When you've found the window's new resting place, release the mouse button and voilà! The window's moved. (I wish sofas were as easy.)

If a window is maximized so it fills your screen, you won't be able to move it around. (I mean, where would it go?) Instead, click on the **Restore** button to restore the window to its previous size, and then move it to wherever you'd like.

If You Feel a Draft, Close a Window

When you "close" a program group, it doesn't actually close (shut down), it is just minimized to an icon at the bottom of the Program Manager window. This makes closing a *program group* a harmless thing. (You'll learn later that closing a *program window* works differently, but let's take one thing at a time.)

To close a program group, you just double-click on the Control-menu box (which has a horizontal line on it; if you need help in identifying it, look back at the last figure). Try this now: double-click on the **Control-menu box** of the Lotus Applications program group. Did it close? Great!

When You're Done for the Day and You Want to Go Home

OOPS!

Later, when we're working in Ami Pro, you'll have to be more careful. If you don't close a program window (that is, a window in which a program is running) correctly, you can lose the document you're working on.

Here comes that logical side of me again. Since I started this chapter showing you how to get into Windows, I thought I'd end by showing you how to get out (how to *exit*).

To exit Windows, exit all your programs first. In other words, close all the windows that programs are running in. (This should be a moot point at the moment, since we didn't start any programs. But later on, when we've got Ami Pro up and running, you'll need to exit Ami Pro first, then Windows. The Surgeon General—who apparently has nothing else to do— has determined that doing this in reverse order could be hazardous to your health.) Once all your widdle biddy programs are safely tucked away, double-click on the Program Manager's **Control-menu box**. This will close the Program Manager window which, in turn, closes down Windows itself.

By the Way . . .

Here's an alternative procedure for closing a window: first, click once on the **Control-menu box**. The Control menu will open, displaying a list of choices. Click on the word **C**lose. To close Windows this way, click once on the Program Manager's **Control-menu box**, and then click on the word **C**lose.

A message will appear, telling you that you are about to end your Windows session. Translation: "Windows is about to close down for the night. Is this okay?" If it is, click on the word **OK**. If not, click on the word

Cancel. If you click on **OK**, you'll exit Windows and return to either your really cool menu or the boring (yawn) DOS prompt. If you click **Cancel**, you'll end up back in Windows as if you never asked to exit.

The Least You Need to Know

Opening windows, closing windows—I'm pretty dizzy from all the stuff we covered in this chapter. Let's look at an instant replay:

- To start Windows, type **WIN** at the DOS prompt and press **Enter**.

- Program Manager helps you switch between programs and customize the way your programs work with Windows.

- To click, press the left mouse button once.

- To double-click, press the left mouse button twice quickly.

- To drag, move the pointer to the starting position. Press and hold the mouse button. Drag the pointer to the ending position, and then release the mouse button.

- To maximize a window, click on the **Maximize** button (the upward-pointing arrow). To minimize a window, click on the **Minimize** button (the downward-pointing arrow). To return a window to the size it was before it was maximized, click on the **Restore** button (the double-headed arrow). To adjust a window to a specific size, drag its edge.

- To move a window, drag it by its title bar.

- To close a window, double-click on the **Control-menu box** (located in the upper left corner of every window).

- To exit Windows, double-click on the Program Manager's **Control-menu box**.

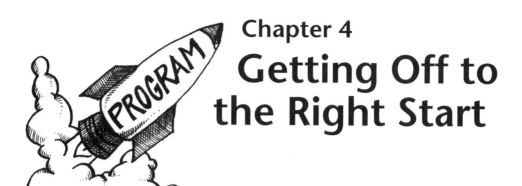

Chapter 4
Getting Off to the Right Start

In This Chapter

- 👉 How to start Ami Pro
- 👉 The basic parts of an Ami Pro screen
- 👉 Selecting commands
- 👉 Navigating a dialog box with ease
- 👉 Working with SmartIcons
- 👉 Changing your mind and undoing a command
- 👉 Shutting down Ami Pro safely

Telling someone what to do is kind of fun. I think that deep down, we all want to be in charge of something. This is one of the things I like most about using a computer—telling it what to do.

The thing I like *least* about using a computer is learning how to use it. Like most kids (and some adults) I know, computers love pretending *they don't understand*. So the trick to using a computer is to learn how to phrase things right. Once you learn that, a computer will do just about anything you tell it to (except the ironing—darn it). In this chapter, you'll learn the simplest and quickest ways to tell Ami Pro what to do.

Launching (Starting) Ami Pro

The steps you use to "launch the Ami Pro rocket" are the same as for any application, so what you learn here, you'll use throughout Windows. As you go through these steps, just keep thinking, "I'm smarter than this stupid hunk of metal."

Ami Pro program icon ——

Lotus Applications —— program group

Other program groups ——

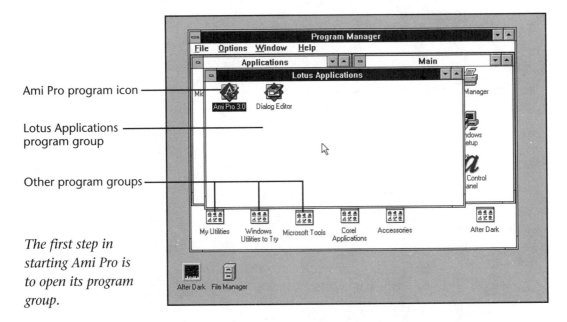

The first step in starting Ami Pro is to open its program group.

First, open the Lotus Applications program group. Hey, didn't you learn to do that in the last chapter? Good timing! (Just double-click on the **Lotus Applications program group icon**—that little picture of a window with the words "Ami Pro" under it.)

Next, double-click on the **Ami Pro program icon**. (Just move the pointer on top of the icon, and click twice real fast.) Ami Pro will start— one small step for the program, one giant step for us!

By the Way...

Using a mouse will feel a bit strange the first few times, but remember that you don't have to be Robin Hood and hit your target dead-center. Just move the mouse pointer towards the thing you want to select, and then click. If it doesn't respond, inch the pointer just a bit closer and click again. If you have to click a few times to get the computer to do something, so what? Nobody's watching. If you start feeling clumsy, just roll the critter off the desk a few times to remind it who's really the boss around here.

Tour de Ami Pro

Once inside the program, you'll notice some familiar friends: the Minimize, Maximize, and Restore buttons, the Control-menu box, and the title bar. Actually, you may think you're seeing double because you're seeing some things twice—but what you're really looking at is one window *inside* another. You see, the big window holds all the controls for the Ami Pro program, and the smaller window inside it holds the contents of the current document

If you can't get the hang of double-clicking, just click one time to highlight the icon, and then press **Enter**. I used to do that all the time in place of double-clicking, until I got used to using my plastic rodent.

(more on this in a minute). Let's look around and see what's new!

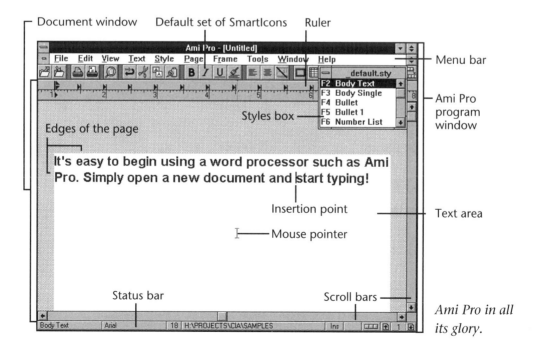

Ami Pro in all its glory.

Program window   This is the window that Ami Pro runs in. Close this window, and you close down (exit) Ami Pro. This window frames the tools and the menus for the Ami Pro program.

Document window   This window frames the controls and information for the document file being worked on. You can have multiple document windows open at one time. For example, you can open a memo to your boss and a letter to Aunt Sally, both at the same time—they'd just be in two different document windows. (You'll learn how to open multiple document windows in Chapter 8.)

Menu bar   Displays a list of menus that contain the commands you'll use to edit documents.

Default SmartIcons set   Presents the most common commands in an easy-to-access form. For example, one of the SmartIcon buttons in the Default set saves your document when you click on it. There are many sets of SmartIcons, each one customized for a particular task. You'll learn more about SmartIcons in this chapter.

Ruler   Use this to set tab stops, indentations, and margins.

Mouse pointer   This vertical line with curls at either end is also called an *I-beam*. The mouse pointer reflects the movement of the mouse. Move the mouse pointer to a particular spot within the text, and then click (press the left mouse button) to move the insertion point.

Insertion point   Vertical line that marks where text will be inserted into the document. To insert text in a different part of the document, move the insertion point there before you type.

Text area   The main part of the document window; this is where the text you type will appear.

Scroll bars   Located along the bottom and right sides of the document window. You use scroll bars to display other areas of the document that are currently hidden (such as the next page).

Status bar   Displays information about your document, while providing an easy method for changing a text's style, font, or size. You can also change from one SmartIcon set to another through the Status bar.

Styles box   Allows you to quickly change the style of selected text. You can display the Styles box too; check out Chapter 7 for the low-down.

> **By the Way...**
>
> If you think that all these screen elements (such as scroll bars, SmartIcons, and so on) just get in the way, you're not alone. Lots of people prefer to enter their text in a nice, clean screen. If you're among them, flip to Chapter 7 and learn how Ami Pro cleans up its act.

Checking the Status of the Status Bar

One neat thing about the Ami Pro status bar is that it's so handy. You'll learn how to change the size and style of text with it in later chapters, but there's one thing I want to show you now.

DOS stores information in files and gives each one a **file name**. Each document you create in Ami Pro is stored in its own file. Anything can be placed in a file: a memo, a budget report, or even a graphics image (like a picture of a boat or a computer).

In the middle of the status bar, the *file name* of the current document is displayed. Click on this button (called the *Document Path* button for those of you who want to know the name of something before you touch it), and it will display the current date and time instead. Real handy if you're working right along but you want to watch the time so you don't miss a big meeting. (Although it should come with a little hammer that reaches out and bops you when it's time to go.) Anyway, click that ol' button again, and it will display the current cursor position, noting its line and column number and its position based on the current ruler settings. (Mine shows 1.50, 1.59, which—because my ruler's set for inches—means that my cursor is 11/2" inches from the left-hand edge of the page, and a little over 11/2" from the top edge.)

Menu, Please

Tucked away at the top of the Ami Pro screen, you'll see something called a *menu bar*. The menu bar is like a salad bar, except instead of choosing from carrots, mushrooms, and radishes, you choose cholesterol-free commands.

SPEAK LIKE A GEEK

A **pull-down menu** contains a selection of menu commands. This type of menu, when activated, is pulled down below the menu bar, the way a window shade can be pulled down from the top of a window frame.

The menu bar lists the main menus, such as File, Edit, View, and so on. Under each of these menus, there are additional selections, but you can't see them until you pull down (open) the menu. (Be patient; you'll learn how to pull down a menu soon.)

Reading the Menu

I have trouble understanding the menus in fancy French restaurants (I took Spanish in high school, which doesn't mean anything since I can't remember a word of it). But I'm sure you'll have no such trouble with the Ami Pro menu system; it follows certain conventions that make it easy to understand:

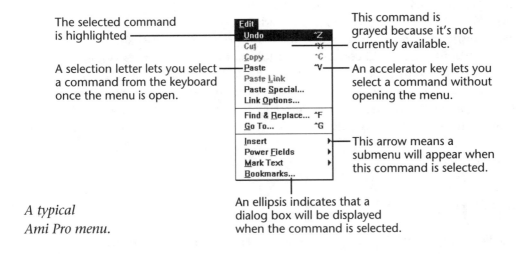

The selected command is highlighted

This command is grayed because it's not currently available.

A selection letter lets you select a command from the keyboard once the menu is open.

An accelerator key lets you select a command without opening the menu.

This arrow means a submenu will appear when this command is selected.

A typical Ami Pro menu.

An ellipsis indicates that a dialog box will be displayed when the command is selected.

☛ **Grayed text**   Commands that are currently unavailable will be grayed (and therefore, slightly depressed) because you can't select them.

☛ **Selection letter**   A single letter of a menu command that is underlined, such as the O in **O**pen. While a menu is open, press this letter to select the command. (As you read along, you'll notice bold letters in this book— they're **not** annoying **g**litches **i**n **t**he **p**rint **q**uality, they're the selection letters for the command you're learning about.)

☛ **Accelerator key**   Sometimes called a *shortcut key*. Like selection letters, these can be used to activate the command with the keyboard. Unlike selection letters, however, accelerator keys work without opening the menu—it's kind of like having somebody bring you a beer so you don't have to leave the sofa. Ami Pro's accelerator keys are displayed next to the menu command, and they usually consist of some key combination (such as Ctrl+O). To use an accelerator key, press and hold the first key (in this case, **Ctrl**), and then press the second key (in this case, **O**). I'll use the plus sign in this book to combine the two keys you have to press (as in **Ctrl+O**); that'll remind you to press them together.

To close a menu you opened by accident, press **Esc** or click anywhere in the document.

A **dialog box** is a special window or box that appears when the program requires additional information before executing a command.

By the Way...

The Ctrl key shows up as a *caret* (^) on the menus—a kind of upside-down v. So if you see **^O** on a menu, it means that you should press **Ctrl+O** to select the command without opening the menu.

If there is an accelerator key for a command, you can press its key combination to activate the command, instead of opening the menu. For example, to select the **Edit Paste** command, you can press the **Ctrl** and **V** keys at the same time.

☛ **Ellipsis**   Three ink blots (dots) following the name of a menu command (as in the File Print... command). When you select a command that has an ellipsis, a dialog box will appear, in which you provide more specific information before the command is executed. In this case, you would need to tell Ami Pro specifics about printing your document.

Take Your Pick: Selecting Menu Commands

It's easy to select menu commands: just point to the menu name, and click. For example, click on the word File to open the File menu. While the menu is open, click once on a menu command to select it.

So that the keyboard doesn't get too jealous, I'll show you how you can use it to select commands. Press **Alt** and the selection letter to open a menu (for example, press **Alt** and **F** to open the File menu). Then press the selection letter alone to choose a command (for example, press **X** to select Exit).

By the Way...

If you see a command with a check mark in front of it, that means the command is "on." For example, if you open the View menu by clicking on it or by pressing **Alt+V**, you'll see a command with a check mark; that's the current viewing mode. If you were to select a different viewing mode, the check mark would move to the mode you selected to indicate that it's "on."

Talking to Your Computer Through Dialog Boxes

When Ami Pro needs more information from you, it displays a dialog box. One of these gizmos will appear whenever you select a menu command followed by an ellipsis, as in the Style Modify Style... command.

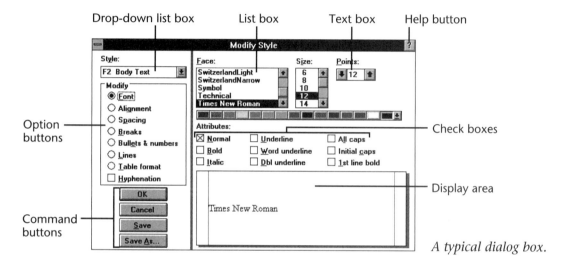

A typical dialog box.

Meet the characters that hang around dialog boxes:

Option buttons   Let you select mutually exclusive options (options that you can select only one of), such as Font, Alignment, Spacing, etc. When an option button is selected, a dot appears inside it.

List box   Presents a list of items to choose from, such as a list of fonts (text styles).

Drop-down list box   Presents a list of items like a normal list box, but this list is not displayed until you activate it by clicking on the downward-pointing arrow. The list is displayed under the main list item, much like a window shade.

Text box   Allows you to type information, such as the size of text (shown here under points—if you don't get the point of this dialog box, peruse Chapter 11 for clues).

Help button   Accesses the Help system for the specific task you're working on. Help is just a phone call (okay, a click) away with this nifty dialog feature.

Check box   Lets you turn on or off such options as **B**old and **I**talic. When a check box is selected, an **X** appears inside it. Unlike option buttons (where you can only choose one), check box groups allow you to choose as many items as you want. So be bold and italic if you feel like it!

Command buttons   Perform some specific command. For example, the OK button tells Ami Pro to perform the selected action, and the Cancel button cancels an operation. To make things fun, some command buttons cause additional dialog boxes to be displayed—for example, the Save As.. button shown here (that darn ellipsis again).

Display area   Shows you how your text will look before you say "OK." After all, we all want to see what we're getting before we pay, right?

To close a dialog box without choosing anything, just press **Esc.**

Making the Right Choice

I like dialog boxes because they give me so many things to play with, such as list boxes and options buttons and the like. (I think it reminds me of all those pinball games I used to play as a child.) Anyway, here's how you flip all those "switches" and press all those "buzzers."

To move around a dialog box, click on any item to activate it. If you want to use the keyboard, press **Tab** until you get to the area you want; use **Shift+Tab** to move backwards from section to section. You can also press Alt and the underlined letter you see on the screen (for example, the i in Italics) to move to a particular place within the dialog box. In this book, those underlined letters will appear as bold.

To display additional options in a list, click on the up or down arrow to scroll one item at a time and click on an item to select it. If you're using the keyboard, use the arrow keys to move through the list.

To open a drop-down list box, click on the arrow to the right of the box. Click on an item to select it. Or, with the keyboard, press **Alt** plus the underlined letter of the list box to activate it, and then use the down arrow key to scroll through the items. If you'd like to see the whole list before making your selection, press **Alt+↓** instead.

To select an option button or check box, click on it to toggle the option on or off. With the keyboard, press **Alt** plus the underlined letter to select an option.

To exit a dialog box, use a command button. You'll meet some standard command buttons while using dialog boxes (such as Cancel, which cancels the choices you have made in the dialog box and returns you to your program). If you want to close the dialog box and execute your choices, click the **OK** button. Sometimes there'll be a Close button, which retains the choices you've made but closes the dialog box without executing those choices. If a command button name is followed by an ellipsis, choosing it will take you to an additional dialog box.

Whew! Can You Give That to Me Again, Only Slower?

Since you'll encounter a lot of dialog boxes whenever you use Ami Pro, here's the bottom line on making your selections:

☞ With a mouse, click on an item to select it or to open a list.

☞ With the keyboard, press **Alt+***selection letter* to select an option, and then use the arrow keys (if necessary) to select something from a list.

I Think Icon, I Think Icon!

SmartIcons are the quickest way for you to select the most common commands. When you start Ami Pro, the Default set of SmartIcons is

Another way to find out about a SmartIcon is to right-click on it with the mouse. Go ahead and try it—move the mouse pointer over a SmartIcon, and click with the right mouse button. Look at the top of the screen, and you'll see a brief explanation. Pretty cool, eh? (If you clicked with the left mouse button, press **Esc** to exit any dialog box. If necessary, click the **Undo** button—the one with the circling arrows—to undo any change that might have happened by accident.)

displayed. There are additional SmartIcon sets in hiding; you'll learn how to get them to come out in just a minute. Each of the SmartIcon sets was designed with a specific task in mind, such as editing, or creating a table (you'll learn about the various SmartIcon sets as we go along). The little squares that make up each SmartIcon set are called (yes, you guessed it) *SmartIcons* because they have an IQ well over 200, and they contain little pictures that represent the task they perform. These boxes are sometimes called buttons because they look as if you're "pressing" them down when you click on them with the mouse.

By the Way...

If you're dying to know what all those buttons are for, turn to the front of this book and check out the reference card. It gives you the unfiltered, unauthorized life story of every button on the Default set of SmartIcons. Parental guidance is suggested.

You can only choose *one* SmartIcon set at a time, so be choosy!

Freedom of Choice

When you start Ami Pro, it displays the Default SmartIcon set. Don't worry—other SmartIcon sets are just a click away. Simply click the **SmartIcons** button located on the status bar. Select a SmartIcons set from the list, and it appears!

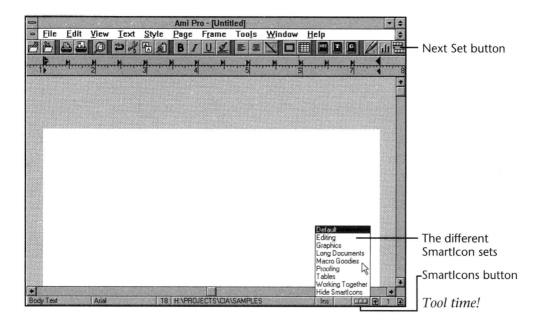

Next Set button

The different
SmartIcon sets

SmartIcons button

Tool time!

If you don't want to display any SmartIcons at all, that's cool. Just click the **SmartIcons** button on the status bar and choose **Hide SmartIcons** from the list. If you want all the screen elements to go away, you can select Show Clean Screen from the View menu (which you'll learn about in Chapter 7). Don't you wish you had a Clean Screen option to remove other annoyances, such as the loud-mouth at the copier, the person in front of you at the bank, or your boss? (Actually, my boss is very nice, and he takes the time to read everything I write, which is why I decided to add this disclaimer.) But feel free to skip to Chapter 7 and give Clean Screen view a try!

To switch between SmartIcons sets as fast as some people switch check-out lanes, click on the **Next Set** button located at the right-hand side of every set.

When SmartIcons Bar Your View

Nine times out of ten when I go to a movie theater, the tallest person in the place sits down right in front of me. (How do they do that? Do they have radar in their heads?) Anyway, you don't have to take that same stuff from your SmartIcon set. If you don't like where it sits, move it! Here's how:

1. Open the Tools menu by clicking on it or pressing **Alt+L**.

2. Click on SmartIcons or press **I**. Be careful, there's a dialog box a-waitin' 'round the bend.

3. Select the **P**osition that suits you. Click on the list to select an item, or press **Alt+P** and use the arrow keys. For some fun, try **Floating**.

4. Select **OK** when you're done.

If you selected Floating, the SmartIcon set is not smack dab in the middle of your screen. Barring any problems, you can simply drag the set wherever you want it.

If you make a SmartIcon set too small, it will display only as many tools as it can. Resize it to display the hidden tools.

Still not satisfied? You can change the shape of a SmartIcon set by dragging one of its edges. Click on an edge and hold down the mouse button. Then drag until the box is the size you want it. As you drag, you may see a ghost—that's the imaginary outline, and it's there to guide you.

Click on the **Hide** button to hide the SmartIcon set. To redisplay it, click on the **SmartIcons** button on the status bar and select that set from the list.

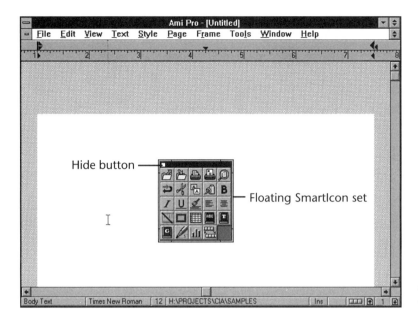

Put it where you want it.

Okay, Have It Your Way

You can customize any SmartIcon set by adding buttons for the commands you use most often. I got used to another program that has a similar feature (they call it a toolbar), and that default toolbar has an icon for New Document. For an entire day I kept forgetting that there is no New Document icon on Ami Pro's Default SmartIcon set. I finally decided I'd had enough, and I took the time to customize it. Here's what you do:

1. First, open the Tools menu by clicking on it or pressing **Alt+L**.

2. Click on SmartIcons or press **I**. You'll see a cute dialog box.

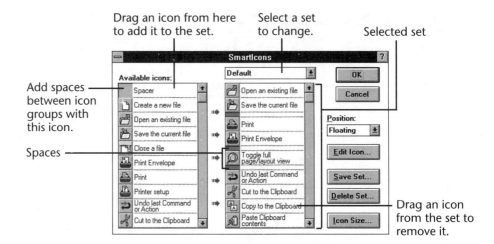

Drag an icon from here to add it to the set.

Select a set to change.

Selected set

Add spaces between icon groups with this icon.

Spaces

Go for it!

3. Select a category from the drop-down list. Click on the down arrow to open the list, and then click on a SmartIcons set to select it.

4. Drag the button out onto the selected set to add it. Click on an icon from the left-hand list, hold the left mouse button down, and drag the icon to the right-hand list.

5. To remove a button, drag it off the selected set. Reverse the process you just did: click on an icon from the right-hand list and drag it to the left-hand list.

6. Click **OK** when you're through having fun. If you want to create your own private set, click on **S**ave Set, type a name, and press **Enter**.

A Good Friend to Know: Meet Mr. Undo

If a command is in progress, you can press **Esc** to cancel it. But what happens if you just finished deleting some text, and it was the wrong text? I can't tell you how many times I've done just that. Well, weep no more. You can restore your deleted text with a little magic button called Undo, located on the Default SmartIcon set.

 Undo undoes your last few actions or commands. If for some reason your last action can't be undone (such as saving a document), Undo becomes unavailable. But how do you do undo? To undo your last action, click on the **Undo** button on the Default SmartIcon set. (Refer to the reference card at the front of this book for the secret location of the Undo button.) If you're a keyboard connoisseur, press **Ctrl+Z** to activate Undo instead of using the mouse (you can also use the Undo command on the Edit menu).

Exit, Stage Right

Here I am with another logic attack: since I began this chapter showing you how to start Ami Pro, I thought I'd end by showing you how to stop it. The technical name for stopping a program is called *exiting*. Here's what you do.

Step one: save whatever you're working on. If you don't, it won't be there when you come back. Computers are very literal, and unless you tell them to save something for you, they don't. You'll learn how to save your documents in Chapter 9.

Step two: exit, stage right. Here you can exercise your own sense of style, because there are a multitude of ways to stop a program:

- ☛ Select the Exit command from the File menu or press **Alt+F4**.

- ☛ Double-click on Ami Pro's **Control-menu box**.

- ☛ Click once on Ami Pro's **Control-menu box**, and then select the Close command.

- ☛ Turn off the computer. Turning off the computer without exiting a program (in this case, two programs: Ami Pro, and Windows itself) is the computer equivalent of taking a hammer and bashing yourself over the head. When you wake up, you're probably not going to remember what hit you, and neither will the computer. If you turn off a computer without first saving your work, it's gone. So, don't turn off a computer until you see the whites of DOS' eyes: the DOS prompt.

When you've exited your program properly (see my diatribe above on how NOT to exit a program), you can probably turn off your computer. How can you tell if it's okay to do that? Look for the DOS prompt (it looks something like C> or C:\>). If you see a menu, choose an exit option to return to DOS, and then turn off the computer.

The Least You Need to Know

Just about everything in this chapter is the least you need to know when using *any* Windows program, such as Ami Pro. Most of these are what I call my Windows life-skills:

☛ To start any program (such as Ami Pro), open the program group it's located in, and double-click on the program's icon.

☛ Check out the status of your document (things such as the current font, point size, and page) by looking at the status bar. You can even make changes with the buttons on the status bar.

☛ To select a menu command with the mouse, open a menu by clicking on the menu name, and then click on the command you want.

☛ To select a menu command with the keyboard, open a menu by pressing **Alt** and the selection letter. Select the command you want by pressing its selection letter.

☛ To select an item in a dialog box with the mouse, just click on it. Click on the down arrow to open a drop-down list box, and click on an item to select it. Clicking on an option button or a check box toggles it on or off.

☛ To select an item in a dialog box with the keyboard, press **Alt** plus the selection letter of the option you want. Use the arrow keys to select an item from a list.

☛ To undo your last command or action, click on the **Undo** button on the Default SmartIcon set, or press **Ctrl+Z**.

☛ SmartIcon sets contain the most often used commands in button form. If a command doesn't exist in a particular SmartIcon set, you can add it.

☛ To exit Ami Pro, use the **Exit** command on the **File** menu. *Be sure to save your document before you exit any program.*

Chapter 5

Getting a Little Help from Your Friends

In This Chapter

- ☞ How to get help when you need it
- ☞ Using the Help index
- ☞ Searching for a particular topic
- ☞ Completing an Ami Pro tutorial

You never know when you'll need help, so getting help when you need it is what this chapter is all about. Help in Ami Pro is as varied as the people who use it. You're sure to find help in some form that you'll like.

Getting the Help You Need

Help for Ami Pro is available 24 hours a day; just press **F1**. Help is *context-sensitive*. In English that means that Help pays attention to what you're doing, so when you press F1, it takes you to a section that explains that specific task. For example, when you select the command to save a document, a dialog box appears, asking for more information (such as a name for the file). If you don't know what to do, press **F1**, and you'll be taken to the section in the Help system that talks about saving your document.

If you're wondering about a particular SmartIcon, move the mouse pointer over it, and click with the right mouse button. A brief description will be displayed in the title bar. For help with a menu command, highlight the command with the arrow keys, and again you'll see a description in the title bar.

Instead of pressing F1 to get help while you're in a dialog box, you can click the **Help** button (that cute little question mark in the upper right-hand corner).

Shoot to Kill (Ignorance)

An easy way to get help with something on your screen, such as a SmartIcon, the scroll bars, or a menu command, is to just "point and shoot."

Press **Shift+F1**, and the mouse pointer transforms itself into the mighty question mark. Move this questionable mouse pointer over the item you're curious about, and then click the left mouse button. You'll be escorted directly to the information you seek.

How Can You Find the Answer When You're Not Sure of the Question?

When you're not sure what to do or where to start, use the **Help** menu. To open the Help menu, click on it or press **Alt+H**. When the Help menu is open, you'll have many things to choose from:

Contents   Here tasks are organized by topic. Use this option when you know generally what task you need help with.

Using Help   This option is perfect for first-time users of the Ami Pro Help system.

How Do I?   Here tasks are organized alphabetically. This option is best when you aren't sure what to call something.

For Upgraders   If you've used Ami Pro before, but you're new to version 3.0, this option is for you.

QuickStart Tutorial   These tutorials are perfect for learning the basics or reviewing what you'll learn in this book. The most popular Ami Pro tasks are presented here in an automated fashion that lets you sit back and relax while you learn.

Macro Doc   This option provides help for writing macros.

Enhancement Products   This option teaches you about other products that work well with Ami Pro.

About Ami Pro   This displays licensing information, as well as information on the amount of *memory* you have left. Why should you care? Well, if you run out of memory, you won't be able to perform really complex tasks, such as creating form letters from a client database, or manipulating large graphics (picture) files.

To choose a command from the Help menu, click on it or use the arrow keys to highlight a topic and then press **Enter**. Once you're inside Help, read the next section for directions on gettin' around.

SPEAK LIKE A GEEK

Memory is an electronic storage area inside the computer, which is used to store data or program instructions temporarily when the computer is using them. The computer's memory is erased when the power to the computer is turned off.

A **macro** is a recorded set of instructions for a frequently used task that can be activated (played back) at a later time by pressing a specific key combination.

Let Your Fingers Do the Walking: Getting Around Help

If you're just sitting in your document wondering how to add a page number (or some such), you can get help in a number of ways. Open the Help menu and you can browse through Contents looking for something about page numbering, or search for the topic "Numbering Pages" under How Do I?. Or you could open the Page menu, select Page Numbering, and then press **F1** from the dialog box to get help (provided you knew about the Page Page Numbering command in the first place). It doesn't matter how you get there—once you get into the Help system, there are some things you need to know about how to get around.

SPEAK LIKE A GEEK

A **jump topic** appears with a solid underline in the Help window. Clicking on a jump topic carries you deeper into the Help system, to that topic.

A **jump term** appears bold with a dotted underline in the Help window. Click on a jump term, and a quick definition or a helpful picture appears.

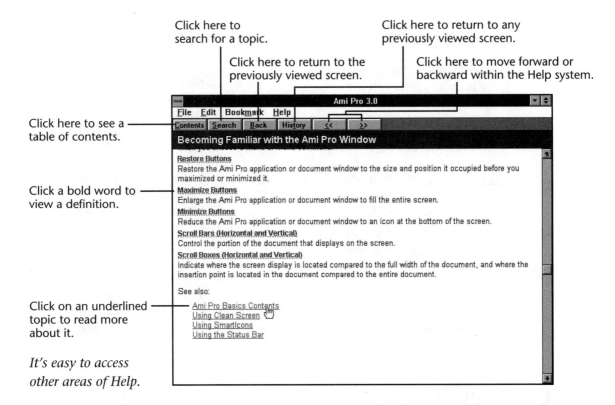

Click here to
search for a topic.

Click here to return to the
previously viewed screen.

Click here to return to any
previously viewed screen.

Click here to move forward or
backward within the Help system.

Click here to see a
table of contents.

Click a bold word to
view a definition.

Click on an underlined
topic to read more
about it.

*It's easy to access
other areas of Help.*

You can access certain
Help buttons quickly: press
Home to access **Contents**;
press **Backspace** to access
Back.

You'll be presented with a lot of choices as you
try to find information on the topic you're interested in. With a mouse, simply click on something
to choose it. With the keyboard, press **Tab** until
you highlight your choice, and then press **Enter**.
To access one of the buttons along the top of the
Help window, press the underlined letter. For
example, to begin a search, press **S**. To move back
one screen in the Help system, press <. To move
forward, press >.

To scroll through long lists, click on either arrow on the scroll bar, or
press **Page Down** to go forward in the list, and **Page Up** to go back.

Searching for Help in All the Right Places

If you know what you're looking for, you can search for a particular topic. With Help's How Do I? feature, you can page through an alphabetical listing of help topics until you find the one you want. If you like life in the fast lane, use the **Search** button within a Help window, and the hunt is on! (Just click on Search or press **S**.)

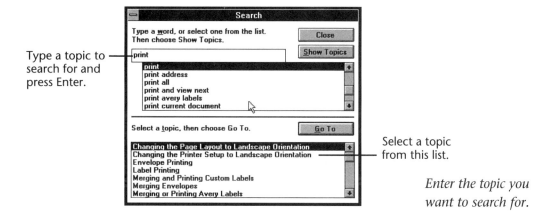

Type a topic to search for and press Enter.

Select a topic from this list.

Enter the topic you want to search for.

In the text box, type the word you want to look up, and press **Enter** or click on Show Topics. Related topics appear at the bottom of this dialog box. Select the topic of your choice by double-clicking on it, or by using the arrow keys to highlight it and pressing **Enter**.

Finding Your Favorite Places

Let's face it—you can't remember everything. And why should you, when Help is as close as the F1 key? However, if you find yourself looking up the same things again and again, mark these help topics with a *bookmark*. (Think of this as putting a paper clip on a favorite page in a book.) Here's what you do:

1. Display your favorite help topic.

2. Click on the Bookmark menu or press **Alt+M**.

3. Click on **Define** or press **D**.

4. If you want to change the title of the topic, type the new name. Then press **Enter** or click on **OK**.

To get to a bookmark you've placed, open the Help menu by pressing **Alt+H** or by clicking on **Help**. Select Bookmark, and when the Bookmark menu is displayed, click on your bookmark or use the arrow keys to select it.

Teacher, Teach Me How to Use an Ami Pro Tutorial

Ami Pro *tutorials* take you step by step through various tasks; think of them as one of those PBS do-it-yourself shows—but without the tools. You can complete an Ami Pro tutorial with the mouse or the keyboard.

If you want to stop the tutorial or change its speed, press **Esc**. Plot dragging? Click on **Speed** or press **Alt+S**, and then use the arrow keys to adjust the reading speed. To start the tutorial again, click on **Resume Tutorial** or press **Alt+R**. To get out of there or to try another channel, click on **QuickStart Menu** or press **Alt+Q**.

First, choose QuickStart Tutorial from the Help menu. Click on a lesson to select it, or press the underlined letter of the lesson you want. (To select the first tutorial, just press **Enter**.) Click on **Begin Lesson** (or press **Alt+B**) to start the show. Quickstart does everything for you; just sit back and relax as it goes through its stuff (popcorn is optional, but recommended). Don't be surprised when you see the mouse pointer move. Your PC's not possessed, it's just the tutorial showing you what to click on to perform some task. When the lesson is over, select another one or click on Exit Tutorial (or press **Alt+X**).

The Least You Need to Know

"Help" me review what we learned in this chapter:

- ☞ To get help while in Ami Pro, press **F1**.

- ☞ To get help with a part of the Ami Pro screen or a specific command, press **Shift+F1**, point the question mark at something, and then click.

- ☞ Jump to an underlined topic by clicking on it. To get a definition for a bold word, click on it. Or, press **Tab** to select it, and then press **Enter**.

- ☞ You can search for a topic by clicking on the **Search** button or pressing **Alt+S** from within a Help window. When the Search window is displayed, type the name of the item you want to search for and press **Enter**. Select a topic with the arrow keys or the mouse, and away you go!

- ☞ Add bookmarks to find often read topics quickly. Open the Bookmark menu from your favorite Help screen, type a reference name, and then press **Enter**. To find the bookmark later, look in the Bookmark menu.

- ☞ To start a tutorial, open the **H**elp menu and select QuickStart **T**utorial. Press its underlined letter or click on a topic to select it. After the tutorial is done, click on Exit Tutorial or press **Alt+X** to return to Ami Pro.

This page is about nothing, absolutely nothing.

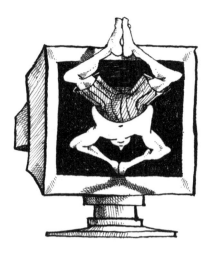

Chapter 6
Diving into a Document

In This Chapter

- ☛ Some simple rules for entering text
- ☛ Understanding what paragraph styles do
- ☛ Moving that darned insertion point
- ☛ Selecting the text you want to edit
- ☛ Inserting and deleting text
- ☛ Copying and moving text
- ☛ Inserting the current date or time
- ☛ Protecting your document against unauthorized changes

Well, congratulations. You've made it to Chapter 6. Sorry about all that preliminary stuff; it seems there's always something you have to learn before you can really "get down to work." Anyway, getting down to work is what this chapter is all about: how to enter text (and how to change it once it's been entered).

Dancing Fingers: How to Enter Text into an Ami Pro Document

When you start Ami Pro, it automatically places your cursor at the top of an empty document window so you are ready to start entering text. (The *insertion point* is a blinking vertical line that acts like the tip of a pencil; anything you type appears at the insertion point.) To enter text into a document, simply start typing. Easy enough. As you type, your words will appear on the screen, like words from a typewriter. Unlike using a type-writer, however, you should *not* press Enter when you reach the edge of the screen. (Make hip and syncopated mouth noises as you read the following line.) Ami-Pro-will-advance-your-text-automatically-to-the-next-line-at-the-appropriate-point. This is called Word Rap—I mean *word wrap*. With word wrap, you just type, and the words take care of themselves. When you get to the end of a complete paragraph, that's when you press Enter.

By the Way...

If you can't see the right edge of your page, change to a different view. Skip to Chapter 7 for info, and then come on back once you can see what you're doing.

With word wrap, words are automatically advanced to the next line of a paragraph when they bump into the right margin. Likewise, you can insert words into the middle of a paragraph, and the rest of the paragraph will be adjusted downward automatically. Likewise, if you change the margins, paragraphs will adjust automatically.

But What If I Make a Mistake?

Correcting typing mistakes in Ami Pro is easy. Simply press the **Backspace** key to back up and erase text, or select unwanted text (selecting text is covered in the next section) and remove that text by pressing the **Delete** key.

Using a Word Processor: Some Rules of the Road

Using a word processor is different from using a typewriter in many respects. So before you take Ami Pro out for a test drive, here are some rules of the road:

☛ **Don't press Enter/Return at the end of every line.** I've said it before, but it's worth saying again. When you use a typewriter, you press the carriage return at the end of a line so you can move down to the next one. When you use a word processor and your text bumps into the right margin, the word processor grabs the last word on that line and places it at the beginning of the next line automatically. Press **Enter** *only* when you reach the end of a paragraph or want to insert a blank line. If you want to divide an existing paragraph into two paragraphs, move the cursor to the dividing point and press **Enter**. To put two paragraphs back together, move to the first letter of the second paragraph and press **Backspace**.

Any grouping of words that should be treated as a unit is considered a **paragraph**. This includes normal paragraphs as well as single-line paragraphs, such as chapter titles, section headings, and captions for charts or other figures. When you press Enter/Return in Ami Pro, you are marking the end of a paragraph.

☛ **Use the Spacebar to insert a space between words or sentences.** Don't use the Spacebar to move the cursor from place to place in a document. (You'll learn how to move the cursor in the next section.)

☛ **Press Tab (not the Spacebar) to indent the first line of a paragraph.** Spaces are not just blank holes on the page; they are characters. Depending on the size of the characters you're using throughout your document, your paragraphs can come out looking uneven if you use the Spacebar to align them. Using the Tab key allows Ami Pro to line up paragraphs for you.

☛ **That gray-green area at the top of your screen represents the page margins.** You'll see a similar gray-green area when you reach the bottom of a page. (At least my area is gray-green; yours could be different. If you're interested in learning why, read the Techno Nerd tip in this section.) If you add text above the gray-green area, the excess text at the bottom of that page will flow onto the next page automatically. You can force the end of a page (before its time)—just read on!

TECHNO NERD TEACHES

The color of the page margins area in Ami Pro depends entirely on your choice of color within Windows. Open the Windows Control Panel from the Main program group by double-clicking it. Double-click the **Color** icon. Click on Color **Palette**, and then select the Screen Element **Application Workspace**. Change the color to whatever you'd like and click **OK**. (This will also change the color of other things, such as the Control Panel window, so be choosy!)

The Demise of a Page— Inserting Manual Page Breaks

A famous actor used to say, "I will serve no wine before its time." Well, what if you type the cover for a report and now you want to start a new page (serve it "before its time")? That's easy—just kill it.

Killing a page (forcing it to end before its time) is called inserting a *manual page break*. To do this, position your cursor below any text you want to keep on the current page. Click on the **Page** menu or press **Alt+P**, and click on **Breaks** or press **B**. You're in luck with this dialog box; it's already set up for page breaks. So just press **Enter**, and congratulations, it's a new baby page!

Shortcut to Styles

When you enter text into an Ami Pro document, it is assigned a *style*. The style of a paragraph defines certain parameters (such as the paragraph's margins, first line *indentation*, and *alignment*).

When a style is assigned to a paragraph, that paragraph changes to fit the definition of the style. For example, if you had a style called Heading that was defined as a center-aligned paragraph, and you assigned that Heading style to a line of text, the line of text would become centered.

By default, Ami Pro assigns the style Body Text to any text you type. The Body Text style is pretty generic; it defines a paragraph that is left-aligned (fits snug against the left margin) and single-spaced. You can switch to other predefined styles as you type, or you can create new styles. You'll learn how to assign paragraph styles, and even how to create new ones, in Chapter 14. For now, just type the your text into a document, and leave the assigning of styles till later on.

Magic Trick: Moving the Insertion Point Without Entering Text

As you type, the little insertion point, or cursor, moves along with you, like a happy puppy at your heels. But suppose you want to insert (or delete, or copy, or move) a word in a previous paragraph? Do you have to back up using the Backspace key and erase everything you've done, so you can retype that sentence? The answer is a big-time "No."

What you do instead is move the insertion point. To move the insertion point with the mouse, just click on the spot where you want it to go. (If you need to move through your document to get to the right spot, see the next chapter for some hints on *scrolling*—a fancy word for moving through a document with a mouse.) If you want to move the insertion point using the keyboard, just keep on readin'.

A **style** includes information for the font, size, margins, and spacing of a section of text. When you apply a style to a block of text, you format it automatically (according to the style's specifications).

Indentation is the amount of distance from the page margins to the edges of your paragraph.

Alignment controls how the text in a paragraph is placed between the left and right margins. For example, you might have left-aligned or centered text.

For People Who Let Their Fingers Do the Walking

Sometimes I hate to have my fingers leave the keyboard just to use the mouse, because they always land back on the wrong keys, and I end up typing garbage.

This table shows you how you can move the insertion point and not your fingers:

To Move . . .	Press . . .
Up or down one line	↑ or ↓
Left or right one character	← or →
One word left or right	Ctrl+← or Ctrl+→
To the next sentence	Ctrl+. (period)
To the previous sentence	Ctrl+, (comma)
Up or down one paragraph	Ctrl+↑ or Ctrl+↓
Up or down one screen	Page Up or Page Down
Up one page	Ctrl+Page Up
Down one page	Ctrl+Page Down
Beginning of the line	Home
End of the line	End
Beginning of the document	Ctrl+Home
End of the document	Ctrl+End

Selecting Text

As you edit your documents, you'll probably begin by modifying only certain sections of text. For example, you may want to move a sentence from the beginning of a paragraph to the end. You can move, copy, delete, and replace text by selecting it and then performing certain commands.

Mousing Around

To select text with the mouse, place the mouse pointer on the first letter in the text to be selected, and press and hold the left mouse button. Drag the mouse until you reach the end of the text you want to select. Release the mouse button, and the text you selected will be highlighted in reverse video.

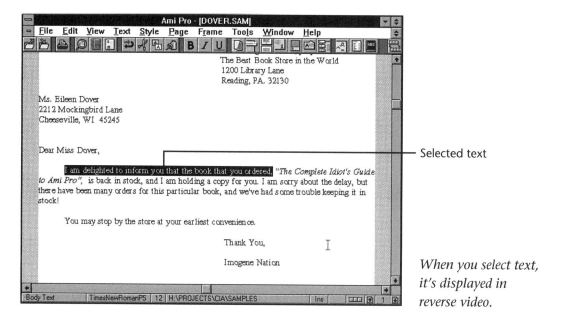

Selected text

When you select text, it's displayed in reverse video.

If you find this method of selecting text a drag, here are some shortcuts you can use when selecting text with the mouse:

Text to Select	Action
Word	Double-click on the word.
Sentence	Press the **Ctrl** key and click on the sentence.
Multiple sentences	Press **Ctrl**, click on the first sentence, and then drag.
Paragraph	Press the **Ctrl** key and double-click on the paragraph.
Multiple paragraphs	Press **Ctrl**, double-click on the first paragraph, and then drag.

To extend your text selection to include more than one word, sentence, or paragraph, simply drag the pointer. For example, to select several words, double-click on one word and drag the pointer over the rest of the words you want to select.

Key Bored

Your keyboard is beginning to think I don't like it, so I'll show you how to select text with the keyboard too. First, move the insertion point to the first letter in the text to be selected, and press the **Shift** key. Then, with the Shift key depressed (and in need of a good shrink), use the arrow keys to reach the end of the text you wish to select. Release the Shift key, and the text you selected will be highlighted in reverse video.

While selecting text with the keyboard, you can use any of those movement keys we discussed a few pages back. For example, to move to the next word, you press Ctrl+→. To select a word, press Shift+Ctrl+→. To select text to the end of the paragraph, press Shift+Ctrl+↓, and so on.

Change Your Mind?

Select the wrong text? Don't worry—just press an arrow key or click anywhere in the document, and watch the text change from reverse video back to normal. This indicates that the text is no longer "selected." The reverse video will also disappear if you select some other text instead.

In with the Good: Inserting Text

Text is always inserted into a document beginning at the insertion point (cursor). To move the insertion point, simply click at the point where you want to begin inserting text, or use the arrow keys.

When you type text into a document, Ami Pro assumes that you want to insert new text, and not type over existing text. Therefore, Ami Pro automatically uses *Insert mode*, in which the text you type appears at the insertion point, and all existing text is pushed to the right. However, if you want to type over existing characters, you can switch to *Typeover mode*.

To toggle between Typeover and Insert modes, press the **Insert** key, or click on the **Typing Mode** button located on the status bar. (That's the part of the status bar that's displaying the word "INS" right now. Go ahead and click on it and see what it does. I know you want to.)

When you are in Typeover mode, "TYPE" appears at the bottom of the screen on the status bar. Remember that the default is Insert mode; when you place the insertion point in text and start typing, words are inserted at that point. To type over (replace) existing text, use Typeover mode (TYPE).

Well, thank goodness we got through that! From now on, the only mode I want to think about is apple pie *à la mode*.

Out with the Bad: Deleting Text

Deleting text is the opposite of inserting. To delete a section of text, select the text you want to delete and press the **Delete** key, or simply start typing text to replace the text you selected.

To delete the previous word, press **Ctrl+Backspace**. To delete the next word (the one to the right) press **Ctrl+Delete**.

You can also delete text as you type by backing up with the **Backspace** key. If you want to delete text and then add it back (in a different place in the document), you *move* it. Moving text is covered in the next section.

But I Didn't Mean to Delete That!

Everyone has a right to change his or her mind (being a woman, I feel I have more of a right to do that.) If you find you've deleted some text you meant to save, open the Edit menu and choose Undo, or just press **Ctrl+Z**. As long as the Undo command is not grayed (meaning that you can't select it), you'll undo your most recent action.

You can also click on the **Undo** button on the Default SmartIcon set to undo your previous action.

SPEAK LIKE A GEEK

The Windows **Clipboard** is a special area inside your computer where data is stored temporarily as it is moved or copied from one place to another. Think of the Clipboard as a kind of invisible way station for data. Using the Clipboard area, a Windows program such as Ami Pro can copy or move data within the same document, from one document to another, or from/to another Windows program.

TECHNO NERD TEACHES

Ami Pro (like a lot of Windows programs) secretly supports the old ways of copying and pasting. So if you learned to copy text by selecting it and pressing **Ctrl+Ins**, and to paste text by pressing **Shift+Ins**, you can still do that in Ami Pro.

By the way, cutting text using **Shift+Delete** is also supported. So why change just because Microsoft decided there needed to be a new standard for Windows applications?

Copying and Moving Text

Copying and moving text is often the key to fine-tuning a document. Because of this, the techniques you'll learn in this section are among those you'll probably use the most. You copy or move text using the Windows *Clipboard*.

Copy Cat!

To copy text, "copy" these steps: first (using the methods you learned earlier in this chapter), select the text you want to copy. Then open the **Edit** menu and choose Copy. The text is copied to the Clipboard.

Next, move the pointer to the place where you want to insert the text, and click to establish the insertion point. Open the **Edit** menu again, and this time choose **Paste**. The text is copied from the Clipboard into the document at the insertion point.

Copying in the Fast Lane

There are some shortcuts you can use to save time copying:

 To copy text, select it and press **Ctrl+C**, or click on the **Copy** button on the Default SmartIcons set.

 To paste text, press **Ctrl+V** or click on the **Paste** button on the Default SmartIcons set.

To place the same section of text in multiple areas of a document, simply repeat the **Edit Paste** command. The contents of the Clipboard are never erased (until you exit Windows); instead, they are overlaid. As long as you have not copied something else to the Clipboard with the **Edit Copy** or **Edit Cut** command, whatever you copied originally is still there, waiting to be pasted over and over again. You can also copy text with the drag-and-drop method; see "By the Way" coming up in this section.

Moving Day

Moving text is very similar to copying. Move along with me here: first (using the methods you learned earlier in this chapter), select the text you want to move. Then open the **Edit** menu and select **Cut**. The text is moved to the Clipboard.

Then move the pointer to the place where you want to insert the text, and click to establish the insertion point. Open the **Edit** menu again, and choose **Paste**. The text appears at the insertion point.

Get a Move On with These Fast Techniques

Here are some shortcuts you can use to save time moving text:

 To move (cut) text, select it and press **Ctrl+X**, or click on the **Cut** button on the Default SmartIcons set.

 To paste text, press **Ctrl+V** or click on the **Paste** button on the Default SmartIcons set.

When you use the **Cut** command, the selected text is removed from the document and placed on the Clipboard. If you copy something else to the Clipboard before you finish moving the text, the text you selected to move will be lost: what used to be in the document has been removed, and what was on the Clipboard has been replaced by what you copied later.

You can switch the order of two paragraphs with these quick keyboard combinations: to move the current paragraph up one paragraph in your document, press **Alt+↑**. To move it down, press **Alt+↓**.

By the Way...

When I want to move text to a place I can see on-screen, I just drag and drop text where I want it to be. To move text with the mouse, first select it, and then press and hold the left mouse button. The cursor will change to a pair of scissors (how cute!). Drag that pointer to the place where you want to insert the text, and then release the mouse button. The selected text is moved to the insertion point. (Incidentally, you can *copy* text instead by pressing **Ctrl** as you drag.)

If you always insert the current date into your documents as I do, add either the Date/Time or the Insert Today's Date icons to one of the SmartIcon sets (see Chapter 4). Then just click the icon to insert a date or time. Now that's my kind of icon!

When Your Document Needs to Know What Time It Is

Even if you never know what day it is, your documents can always be timely. You can insert the current date or time, and even have them automatically updated whenever you make a change to a document. And the best news is, it's a lot easier than setting your alarm clock.

First, move the insertion point to the place where you want to insert the date or time. Then open the Edit menu and select Insert. (Click on the commands or press **Alt+E** and then **I**.) Select Date/Time off the submenu. (If you're using a keyboard, press **D**.) Now you've got to make a selection:

Today's date   Inserts today's date. Doesn't update.

System **date**   Inserts today's date, but updates it whenever the document is reopened at a later time.

System time   Inserts the time, but updates it whenever the document is reopened at some later time.

Date of last **revision**   Inserts the date on which the document was last revised (saved). Doesn't update.

Date created   Inserts the document's creation date. Doesn't update.

To make your selection, click on it or press **Alt** plus the selection letter. You can change the format of the date with the **S**tyle list. If you're using a keyboard, press **Alt+S** and use the arrow keys to select a format. Press **Enter** or click **OK** when you're through, and your document's got a date!

Don't Change a Word for Me (Protecting Your Prose)

Ami Pro can help protect you from over zealous word critics and even yourself, if you need it. With text protection turned on, you will not be able to move the insertion point into the protected text. Therefore, deleting or changing text while it's protected is difficult.

To protect your prose, select it and then open the Edit menu (press **Alt+E**). Select Mark Text (press **M**), and then select Protected Text (press **P**). To unprotect it later on, just repeat these steps.

Changing or deleting protected text is difficult, but not impossible. You can still select the text by pressing **Shift** and one of the arrow keys, or by selecting the text beginning at an unprotected point. So if something is really important, keep a copy of it on disk.

The Least You Need to Know

Editing is the most important processing you do when creating any kind of document, so here's a quick review of what you'll need to know to make your documents perfect:

- ☛ Text is always inserted at the cursor, otherwise known as the insertion point. To type over existing text, press **Insert** to turn on Typeover mode (and do the same to get back to Insert mode).

- ☛ To move the insertion point with the mouse, just click on the place where you want it located.

- ☛ When entering text using a word processor, press Enter only at the end of a paragraph. Only use the Spacebar once between words, and once or twice between sentences. Use the **Tab** key, not the Spacebar, to indent paragraphs.

continues

continued

☞ Text you enter is assigned a *style*, which determines its indentation, alignment, and text attributes. You change the style of a paragraph with the Styles Box. You can change the characteristics of selected text with commands in the **T**ext menu.

☞ To end a page before it is full, insert a page break. Open the **P**age menu and select **B**reaks. When the dialog box appears, press **Enter**.

☞ To select text with the mouse, press and hold the left mouse button, and drag the mouse over the text. To select text with the keyboard, press and hold the **Shift** key as you use the arrow keys to highlight the text.

☞ To delete text, select it and press **Delete**.

☞ To copy text quickly, select it and press **Ctrl+C** (or use the **Copy** button). Paste text in a new location by pressing **Ctrl+V** or by clicking on the **Paste** button.

☞ To move text quickly, select it and press **Ctrl+X** or use the **Cut** button. Paste text into a new location by pressing **Ctrl+V** or by clicking on the **Paste** button.

☞ To use drag and drop to move text, select it and drag it with the mouse. To copy text using drag and drop, press **Ctrl** as you drag.

☞ Insert the date or time into a document by opening the **Edit** menu and selecting **I**nsert. Choose the type of date or time you want to insert and press **Enter**.

☞ To protect important text or data, select it. Then open the **Edit** menu, select **Mark Text**, and select **Protected Text**.

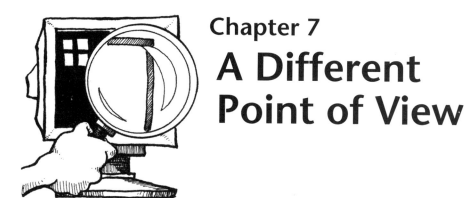

Chapter 7
A Different Point of View

In This Chapter

- ☞ Scrolling through a document
- ☞ Displaying the Styles Box or the Ruler
- ☞ The many ways you can view your document
- ☞ Creating a document outline
- ☞ Using a document's outline to quickly rearrange a long document

This chapter is all about points of view: what you see on your screen when you look at your document, and—more importantly—what you don't see. There is a perfect document view for each task you perform: editing (Custom or Standard views), looking at an entire page (Full Page view), getting up close and personal (Enlarged view), or comparing the design of two adjoining pages (Facing Pages view).

As if this weren't enough, Ami Pro offers different viewing modes which affect the level of detail that you see. For example, in Layout mode, everything's displayed as it will print; in Outline mode, paragraphs are collapsible so you can study the organization of an entire document; and in Draft mode, certain elements aren't displayed exactly as they will print, which allows Ami Pro to edit your document faster.

Whew! Before we get to the main topic in this chapter (changing your view of things), let's cover something a bit easier—scrolling.

Taking Your Document Out for a Scroll

When I'm editing, I tend to move around the document a lot: making changes, reading, and rereading, until I find just the right words or just the right look. Such jumping around is called *scrolling*. You can move (scroll) through a document word order using a mouse or the keyboard.

The fastest way to scroll through a document is with the mouse and the scroll bars. You'll find the *vertical scroll bar* lurking along the right-hand side of the document window. This scroll bar looks like an elevator shaft with a tiny elevator suspended in it. That "elevator" is called the *scroll box*, and it lets you know where you are. For example, if the scroll box is close to the bottom of the scroll bar, you're almost at the end of your document.

You'll also see a scroll bar along the bottom of the window. It's called the *horizontal scroll bar*, and it tells you where you are in relation to the right and left margins of your document. Here's how to take your document "out for a scroll."

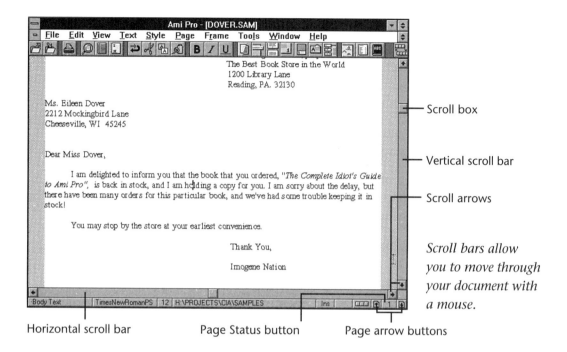

Horizontal scroll bar   Page Status button   Page arrow buttons

Here's how you scroll with the mouse:

To move . . .	Click . . .
Up or down one line	On the up or down arrow of the vertical scroll bar.
Left or right	On the left or right arrow of the horizontal scroll bar.
Up or down one screen	Above or below the scroll box in the vertical scroll bar.
A portion of the document length	On the vertical scroll box, and drag it up or down a proportionate distance.
A portion of the document width	On the horizontal scroll box, and drag it left or right a proportionate distance.

You can jump to the next page or to the previous one by clicking the appropriate **Page arrow** buttons located on the status bar. Not quick enough for you? Try the Page Status button. When you click on the **Page Status** button, a dialog box appears. Then simply enter the page number you want to go to, or click on **First** page or **Last** page to jump to the beginning or the end of a document.

Keep in mind that scrolling with the mouse simply changes the part of the document you're looking at; your insertion point remains where you left it. If you want to start editing, click within the document to move the insertion point. If you missed the awarding-winning documentary "Magic Trick: Moving the Insertion Point without Entering Text" when it was on PBS, see Chapter 6 for a quick review.

Most Windows programs do not display the scroll bars unless some portion of your document is currently out of sight (if the right margin is hidden, for example, you see a horizontal scroll bar you can use to scroll right). Ami Pro does not follow this unwritten rule; instead, it displays both the horizontal and vertical scroll bars at all times, unless you turn the horizontal scroll bar off. (Sorry, you can't turn off the vertical scroll bar.)

To turn the horizontal scroll bar off, open the View menu and select View **Preferences**. (Press **Alt+V** and then **P**.) Select **Horizontal** scroll bar (press **Alt+O**), and then click on **OK** or press **Enter**. To return the horizontal scroll bar to the screen for your viewing pleasure, repeat these steps.

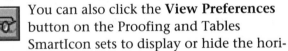 You can also click the **View Preferences** button on the Proofing and Tables SmartIcon sets to display or hide the horizontal scroll bar.

Scrolling with the Keyboard

To scroll through a document with the keyboard, simply press **Page Down** to move one screen forward in the document. Press **Page Up** to move one screen back. You can get nowhere fast by scrolling one line at a time with the up and down arrow keys.

Unlike when you use the mouse and the scroll bar, scrolling with the keyboard *does* move the insertion point, so you don't have to unpack your editing bags when you get there—you're ready to edit.

Displaying the Styles Box or the Ruler

If Ami Pro doesn't display enough on the screen to suit you, you can add more. (In the next section, you learn how to remove all the clutter from the screen and focus on just text; but for now, let's learn how to make an even bigger mess!)

I know it's weird that the Page Up and Page Down keys don't move you one whole *page* in your document (like from page 1 to page 2), but the computer's "page" is its screen, so that's why the keys work that way.

The Ruler, when it's displayed, appears at the top of the screen just under the SmartIcon bar. You use the Ruler to change the margins, indentations, and tab settings of individual paragraphs. (You'll learn how to use the Ruler in upcoming episodes—so don't touch that dial!) To display the Ruler, open the View menu (press **Alt+V**) and select Show **R**uler (press **R**).

You can also click the **Show/Hide Ruler** button on the Default SmartIcons set to display the Ruler.

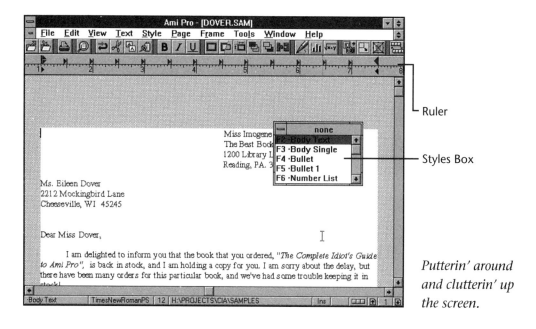

Ruler

Styles Box

Putterin' around and clutterin' up the screen.

To jump to any page in a document, press **Ctrl+G**, type the number of the page you want to go to, and press **Enter**. To jump to the first page, press **Alt+F** instead of typing a number and press **Enter**; to jump to the last page, press **Alt+L** and press **Enter**.

As you learned in Chapter 6, when you enter text into an Ami Pro document, it is assigned a *style*. The style of a paragraph defines certain parameters (such as the paragraph's margins, first line *indentation*, and *alignment*). You can change the style of a paragraph using the Styles Box. You'll learn the details of this little maneuver in Chapter 14; but for now, to display the Styles Box, simply open the View menu (press **Alt+V**) and select Show Styles **B**ox (press **B**). If you want to move the Styles Box around, click on its title bar, hold the mouse button down, drag it wherever you want, and then release the mouse button.

The Case of the Disappearing Menus

Now that we know how to display lots of stuff on the screen, let's learn how to get rid of it. Take a good look at this picture. Can you list everything that's missing?

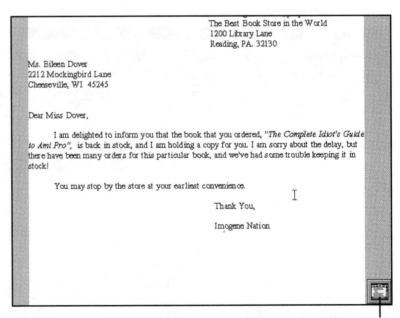

The Best Book Store in the World
1200 Library Lane
Reading, PA. 32130

Ms. Eileen Dover
2212 Mockingbird Lane
Cheeseville, WI 45245

Dear Miss Dover,

I am delighted to inform you that the book that you ordered, *"The Complete Idiot's Guide to Ami Pro"*, is back in stock, and I am holding a copy for you. I am sorry about the delay, but there have been many orders for this particular book, and we've had some trouble keeping it in stock!

You may stop by the store at your earliest convenience.

Thank You,

Imogene Nation

Now where did everybody go?

Return icon

The Five Million Dollar Answer: If you said the scroll bars, the menu bar, the SmartIcon set, the status bar, and the Ruler, you're right. If these things are just a collection of junk that gets in the way of your typing, get rid of them! In Ami Pro, you have the option of removing everything from the screen so you can do your typing in peace. This option will be especially welcome if you switched from WordPerfect, where the normal operating environment does not include any clutter.

So, whether you're a former WordPerfect user, or you just want to give this a try, here's what you do: open the **View** menu and select Show Clean Scree**n**. (If you use the keyboard, press **Alt+V**, and then **N**.)

Maybe having no menu bar is not such a good thing, at least when it comes time to issue a command. Not to worry—you can still use the Alt+selection letter keyboard commands to open menus if you need to, clean screen and all. If you want to display the menu bar whenever you use Show Clean Screen, read the Techno Nerd tip in this section.

To return to "normal" clutter, click on the **Return** icon, or press **Alt+V** and **N** again.

 You can also switch to Clean Screen mode by clicking the **Show/ Hide Clean Screen** button, located on the Editing SmartIcons set.

Coming into View

When it comes to viewing your document, Ami Pro offers almost as many choices as an ice-cream store. Here's the scoop:

You can use Full Page view only while in Layout mode. See the section, "Mo' Viewing Modes" for info.

Full Page   Displays an entire page by reducing the text to tiny, illegible glop. Good for getting a "lay of the land" picture. You can edit text in this view (if you can see it).

Custom   The default view, which is normally set at 91% of Standard view. You can change the percentage to see exactly what you want to see on-screen. For example, 150% would enlarge the text more than Standard view (which is considered 100%), but less than Enlarged view (which is set at 200%). This is a good view for getting exactly what you want, and you can edit to your heart's delight.

Working in a screen without the normal distractions of a menu bar, scroll bars, etc., can be a relaxing and speedy experience, since Clean Screen mode requires less time to update than other modes. If you're a fast typist (or you simply hate clutter), Clean Screen mode is for you.

If you want to have your cake and eat it too, you can still enjoy the benefits of Clean Screen mode without removing all the clutter. Simply open the **View** menu and select View **Preferences**. Click on Clean **S**creen Options and select whatever you still want to see on-screen after you use Clean Screen. Click **OK**, and then click **OK** again, and the next time you use the Clean Screen mode, you'll be all set.

 You can also click the **View Preferences** button on the Proofing and Tables SmartIcon sets to change the Clean Screen options.

Standard   Sets the text size to the same size as displayed in other Windows applications. It's okay, but personally I like Custom better because I can see both sides (the left and right margins) of the page without scrolling.

Enlarged   BIG TYPE! What else can I say? This view is good for getting in close and making small changes to drawings.

Facing Pages   When one page isn't good enough, use this viewing mode. You'll see two, two, two pages at once! Again, you can edit, but the text might be too tiny.

So how do you change from one viewing mode to another? I knew you'd ask that, but I've decided to wait until the next section to tell you. (This is called a teaser. In television, a teaser compels the viewer to continue to watch complete drivel because there is something about the human psyche that makes us naturally curious about everything, including disappearing rock stars, bald cross-dressing chefs, Joey Buttafucco, dogs that fetch fish for lazy fishermen, Elvis, and stuff that slices, dices, and makes julienne fries.)

Changing Your Point of View

Okay, here's what you've been waiting for: to change to a different view, just open the View menu and select the option you want. (Keyboarders: press **Alt+V**, and then press the underlined letter of the command you seek.) It's that simple.

Click on the **Full Page/Layout** button on the Default or the Editing SmartIcon set to switch between Full Page and other views. (Read the EZ tip in this section for a way to use the keyboard to do the same thing.)

To switch to Facing Pages view, open the **V**iew menu and select F**a**cing Pages (just like any other view). What's weird is getting back from Facing Pages view. You can get back to the previous view by clicking the **Cancel** button or pressing **Esc**.

Mo' Modes of Viewing

As I said before, Ami Pro offers more ways to view your documents than you could imagine. In addition to the different document views (they were described in the last section for those of you who fell asleep while reading it), Ami Pro provides different *viewing modes*.

The default viewing mode is Layout, which displays your document as it will look when printed, warts and all. By the way, this type of viewing mode is known in the trade as *WYSIWYG* (**W**hat **Y**ou **S**ee **I**s **W**hat **Y**ou **G**et). Use that in a sentence and impress your co-workers—"Ami Pro is cool. It provides perfect WYSIWYG." In Layout view, *headers*, *footers*, imported pictures (*graphics*), and text all show up exactly as they will look when you print that page. All in all, it's a pretty handy viewing mode, which is why it's the default.

For a fast change to **Full** Page view, press **Ctrl+D**. (Don't ask me why they chose "D"; it's just one of those mystery programming things.) To return to the mode you were using before, just press **Ctrl+D** again.

TECHNO NERD TEACHES

You can change the Custom view percentage to create a view that's perfect for working with a particular document. After that, I usually change it back because I like the default percentage of 91%. Anyway, open the **View** menu and select View **P**references. (Press **Alt+V**, and then **P**.) Choose Custom vie**w** (**Alt+W**) and enter a number. Click **OK** or press **Enter** when you're done. To change Custom view back to its old percentage, repeat these steps.

 You can also click the **View Preferences** button on the Proofing and Tables SmartIcon sets to change the Custom view percentage.

To fit the current document so that its left- and right-hand edges fit the screen, click the **Fit to Screen** button on the Macro Goodies SmartIcons set.

WYSIWYG stands for **W**hat **Y**ou **S**ee **I**s **W**hat **Y**ou **G**et, and it's a type of viewing mode where all elements of a document (headers, footers, graphics, and the like) are displayed as they will appear when printed.

A **footer** is printed at the bottom of every page within a document.

A **header** is printed at the top of every page within a document.

The term **graphics** describes any picture that can be imported into Ami Pro (or a picture that you draw yourself using Drawing mode).

However, pretty comes with a price it seems. To display everything as is, that computer of yours is working overtime. As you move back and forth through your document, the computer is constantly redrawing what is being displayed on your screen. Think of trying to do a pencil sketch of a tennis match: although a computer is very fast, if your document contains complex graphics (pictures) or other detailed information, this redrawing process can take longer than you'd like. Unless you're sitting there with a stopwatch, you probably won't notice the difference much. But if you feel like you're working with a turtle, change Ami Pro into a hare by switching to Draft mode. (Be patient—you'll learn how in a minute.)

Draft mode is no angel either. Although it's faster than Layout mode, it doesn't display headers or footers, or most *frames*. (That's why it's faster—it doesn't display as much.)

The last contestant in the viewing mode wars is Outline mode. This mode allows you to condense all that fluff (otherwise known as paragraphs) in your document into a neat outline that displays only headings. Reorganize huge documents with a click here and a click there. It's a great tool, which you'll learn more about in a special section called "Just a Little Reorganization."

Changing Modes

To change to any mode, the instructions are the same: open the View menu and select the mode you want. (With the keyboard, press **Alt+V** and the selection letter of the command you want.)

You can also switch between Draft and Layout viewing modes by clicking on the **Draft/Layout** button, conveniently located on the Long Documents and Proofing SmartIcon sets.

 You can switch between Outline and Layout viewing modes by selecting the command or by clicking the **Outline/Layout** button, located in lots of SmartIcon sets: Editing, Long Documents, Proofing, and Working Together.

Frames are small boxes in which you place text or pictures so you can maneuver them easily within your document.

To switch to Draft mode quickly, press **Ctrl+M**. Again, there's no real explanation as to why Lotus picked the letter M, instead of the letter D, which you might actually remember and use. Except that (for those of you who do read all these things) you might remember that Ctrl+D switches you to Full Page view. Go figure.

Just a Little Reorganization

When you need to move several sections of a long document, use Outline mode. When you work in Outline mode, you'll see just the section headings of your document. You can change the headings themselves, or copy, move, and delete them. When you copy, move, or delete a heading, you can copy, move, or delete the entire section that's attached to it. Or, if you prefer, you can copy, move, or delete just a heading, leaving the subordinate text intact and in place.

Switching to Outline Mode

To change to Outline mode, click on the **Outline/Layout** button on the Editing, Long Documents, Proofing, or Working Together SmartIcon sets, or open the View menu and select Outline Mode. To change your view, adjust heading levels, and move headings or other text, you can select buttons on the Outlining bar.

Outline Level icons

Click here to switch back to Layout mode.

Outline Command icons

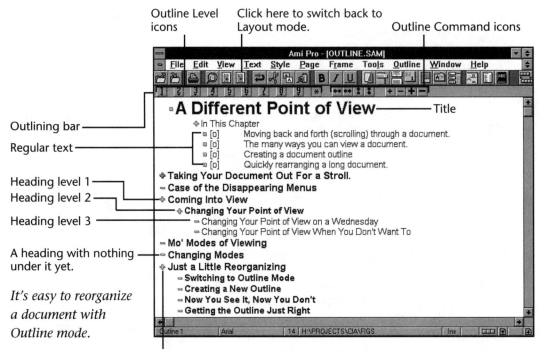

Outlining bar

Regular text

Heading level 1

Heading level 2

Heading level 3

A heading with nothing under it yet.

It's easy to reorganize a document with Outline mode.

A heading with sub-headings and/or text.

A plus sign in front of a heading indicates that the heading has either subheadings or paragraphs under it. If those subheadings/paragraphs are currently displayed, the plus sign is clear. If they're hiding, the plus sign is filled in. A minus sign indicates a heading with no subheadings or paragraphs. A dot indicates a regular ol' paragraph.

If you select an outline style sheet that contains sample text, you'll need to type over it by pressing the **Insert** key or clicking on the **Typing Mode** button on the status bar.

Outline mode is great for working with the structure of a long document. Although you can enter regular text while in Outline mode, switch to Layout view if you want to do any heavy formatting.

Creating a New Outline

Before we type the outline for the Great American Novel, let's get some basics straight. Ami Pro provides outline styles for each level of an outline, up to nine levels deep. The top level of an outline is a *style* called **Outline 1** (sometimes called **Level 1**). The next level down (indented) is **Outline 2**. The next level down is **Outline 3**, and so on. (You'll learn more about paragraph styles and how they work in Chapters 14 and 15.)

 To create a new outline, open the File menu and select New. Select an outline style sheet, and then click **OK**. Switch to Outline mode and start typing the title. To type the first heading in your outline click on the **Demote** button (right arrow) or press **Alt+→**. To enter a lower-level heading in your outline, click again on the **Demote** button or press **Alt+→**.

 To type a higher-level heading (to type an Outline 1 after entering an Outline 2, for example), click on the **Promote** button (left arrow) or press **Alt+←**.

> ### By the Way . . .
>
> Use Outline mode to create your outline first; then switch to Layout view to enter your text. To enter text, press **F2** or switch to Body Text style. (You'll learn more about paragraph styles in Chapters 14 and 15.)

Now You See It, Now You Don't

 After you've created your out-line—and maybe even entered some text—you can use Outline mode to control the level of subheadings and the amount of the underlying text that you see. To expand a heading so you can see the

You can expand and collapse a heading by double-clicking on its plus sign within the outline.

subheadings, select the heading by clicking on it. Then click on the plus sign. To collapse a heading so you do not see subheadings, select the heading and click on the minus sign. You can even expand or collapse an outline to just the next level by clicking on the small plus/minus signs.

 To expand the outline to a particular heading level, click on the appropriate number. For example, to expand an outline to heading level 3, click on the **3** button on the Outlining bar. To expand the complete outline, click on the asterisk on the Outlining bar.

You can print the outline of your document at any time, simply by switching to Outline mode and selecting the **File Print** command. You'll learn more about printing in Chapter 10.

Getting the Outline Just Right

When I start out to write a book (or anything else, for that matter), I try to get organized by creating an outline right off. Then I proceed to ignore my outline and write what I want. Okay, it's not really that bad, but I find that during the course of creating any long document (such as a chapter, report, or manual), changes in the structure of the original outline are inevitable. (At least that's what I tell my editors!)

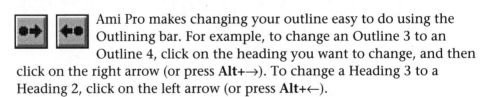 Ami Pro makes changing your outline easy to do using the Outlining bar. For example, to change an Outline 3 to an Outline 4, click on the heading you want to change, and then click on the right arrow (or press **Alt+→**). To change a Heading 3 to a Heading 2, click on the left arrow (or press **Alt+←**).

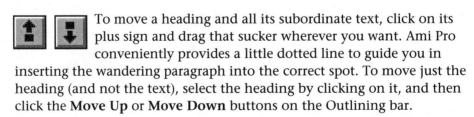 To move a heading and all its subordinate text, click on its plus sign and drag that sucker wherever you want. Ami Pro conveniently provides a little dotted line to guide you in inserting the wandering paragraph into the correct spot. To move just the heading (and not the text), select the heading by clicking on it, and then click the **Move Up** or **Move Down** buttons on the Outlining bar.

The Least You Need to Know

Depending on your "point of view," these may or may not be the highlights of this chapter. Here goes:

☛ To see something in another part of your document, scroll with the scroll bars and a mouse.

☛ If you want to scroll using the keyboard, press **Page Up** or **Page Down** or use the arrow keys.

☛ If you want to remove everything but the text area from your screen, use the **View Show Clean Screen** command.

☛ There are five views: Full Page (shows an entire page), Custom (you choose how much to show), Standard (shows text in the same size as other Windows applications), Enlarged (200% of Standard), and Facing Pages (two pages at once).

☛ To change views, open the **View** menu (press **Alt+V**) and select a view.

☛ There are three viewing modes: Layout (shows the document as it will print), Draft (shows the document with headers, footers, and some frames missing), and Outline (shows a document condensed to headings). To switch viewing modes, open the **View** menu (press **Alt+V**) and select a viewing mode.

☛ Click the **Show/Hide Ruler** button on the Default SmartIcons set to display the Ruler.

☛ To display the Styles Box, open the **View** menu and select Show Styles **B**ox.

☛ Outline mode is great for reorganizing long documents. Click the **Outline/Layout** button on the Editing, Long Documents, Proofing, or Working Together SmartIcon sets, or select the **View O**utline Mode command.

continues

continued

To change the level of a heading within an outline, click on these buttons.

To display or hide lower levels in an outline, click the plus or minus signs in front of a heading.

To expand the outline to a particular heading level, click on the appropriate number. To completely expand an outline, click on the asterisk on the Outlining bar.

To move a heading and all its subordinate text, click on its plus sign and drag that sucker wherever you want. To move just the heading (and not the text), select the heading by clicking on it, and then click the **Move Up** or **Move Down** buttons on the Outlining bar.

Chapter 8
Juggling Documents

In This Chapter

- ☞ Creating a new document
- ☞ Creating documents automatically with style sheets
- ☞ Opening an existing document
- ☞ Finding little lost documents
- ☞ "Paneless" ways to work with multiple documents
- ☞ Working in two places in a document at the same time

Maybe it's not so wonderful to have to juggle changing priorities and multiple projects, but at least Ami Pro works the way people really do: that is, on more than one thing at a time. As you work in Ami Pro, you'll find yourself opening old documents and starting new ones. You may even want to have several documents showing on your screen at the same time, or two parts of the same document. This chapter will show you how to do all this and more.

Starting A-New

When you first start Ami Pro, it assumes you want to begin something new, so it accommodates you by giving you a blank screen. But what do you do when you've just finished one document, and you want to start "a-new" while you're still in Ami Pro? How do you get an empty window so you can start typing?

Well, open the File menu and select the New command (press **Alt+F** and then **N**). A dialog box opens. You can basically ignore this box and press **Enter**, unless you want to base your new document on some style sheet other than the default *style sheet*. (Be sure to read the next section if you're interested in using style sheets.)

If you're done with your current document, select the option Close current file, and Ami Pro will close your old document for you (such service!). If you don't select this option, your new document will be opened in a new window. (And how convenient for you that the instructions for dealing with multiple documents are included right here in this chapter! Now that's really service!)

Now We're Stylin'

When you start a new document, you use a default style sheet (called _DEFAULT.STY) that defines margin settings, page orientation, and so on for the document. The default style sheet also includes some pre-defined paragraph styles, which you can use to format your text.

Ami Pro comes with additional style sheets that you can use to create specialized documents, such as memos, proposals, overheads, faxes, and mailing labels. If you want to use one of these specialized templates, select the File New command. Then click on the style sheet you want to use, or press **Alt+S** and using the arrow keys to highlight one.

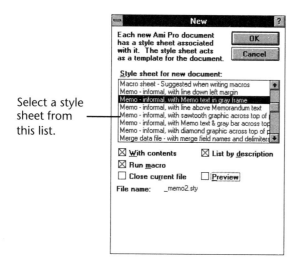

Select a style sheet from this list.

Why do all the work, when the right style sheet will do it for you?

Some style sheets contain dummy text (boilerplate text), pictures, and/or tables. Select **W**ith contents or press **Alt+W** to include this data in your new document. Flying blind? You don't have to—just click on **Pre**view or press **Alt+P** to see what you're gonna get before you get it. When you're done choosing your options, press **Enter** or click **OK**, and your new document awaits your commands.

Macro Magic: Creating Documents Automatically

Ami Pro macros take the idea of using style sheets one step further, by automating the tedious task of actually typing text. (Now if only it would do the laundry!) Anyway, in the New dialog box, select Run **m**acro before you press **Enter** or click **OK** to close it. You'll be greeted with a series of dialog boxes, prompting you to input basic data for the document.

If you create new documents a lot (I mean, isn't that why you got Ami Pro in the first place?), you'll want to add the New document icon to one of the SmartIcon sets. (I added mine to the Default set.) Open the Tools menu and select SmartIcons. Find the New document icon on the left-hand side of the dialog box, and drag it onto the Default SmartIcon set displayed on the right-hand side. Click **OK**, and now you're livin' the easy life.

The Surgeon General warns that some style sheets are not equipped with macros, and as such, are dangerous to your health.

For example, if you selected one of the memo style sheets, Ami Pro would prompt you for your name (the sender), the recipient's name, and the memo's subject. Just type in the needed data, press **Enter**, and away you go! Makes even something as boring as writing a sales proposal a little more fun.

Document Déjà Vu: Opening an Existing Document

Ami Pro remembers the last four (or more) documents you worked on so that you can get to them easily. If the document you want to work on (open) is a recent one, it'll be displayed at the end of the File menu. To open it, open the File menu and click on the document you want, or press the number next to the document name. (I use this method to open existing documents more often than any other method.)

If you haven't worked on a document in a while, you'll have to open it the long way. Open the File menu and select the Open command, or press **Ctrl+O**. You can also click on the **Open** button on the Default SmartIcon set. Another one of those boxes will appear (oh, goody). Either type the name of the file you want to open, or (using the scroll bars or the up or down arrow keys) scroll through the list.

You can have Ami Pro display more (or less) than the last four documents at the end of the File list. To change this setting, select the **Tools User Setup** command. Click on **Recent** files or press **Alt+R** to select it. Enter a number between 0 and 5, and then press **Enter** or click **OK**.

If you can't find your file, change to a different *drive* or *directory*. (To move to Directories with the keyboard, press **Alt+D**; to move to Drives, press **Alt+V**. Then use the arrow keys to select an item.) Select a different disk drive from the drop-down list box by clicking on the down arrow and then clicking on a different drive. If you need to change to another directory, click on that directory.

Enter the name of file to open, or select from list.　　Preview a file before opening it.

Change directories.　　Change drives.

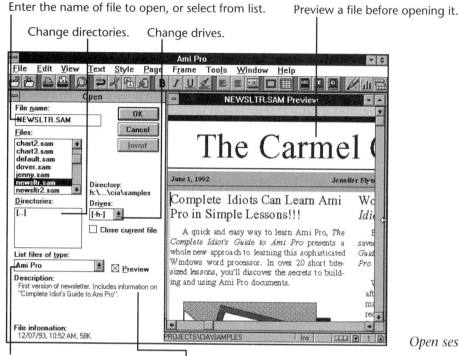

Open sesame!

List files created with another　　Identify a file based on its description.
word processor.

If you're trying to open a document that was created in another program (such as WordPerfect), select that program from the List files of **t**ype drop-down list box by clicking on the down arrow and then picking a type. If your file type is not listed, select **All Files**.

You can close your current document before you open a new one by selecting Close current file (press **Alt+R**). When you're done making choices, select **OK** or press **Enter** to open the file. (If you'd like to preview the document to be sure it's the right one, jump to the next section before pressing Enter.)

When you open a foreign-format document (such as a WordPerfect file), Ami Pro attempts to convert it. Expect to lose some formatting; no conversion process is absolutely perfect.

SPEAK LIKE A GEEK

Disk drive A type of computer storage device that reads and writes on a magnetic film. Think of a disk drive as being like a cassette recorder/player. Just as the cassette player can record sounds on a magnetic cassette tape and play them back, a disk drive can record data on a magnetic disk and play back the data. Most computers have two types of disk drives: a **hard disk drive**, which stores vast amounts of data on permanently mounted disks, and a **floppy disk drive**, which records smaller amounts of data on portable disks.

Because large hard disks can store thousands of files, you often store related files in smaller, separate groups or **directories** on the disk. Think of your disk as a filing cabinet, and think of each directory as a drawer in the filing cabinet. By keeping files in separate directories, it is easier to locate and work with related files.

Look Before You Leap: Document Preview

I hate packages that don't let you see what you're getting before you buy something. So that's probably why I like to use the preview feature in the Open dialog box. After you choose **File Open**, just select **Preview** (or press **Alt+P**), and you'll be greeted with a picture of the first page of the selected document. (Look back at the last figure for a review of preview.)

You can even scroll through the document preview until you're sure you've identified it. If your memory of how to scroll has faded like yesterday's blue jeans, look back at Chapter 7 for a refresher.

Besides scrolling, you can copy text from a previewed document (see Chapter 6), and/or print it if you want (see Chapter 10)—all this without even opening the document!

A Paneless Way to Work with Multiple Windows

You can open multiple documents at one time, with each of your "children" running around in its own document window. Once several documents are open, you can copy or move text between them, or simply refer to one document as you edit another. You can scroll through each document, and make changes as you would at any other time. However, you can only make changes to one document at a time—the *active document*.

Doing the Document Shuffle

Normally, the active document takes up the entire screen, but you can divide the screen equally among all open documents by opening the Window menu and selecting either Tile or Cascade. Jump between documents using one of these two methods:

☞ Open the Window menu and select the document from the list displayed at the bottom.

Or

☞ If more than one window is displayed on-screen, click inside a window to make it active. You can also press **Ctrl+F6** to move back and forth between displayed windows.

You close document windows in the normal way, by saving the file, and then closing the window. You'll learn how to do this in the next chapter.

Seeing Double

Sometimes you want to work in two sections of the same document at the same time. For example, if you wanted to move or copy text within a long document, scrolling back and forth would be a waste of time. Instead, just open two windows of the same document. With the document already open, open the Window menu and select New Window (press **Alt+W**, and then **N**). A message will appear, telling you that the document is already open.

The document that you are currently working in, the **active document**, contains the insertion point. If more than one document window is being displayed on-screen, the active document's title bar appears darker than those of the other document windows.

Tiled windows are arranged so that they divide the screen into equal parts. For example, two tiled windows would each occupy one-half of the screen.

Cascaded windows are arranged so that they overlap, with each window's title bar clearly displayed.

You can resize and/or move document windows to get them "just right." If you need a quick review, see Chapter 3.

Only one of the two windows will contain an editable copy of the document. You will not be able to make changes within the window whose title bar contains "Read Only."

Click **OK**, or press **Y**. Arrange the two windows with the **W**indow **Ti**le or the **W**indow **C**ascade command.

To move between the two windows, click inside a window to make it active, or press **Ctrl+F6** to toggle back and forth. You can get really fancy and select different views for each window (see Chapter 7 for more information).

The Least You Need to Know

Congratulations! You now have your Document Doctorate. Let's review what you learned:

- ☞ To open a new document window, use the **File N**ew command.

- ☞ To open an existing document, click on the **Open** button on the Default SmartIcons set or use the **File O**pen command.

- ☞ If you're not sure you have the right document, read its description or use **P**review to view the document before you open it.

- ☞ You can open up to nine documents at the same time. To move to another document window, open the **W**indow menu and select the document you want. If more than one window is displayed on-screen, you can click on a window or press **Ctrl+F6** to make another window active.

- ☞ You can work on two sections of the same document with the **W**indow **N**ew Window command. You can even change how you view each section of the document.

Chapter 9

Saving Your Docs for a Rainy Day

In This Chapter

- ☛ How to save a new document
- ☛ Valid names for your files
- ☛ Creating a copy of a document
- ☛ Saving your documents automatically
- ☛ Saving backups of your documents onto diskettes
- ☛ Closing document windows

Save a document, save a life. Okay, maybe it's not that dramatic, but by saving your documents often, you can save yourself a lot of time and trouble when something happens to your computer (such as a power failure). Notice I said "when," not if. These things happen to all of us—it's inevitable—so you might as well be prepared.

If you don't want to bother with remembering to save files regularly, you can configure Ami Pro so it saves your files at *periodic intervals*.

> **By the Way . . .**
>
> I like that term "periodic intervals," don't you? I try to use it often to make me sound smart: "In the morning, I need coffee at *periodic intervals.*" Feel free to try it yourself: "Before I found this wonderful book to help me, I used to toss my computer against the wall at *periodic intervals.* Now I toss my computer manual."

When Should I Save a Document?

You'll always want to save your document before you exit Ami Pro (because otherwise, it's gone-o!). But you may also want to save the document periodically during a long work session.

Any time is a great time to save your documents, but I like to save them just before I attempt some complicated task, and again when I finish that task correctly. I also save documents just prior to printing.

Knowing that you should save your documents frequently is one thing; remembering to do it is another. You can set Ami Pro to save your work for you at (ahem) periodic intervals. Stay tuned; you'll learn how it's done later in this chapter.

DOS stores information in **files**. Anything can be placed in a file: a memo, a budget report, or even a graphic image (like a picture of a boat or a computer). Each document you create using Ami Pro is stored in its own file. Files always have a **file name** to identify them.

A Document by Any Other File Name Would Still Spell as Sweet

Shakespeare would argue that there's not much in a file name, but I have to disagree. Naming your documents so you can identify them easily will save you lots of time and trouble when you go to locate them. DOS must agree with Shakespeare, though, because DOS gives you very little room to be informative when naming your files.

Each file has a first and a last name. The last name (called the *extension*) helps to identify the file's type: Ami Pro uses the extension .SAM to identify your Ami Pro files. You give your documents their first names, which can be as long as eight characters. Let me give you some examples:

93BUDGET.SAM

TO_DO.SAM

4THQTR.SAM

COVLETTR.SAM

WHATS_UP.SAM

RESUME.SAM

By the Way . . .

Most word processors use the extension .DOC to identify their files as *documents*. Ami Pro decided to stake its own claim by using the unique .SAM extension. What .SAM stands for is anyone's guess—could it be someone's initials, or the name of the programmer who created Ami Pro? Or could it be the name of someone's dog, or a long lost love, "Please come back to me, Sam!" My guess (although it's rather boring) is that .SAM stands for **S**tandard **AM**i Pro document, but feel free to make up something more exotic.

You can use letters and numbers, and even an underscore as a substitute space (you can't use actual spaces in file names), but you can't use more than eight characters (bummer). If you forget and type a twelve-letter name, for instance, Ami Pro just ignores the last four letters. Don't worry about the extension; Ami Pro adds the .SAM extension for you.

Now that you know how to name your files, let's get down to the business of saving them.

There's a First Time for Everything: Saving a Document

Saving your document for the first time is a little bit more complex than saving it later on because you must answer some basic questions (such as "What do you want to call this thing?") before Ami Pro can save your work. Here's the play-by-play:

First, click on the **Save** button, which appears on just about every SmartIcon set, or, if you have time to kill, select **File** from the main menu and choose **Save**, or press **Ctrl+S**. Then type the name for your file. Remember not to use more than eight characters. Also, you don't have to add the .SAM extension—but if you do, separate it from the file name with a period, as in CH09.SAM.

Type a name for your file.

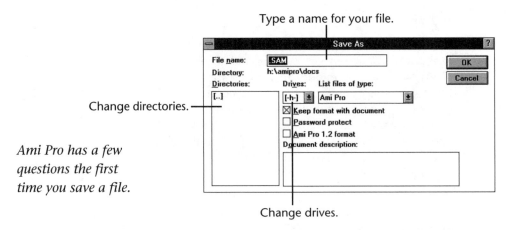

Change directories.

Change drives.

Ami Pro has a few questions the first time you save a file.

If a file with the name you want to use already exists, Ami Pro will ask whether you want to replace the existing file. If you don't, type a different file name.

If you want to save your file in a different drive, select a different disk drive from the drop-down list box. If you need to change to another directory, click on that directory, or press **Alt+D** and use the down arrow key to select the directory.

You'll learn about some other options in a minute, but if you're done saving your file, press **Enter** or click **OK** to close the dialog box and save your file.

Know Your Options

There are some additional file saving options you should get to know. To protect your document against changes, use the **Password** protect option. If you make a document *password protected*, no one (including you) can open the document without the secret knock or the password of up to 14 characters.

Here's what to do to password-protect a document: from the Save As dialog box, press **Alt+P** or click on **Password** protect. Click **OK** or press **Enter** to close this dialog box, and another one appears. Type a password (make it one that you can remember) and press **Enter**. Type the same password again to verify it, and then press **Enter**.

> ### By the Way . . .
>
> You cannot open a protected document without the password, no matter who you are—so be sure to write it down!
>
> Also, if you want to "unprotect" the document later on, you have the right to do so. Just use the File Save **As** command, and verify that the Password protect option is *not* on. Click **OK** or press **Enter** to save the file with its same name. You'll be asked if you know what you're doing, so just answer **Yes** (or press **Y**). The file will then be saved unprotected.

You can also enter a description for your document when you save it. This description makes it easier to identify the document later on, and can make up for the short file name. For example, I might type the description "Home Budget for 1993," which tells me a lot more than the file name HOBUD93.SAM does.

To enter a description, press **Alt+O** or click inside the Document description area. Then type a short note to yourself. When you open the document later, the description will be displayed at the bottom of the Open dialog box, making it easy to figure out whether or not this is the document you want.

Don't leave document windows open if you're done with them; they just add to screen clutter and make it more difficult to work. (I'm writing this as I search for a disk under tons of paper and other stuff on my desk. I thought you'd appreciate the irony.) Close document windows when you're through (after saving them first, of course!). Also, if you continue working on your document after you save it, remember to save the file *again* before you exit Ami Pro or close the document's window.

To close a document's window, save the document first (okay, enough already!), and then open the **File** menu and select **Close**, or double-click on the document's **Control-menu box**.

Saving Once, Saving Twice

After a file has been saved for the first time, whenever you use the File **S**ave command or the Save button, your document is simply saved to the disk with the same name you used when you first saved it. This process updates the existing file with the changes you've made.

But what if you're creating a revision to a document, and you want to save this version under a new name? To save a document under a different file name, you need its birth certificate, Social Security card, several IRS tax forms, and the Save As command.

Select **F**ile from the main menu, and choose the Save As command. If you use a keyboard, press **Alt+F** and A. (*Do not use the Save button on the Default SmartIcon set, because it saves the file without allowing you to make any changes.*) Now don't think you've gone crazy; this is the same dialog box that appears when you first save a file. Why should Ami Pro use two boxes when one will do?

Type the new name for your file. Remember not to use more than eight characters. As before, you don't have to add the .SAM extension, but if you do, separate it from the file name with a period, as in CH09.SAM.

If you want to save this copy of your file in a different drive or directory, select a different disk drive from the Drives drop-down list box. If you need to change to another directory, click on that directory, or press **Alt+D** and use the down arrow key to select a directory.

Since this is the same dialog box, if you want to protect your document against changes or add a new description, follow the directions given earlier. When you're done, press **Enter** or click on **OK**, and Ami Pro saves the document with the name you specified.

Living in a Worry-Free World

Earlier on, I mentioned being careful by saving your documents often. When you save your documents, usually you save them to the hard disk; but if your computer itself goes on vacation, what do you do? Well, as part of your daily regimen, you should back up your files (a fancy way of saying "Make a copy of them") onto diskettes. These diskettes could be used on another PC while yours is in the shop, and later they could be used to restore any broken data on your PC. For example, when you get your PC back from the shop and you try to open a document, you may or may not have trouble doing so—it depends on what the problem originally was. Anyway, to live in a worry-free world, copy your documents onto diskettes so you don't lose them.

How to do that? Well, what I do is copy them onto diskettes once a week. (You can do your backups more often if you've got the time—believe me, you can never be too careful.) I open the File menu and select File Management (press **Alt+F** and then **F** again). Whoopee! A dialog box we've never seen before! Actually, this is more than a dialog box, it's a miniature program called the Ami Pro File Manager.

You can use File Manager to manage your documents (copy them, delete them, and so on). Start by changing directories to locate your documents. Click on the documents you want to back up (copy to diskette), and then open the File menu again and select Copy (press **Alt+F** and then **C**). A dialog box will appear. Insert a diskette into one of your diskette drives and under **To**, type either **A:** or **B:** (the letter depends on which diskette drive you're using). Then click **OK** or press **Enter**. You may see a little box asking you what options you want to use (for example, if your document contains a picture, do you want the picture file copied to the disk too?). Click on the options to select them, and then click **OK** or press **Enter**. That's it until next week! Open the File menu and select Exit (press **Alt+F** and then **X**) to return to your regularly scheduled program—Ami Pro.

Putting Ami Pro on Automatic

You won't have to worry when a storm shuts down your computer's power if you've saved your data recently. But if you're the kind of person who gets so involved in working that you forget to save, you may want to have Ami Pro save your changes automatically. Use this option to put Ami Pro on "automatic." Just open the Tools menu (press **Alt+L**) and select User Setup (press **U**). In the dialog box, click on Auto timed save or press **Alt+A**. Enter the number of minutes you want Ami Pro to wait between automatic saves. (Press **Tab** or click inside the box to enter a number.) You can enter any number between 1 and 99, but I recommend 10 or 15 minutes. When you're through, press **Enter** or click **OK**.

Before closing a document, you should save it. When you exit Ami Pro, all files are closed automatically, so you should save your files before you quit.

Reverting to the Last Saved Version of a Document

Well, now you're a saving maniac. You know how to save a document—and when. But what do you do if you've saved a document, and then moved or copied some text or added a graphic that looks horrible? How do you get back to the pretty document you had before you mucked it up?

This happens to me more times than I care to mention—so I've learned how to fix it. That's why I save my documents whenever I have something that I like, before I edit some more and mess it up. To get back to the last saved version of a document, open the File menu (press **Alt+F**) and select Revert to Saved (press **R**). The magic Ami Pro fairy will undo any changes you've made since you last saved the document.

Closing a Document and Going Home

My mom was always yelling at us to close the door: "Are we trying to heat the outside?" Just like doors, you should close document windows after you're finished working with them. Of course, you probably won't have your mother to remind you, but remembering to close windows when you're through will eliminate clutter and make it easier for you to work.

> Be careful not to double-click on the bigger square just above the document window Control-menu box; that will cause you to exit Ami Pro.

To close the active document window, double-click on its **Control-menu box** (that's the square with a dash in it, in the upper left corner of the document window). If you are using a keyboard, press **Ctrl+F4** to close the active document window. If you've made some changes, you'll be asked if you want to save them. Click **Yes** or press **Y**.

If you have more than one document open, the other windows will be unaffected by your actions.

The Least You Need to Know

As we bring this chapter to a "close," let's review what we've learned:

- Always save your documents before exiting Ami Pro, and before and after any complicated task. It's also a good idea to save your document prior to printing.

- File names consist of up to eight characters, with a three-character extension. Ami Pro documents use a .SAM extension, as in CH09.SAM.

- To save a document, click on the **Save** button on the Default SmartIcon set.

continues

continued

☞ You can save a copy of your current document under a new name with the Save **As** command on the File menu.

☞ To set up Ami Pro so it saves documents automatically, open the Tools menu and select **U**ser Setup. In the dialog box, click on **A**uto timed save and enter the number of minutes you want Ami Pro to wait between automatic saves. When you're through, press **Enter** or click **OK**.

☞ You can close a document window after you've saved the file to get it out of your way. To close a document window, double-click on the window's **Control-menu box** or press **Ctrl+F4**.

Chapter 10
Hold the Presses, It's Time to Print!

In This Chapter

- ☞ Printing your document
- ☞ Selecting certain pages or text to print
- ☞ Printing just the current page
- ☞ Printing multiple copies of a document
- ☞ Changing the orientation of the printed page
- ☞ Printing an envelope
- ☞ What to do when your printer is having a bad day
- ☞ Selecting which printer to use if you have more than one

After I've wrestled with Ami Pro for hours trying to get a document to look exactly the way I want it to, I sometimes get this overpowering urge to jump up and say, "See? I did this!"

You might be experiencing something like that now since your document is just about ready to print. With the help of this chapter, you'll soon be holding your new document, and if you experience any problems along the way, there's a troubleshooting section at the end of the chapter to help you out.

A Sneak Preview Before You Print Is a Good Idea

Before you print your document, you should look at it using Layout Mode. As you learned in Chapter 7, Layout Mode displays your document in a format matching what actually prints on the page. Layout Mode is the default display mode for Ami Pro, so you may not need to do anything before you print. But if you've been using Draft Mode or Outline Mode to make speedy changes to your document, you'll want to switch to Layout Mode now. How do you do that? It's easy: just open the View menu and select Layout Mode (press **Alt+V**, and then **L**.)

 You can also switch between Draft and Layout viewing modes by clicking on the **Draft/Layout** button, conveniently located on the Long Documents and Proofing SmartIcon sets.

 You can switch between Outline and Layout viewing modes by clicking the **Outline/Layout** button, now playing at a SmartIcon set near you (the Editing, Long Documents, Proofing, and Working Together SmartIcon sets).

 If you want to see a full page or maybe two pages at once, select Full Page or Facing Pages from the **View** menu. You can also click on the **Full Page/Layout** button on the Default or the Editing SmartIcon set to change to Full Page view.

The Printed Word

 It's always a good idea to save a document before you print it, in case you run into printer errors or other problems. Click on the **Save** button on just about any of the SmartIcon sets or use the **Save** command on the File menu. (You can also press **Ctrl+S** to save the current document.)

Printing the active document is easy, especially if you want to print the entire document, and you want only one copy of it. Later in this chapter, you'll learn how you can be selective in what you're printing. But for now, let's start with the basics.

To print a document with the mouse, just click on the **Print** button located on just about all of the SmartIcon sets. The active document will start printing according to the print defaults—Ami Pro's out-of-the-box settings which specify printing for just one copy of the entire document. If you want to print more than one copy (or less than the entire document), you'll need to use the **File Print** command described next.

To print the current document using the keyboard, select the **Print** command on the **File** menu, or press **Ctrl+P**. A dialog box appears, allowing you to change the print defaults (such as the number of copies you want). In later sections of this chapter, you'll learn what each of these options is for—but if you just want to print one copy of the entire document, press **Enter**, and that's it!

If you have problems printing, check out the troubleshooting section later in this chapter.

If you need to stop the print job while Ami Pro is still processing it, press **Esc**. If the printer runs out of paper, a dialog box will appear and tell you so. You'll be able to choose Retry or Cancel. Load more paper and choose **Retry**.

Printing Only Part of a Document

You can print only certain pages in a document if you want. For example, maybe one page was misprinted and you want to reprint it with corrections, or perhaps you need only one section of a complex document. Here's what to do.

Select the **Print** command from the **File** menu. (Do not use the Print button on the SmartIcon sets; by default, it prints *all* the pages of a document.) Surprise! It's a box.

You can print only part of a document if you want.

Choose which pages to print from your selection.

Enter the first page number you want to print.

Enter the last page number you want to print.

First, click on From or press **Alt+F**, and enter the number of the first page you want to print. Press **Tab** or click in the To box, and enter the number of the last page you want to print. (If you want to print to the end of the document, just skip this step.) When you're done, press **Enter** or click **OK**.

As an alternative, you can print the current page only by choosing Current page or pressing **Alt+C**. You can print only odd or even pages within the selected range by choosing Even pages (press **Alt+E**) or Odd pages (Press **Alt+D**).

If you have a printer that allows you to select the number of copies to print on some kind of control panel, you may want to use that option instead of having Ami Pro print your copies for you. When Ami Pro prints multiple copies, it reprocesses the document over and over, using more time than your printer would to print the same number of copies.

I'll Take Two!

If you need more than one copy of your document, Ami Pro can print multiple copies for you, saving you the time of standing in line at the copier.

Start out by selecting the **Print** command from the File menu. (Do not use the Print button in the SmartIcon sets; by default, it prints only one copy of a document.) When that dialog box appears, type the number of copies you want under Number of copies. If you're using the keyboard, press **Alt+N** to move to Number of copies, and then type your number.

With **Collate**, Ami Pro not only slices and dices, but it collates, too—by printing all of one copy first, and then all of the next. First, access the print options by clicking on **Options** or pressing **Alt+O**. Then select Collate by clicking on it or pressing **Alt+C**. When you're completely finished, choose **OK** or press **Enter**. Press **Enter** again, and your document will start to print.

The Great American Landscape Mode

You can print your document in *Portrait* mode or *Landscape* mode. To change the orientation of pages within your document, just follow along with me.

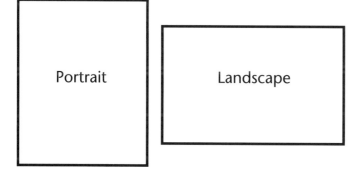

Have it your way: landscape or portrait

First, open the **Page** menu and choose the **Modify Page Layout** command. Keyboarders, press **Alt+P**, and **M**. Next, click on **Page** settings or press **Alt+P**. Now it's time to pick a page orientation. Click on either the **Portrait** or the **Landscape** option button. If you're using a keyboard, press **Alt+P** or **Alt+L**. When you're finished, choose **OK**.

Honorable Mention: Some Interesting Print Options

There are some additional print options you may want to use from time to time, if for no other reason than that they're cool.

When you use **portrait orientation**, your document is oriented so that it is longer than it is wide, as in 8 ½ by 11 inches. This is the normal orientation of most documents.

When you use **landscape orientation**, your document is oriented so that it is wider than it is long, as in 11 by 8 ½ inches.

When you change the orientation of a page, it changes all the pages within your document. You may find this inconvenient (read: annoying). For instance, let's say you're trying to print a report with portrait pages, and you have a chart at the end that you want to print in landscape orientation. Well, you can do this by inserting a new page layout within your document, on the page with the chart. So don't despair; you'll find out how to insert page layouts in Chapter 16.

A **frame** is a small box in which you place text or pictures so you can maneuver them easily within your document.

Power fields are codes that update information in a document based on changing conditions, such as changing data, page numbers, figure references, and so on.

Here's a listing:

Reverse Order   Prints the document last page first, first page last.

Collate   We've already used this one, so get out of here. Okay, just kidding. Use this option when you print multiple copies to print each copy completely, one at a time, so you can keep them in order.

Crop marks   Useful in typesetting, this option prints crop marks 1/2 inch outside of the margins.

Without pictures   Prints only the actual text, without any pictures. The places where pictures would appear are marked by boxes called *frames*.

With notes   Prints on the last page any notes that are attached to the document.

With doc description   Prints the document information as the first page.

On preprinted form   When you use this option, Ami Pro prints only text, and not the additional lines and shading you may have used to create a nice looking document.

Update fields   Updates the results of any *power fields* prior to printing.

Bin Options   Select either the upper tray, lower tray, or the manual feed areas of your printer. You may also send the first page of your document to a different print area from the rest of the document, in case you want to print the first page on letterhead and the rest of the document on plain paper.

To select any of these print options, just select **O**ptions from within the Print dialog box. (If you're using a keyboard, press **Alt+O**.) Select an option by clicking on it or pressing Alt plus the underlined letter (shown here in bold). Click **OK** or press **Enter**, and you'll be returned to the Print dialog box. Click **OK** or press **Enter** again, and your document will start printing.

The Envelope, Please

Ami Pro makes it incredibly easy to prepare an envelope for a letter. The only thing that you'll find hard about this is getting your printer to print the darn thing—so I'll give you some tips in a moment. First, the easy part.

If you've included more than one address in your letter, start out by selecting the delivery address. If you didn't include an address in your letter (or if you included just the delivery address), that's okay—just skip this step.

Click on the **Envelope** button on the Default SmartIcon set, or select the Print Envelope command from the File menu (press **Alt+F**, and **V**). When the dialog box appears, if you didn't select an address earlier, Ami Pro will select the first address it finds. If that's not the right one, click on **Cancel** or press **Esc**, and then select the delivery address yourself.

Select an envelope size by clicking on it or by pressing **Alt** plus the selection letter. Got an odd-sized envelope? That's okay; just open the More envelope sizes list box, and select a size or enter the dimensions of the envelope yourself.

To print your address on the envelope, click on **P**rint return address or press **Alt+P**. Your name will appear in the **R**eturn address area, but if this is your first envelope, you'll have to enter your address. Just press **Tab** or click in the **R**eturn address area and type your address (press **Delete** to delete the message that appears there). To save your new address, click on Add Address or press **Alt+A**. Whenever you use the Print Envelope option from now on, your address will already be there, so you will be able to skip this step. You can add other addresses, and then select them at the time of printing with the Return address **n**ames list box.

Before we print our envelope, let's check some of the options. Click on the Options button or press **Alt+O**. If you want, you can change the printer you want to use, and/or the feed location for the envelope. Click on the appropriate option, or press **Alt** plus the underlined letter. Click **OK** or press **Enter** to return to the Print Envelope dialog box. Click **OK** or press **Enter** to print your envelope.

Some Quick Tips for Printing Envelopes

If you have a laser printer:

☞ You basically need a special thing called an *envelope feeder*. If you don't have one, check your manual for instructions on how to feed an envelope in some kind of "straight-through" path that bypasses the nasty twists and turns that normal paper takes through your laser printer. With my HP Laserjet IIP, I press a little switch on the right-hand side marked with little symbols indicating the path that the paper will take. By choosing the path that looks like a U, the envelope feeds in and then right back at me, which causes it to get less wrinkled.

☞ Check your manual to see if the envelope is supposed to be inserted in the center of the feed slot or against one edge (lasers vary on how they want this done).

☞ Most important of all: don't skimp on quality. Buy envelopes that are made for a laser. Other envelopes practically melt from the heat, and really gum up the works (if you don't mind the pun).

If you have a dot-matrix printer:

☞ Line up the left edge of the envelope against the left edge of the paper feed.

☞ Move the tractor feed so the top edge of the envelope is even with the print head. Ami Pro will move the envelope up about a half inch before it prints anything, so don't worry that your address will fall off the edge.

Printer Jams and Other Problems You Might Encounter

There is probably nothing more frustrating than coaxing a reluctant printer to spit out some text. After putting all your hard work into creating the perfect report, the last thing you want to deal with is a problem printer. If you encounter problems, check the printer cables to be sure they're plugged in tightly, and verify that the printer is on and on-line (look for a button labeled *on-line, ready,* or *select,* which controls this). Here are some other things to watch out for:

If you get a message from Ami Pro asking if you want to retry, examine the reason for the error. If the printer wasn't on, turn it on and then retry the print job. If the printer ran out of paper, replace it and retry. If the printer jammed, retry if you have a laser, but cancel if you have a dot-matrix. (A laser printer has a better memory than a dot-matrix, and can pick up where it left off.)

If you get something to print, but it looks like the printer is on drugs, you may not have the printer set up for use with Windows. Or if you have more than one printer, you may have chosen the wrong printer for this document. An upcoming section talks about how to choose a printer.

Now here are some specifics you can try, depending on the type of printer you have.

If You Have a Laser Printer

Use the right paper and load it correctly. Use special laser paper (I recommend 20-lb. and not a cheaper type of paper). Laser paper has a texture that is easier for the laser printer to grab as it moves through the printer. Do not use stuff that isn't specifically designed for a laser printer; use *laser* labels, *laser* transparencies, etc. Colored paper is okay, but avoid papers with dusty surfaces.

When the paper gets jammed (stuck), remove it. Pop it open and carefully remove the errant page, just as you would with a copier.

My laser printer seems okay, but nothing is coming out. You may need to form-feed (eject) the paper by taking the printer off-line (press the **On-Line** button) and then pressing the **Form Feed** button. Then press the

OOPS!

Watch out for hot parts—a laser printer is full of them. Most are labeled with warnings, but be safe: try not to touch any part unless absolutely necessary.

Usually laser printers will only eject a page when that page is full. (I wish someone had told me that when I first got my laser!)

Ami Pro does have to do some work before it turns over your document to Print Manager, and that preparation time may take anywhere from a few seconds to a few minutes depending on the complexity of your document. While it's preparing the document, you just sit and wait. If you're one of those "gotta go" types, select background printing, and Ami Pro splits its time between your editing tasks and processing the printer information. Let Ami Pro do its stuff, and you can get back to work (although a bit more slowly).

To enable background printing, open the Tools menu and select User Setup. Click on Options and select Print in background. Click OK twice. Now any document you print will be printed in the background. To turn this option off later, follow these steps again, and deselect Print in background.

On-Line button again to put the printer back into service. This should get the paper to come out.

If You Have a Dot-Matrix Printer

Use the right paper and load it correctly. Be sure that the continuous-feed paper (if you use it) is not caught on anything, and that the perforation between pages is just barely above the print head when the printer is turned on.

When the paper gets jammed (stuck), remove it. If you have a dot-matrix printer, turn it off first, and then use the print knob to back the paper out. (Turning the knob while the printer is on may lead to expensive repairs later.) Avoid the urge to rip the paper out. It'll tear and you'll spend the rest of the day with a pair of tweezers trying to pick out the last remnants.

Everything is printing on one smeary line of ink. Your printer isn't getting the order from the computer to advance the paper before it prints the next line. You can fix this by flipping a small switch called a *DIP switch*. The DIP switch is usually located in some "convenient location," such as the back of your printer, or even inside. Look in your manual for the location of the DIP switches. Each switch has a particular purpose, and the one you're interested in is called "LF after CR" or "Add linefeed" or some such. Turn your printer off, flip the switch, and then turn the printer on and try again.

Everything is coming out double-spaced even though it's single-spaced in Ami Pro. This problem is the opposite of the single smeary line of ink. Only this time, the computer is sending the order to advance the paper, and the printer is adding its own advance. Locate the "LF after CR" or "Add linefeed" DIP switch, turn your printer off, flip the switch, and then try printing again.

Printers and the Wonderful World of Windows

All the printing for Ami Pro is actually handled by another Windows program, the Print Manager. When you installed Windows, you told the Print Manager what kind of printer you had. When you print a document in Ami Pro, it simply packages it up and sends it to the Print Manager, and the Print Manager sends it to your printer.

When you're printing a document within Ami Pro, and the **Printing** message disappears from the screen, your print job has been turned over to Print Manager. So if you have any further problems, you need to go there to handle them.

The Print Manager's best feature is that you can pretty much forget about it. Once a printer is set up for Windows, it's set up for *all* Windows-based programs, including Ami Pro. Print Manager also is adept at handling multiple print jobs, so you don't need to wait until a printer is done printing before you start working again or print another document.

Although this book is not about how to use Windows, it's kind of hard to avoid the subject, since you're using a Windows program. Here are some quick steps for cancelling a print job within Print Manager—but if you "don't do Windows," refer to Chapter 3 for help in deciphering these instructions.

From within Ami Pro, press **Ctrl+Esc** to bring up the Task List. Select **Print Manager**. All the current print jobs will be displayed. If you want to start a print job over because the paper jammed (or for some other reason), just highlight the job you want to cancel and then click on **Delete**.

Ami Pro prints all documents in the background until that option is turned off.

Print Manager starts itself when you print a document, and closes itself when the document is done printing. However, there's an exception to this rule. If you open the Print Manager window (by double-clicking on its minimized icon, or by selecting it from the Task List), and then re-minimize it after the print jobs are completed, Print Manager will remain open and minimized until you close it or exit Windows. Why? Who knows? It's just one of those things.

You can do other fancy stuff while you're here—such as reordering the priority of print jobs (just drag the print job to wherever you want it to be in the print queue), or temporarily stopping and resuming the operation of the printer (use the **Pause** and **Resume** buttons).

Minimize the Print Manager window when you're done (click on the **Minimize** button). CAUTION: If you *close* Print Manager at this point, you'll cancel all the jobs waiting to be printed.

By the Way...

While Print Manager still has print jobs waiting to print, its little tiny icon will appear at the bottom of your Windows desktop. So, as an alternative to using the Task List, you can open Print Manager from your desktop. Double-click on that icon to open the Print Manager window just as you would any other window.

The **default printer** is the printer that was set up when Windows was installed.

Embarrassment of Riches: Choosing from Several Printers

If you're lucky enough to have a choice of printers to use, you should tell Ami Pro when you *start* a new document which printer you'll want to use later when you print. If you don't specify, Ami Pro will use the default printer.

To change the default printer that's used with Ami Pro, open the **File** menu and choose the **Printer Setup** command, or press **Alt+F** and **T**. When the dialog box appears, click on the printer you wish to use, and then click **OK**. If the printer you want to use is not listed, you will need to install the printer through the Windows Control Panel. Get someone to help you.

The Least You Need to Know

Sometimes getting your document to print can be pretty irritating, but the whole process will go a bit smoother if you remember these things:

- ☞ Before you print your document, you may want to view it first in Layout Mode.

- ☞ Also before you print, save your document by clicking on the **Save** button on the Default SmartIcon set.

- ☞ To print one copy of all pages of the document, click on the **Print** button on the Default SmartIcon set.

- ☞ Use the **P**rint command on the **F**ile menu to print selected pages or text within a document.

- ☞ You can also use the **P**rint command on the **F**ile menu to print multiple copies of your document.

- ☞ Use the **M**odify Page Layout command on the **P**age menu to change between portrait and landscape orientations for all pages of a document.

- ☞ Click on the **Envelope** button on the Default SmartIcon set, or use the Print Envelopes command on the **F**ile menu to prepare an envelope for your letter.

- ☞ If you want to cancel a print job or change the priority of a print job, use Print Manager.

- ☞ If you have more than one printer available, select the printer to use with the **F**ile Printer Setup command. After the dialog box opens, select the printer you want to use and click **OK**.

This page suitable for doodling.

Part II
Document Makeovers

The irony about using makeup is that most women spend hours trying to look as if they haven't done anything at all. I think of formatting as "makeup" for a document, and in this section I'll show you how to "apply it." And believe me, if you spend two hours formatting a document, someone will definitely notice.

Chapter 11
Developing Your Character(s): Changing How Text Looks

In This Chapter

- ☞ Choosing the font (typeface) of text
- ☞ Quick ways to change the size of text
- ☞ Selecting various character formats, such as bold or underline
- ☞ Changing multiple formats at one time
- ☞ Copying character formatting to other text

Character formatting is the process of changing the appearance of text. For example, through character formatting you can make a word bold or underlined. You can also change the size of text (its *point size*), making it bigger or smaller, and you can change its style by choosing a different *font*. Sometimes Ami Pro refers to a text's font as its *face* (from the word typeface); but the two terms mean the same thing.

Character formatting can be used to make titles, headings, and individual words stand out. Use character formatting to emphasize a point, create a mood, and visually organize your documents. (End of commercial; we now return you to our regularly scheduled chapter.)

Paragon font

Ariel font

Paradise font

Mystical font

The font you select should reflect the mood of your document.

SPEAK LIKE A GEEK

A **font**, sometimes called simply a face, is any set of characters that share the same **typeface** (style or design). Examples are Times Roman and Arial. Technically, "font" describes the combination of the typeface and the point size of a character, as in Times Roman 12-point, but many people use it to describe only a character's style or typeface.

Point size describes the type size of a particular character. There are 72 points in an inch.

Applying Makeup to Your Text

You can change text formatting in one of three ways:

☛ **By changing to a particular paragraph style.** The *style* of a paragraph defines its characteristics, such as its margins, indentations, and tab settings. The style also defines the type of font used, the point size of text, and other text characteristics (such as bold and underlined). So if you want to change the font used in several paragraphs (all with the same style), just change the style definition and you change all the related paragraphs. You'll be stylin' by Chapter 14.

☛ **By changing the text as you type.** You can apply character formatting as you type a word or a heading, or you can go back later and select the text and change its formatting. (I use both methods, depending on my mood.) If you change character formatting as you type, remember to turn it off when you finish typing the text you want to affect. (Think of it as a light switch; if you turn it on, you have to turn it off.) If you don't turn formatting off, the formatting you turn on will apply to the rest of the document until you turn it off. Turn off the text format by selecting it again; you can then continue typing.

☞ **By selecting the text you want to change after you type it** and applying different formatting. If you go back and select text after you've typed it, only the text you select is changed. So if you want formatting to apply to some particular text, first select it. Drag the mouse over the text to select it, or press and hold the **Shift** key as you use the arrow keys to highlight the text. Then choose the formatting you want. More about this in a minute.

You can use either the mouse or the keyboard to change character formatting. Again, I use a combination of both, depending on what I'm doing at the time.

Font Memories: Changing the Text Style

The type of font you use helps to set the style of your document: is it fun and light, or crisp and businesslike? One tip if you're new to fonts— don't overdo it (it's very easy, believe me). At most you want to use only two or three font styles: one or two for different headings, and one for text. Vary the size of text (point size) to create sections in your document, rather than choosing a different font (typeface).

Department Budget Report

This month, we managed to take more calls, handle more special requests, and yet we didn't use a lot of overtime. I think you'll be pleased with the numbers: (see Attachment.)

As you can see, we did very well at increasing our volume while decreasing our costs. How did we do it? With the training I was able to provide my employees, they responded by handling calls faster and more efficiently. Jane, Pat, and Bill did an especially outstanding job.

How Can We Maintain This Trend?

I propose that we install a new telephone messaging system, such as the Caller 2000. This will allow me to direct the volume of calls to the fastest workers, increasing the chances of our clients reaching a representative. Also, with the Caller 2000, a customized message system will allow the caller to pick and choose from several options, so they reach the department they want with the least amount of hassle.

Too many fonts. Arghh!

One font for the headings, one for the text. Ahhh.

DEPARTMENT BUDGET REPORT

This month, we managed to take more calls, handle more special requests, and yet we didn't use a lot of overtime. I think you'll be pleased with the numbers (See Attachment.)

As you can see, we did very well at increasing our volume while decreasing our costs. How did we do it? With the training I was able to provide my employees, they responded by handling calls faster and more efficiently. Jane, Pat, and Bill did an especially outstanding job.

How Can We Maintain This Trend?

I propose that we install a new telephone messaging system, such as the Caller 2000. This will allow me to direct the volume of calls to the fastest workers, increasing the chances of our clients reaching a representative. Also, with the Caller 2000, a customized message system will allow the caller to pick and choose from several options, so they reach the department they want with the least amount of hassle.

I'm not fond of using too many fonts.

By the Way . . .

If you have more than one printer, make sure you select the correct printer before you start working; the printer that's selected determines what fonts will print correctly. Change from printer to printer with the **File Printer Setup** command. Back up to the previous chapter for more details.

Select a font from this box.

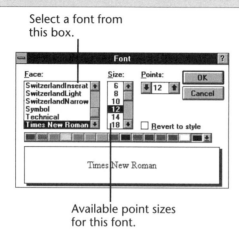

Available point sizes for this font.

Use this dialog box to change the font and point size of text.

Remember that you can change the font and point size of text—either before you enter it, or after the fact. First select the text you want to change. Open the Text menu and select Font (press **Alt+T** and **F**). Change the font (remember that Ami Pro calls this the "face") by clicking on a font, or by pressing **Alt+F** and using the arrow keys to highlight one. Change the point size by either selecting one from the **S**ize list or entering a number under **P**oints.

 You can easily change the font and/or point size of text with the Face and Point Size buttons located on the status bar, or with the Font button located on the Editing SmartIcon set.

 You can also use the Increase Size and Decrease Size buttons on the Macro Goodies SmartIcon set to increase or decrease selected text by one size. If you're typing text, remember to change the font and point size back to normal later on. Just repeat these steps to change it back.

Getting Back to Normal

If you want to remove all character formatting from a section of text, select it, and reverse what you did. For example, if you changed some text from 12 point to 24 point, follow the instructions given here to change it back to 12 point.

You can also press **Ctrl+N** or select the Normal command on the **Text** menu to remove formatting. Your text will take on the characteristics of the paragraph's style, and will lose all the additional formatting you may have applied using these instructions. You'll learn more about styles in Chapters 14 and 15.

Making a Bold Statement (or Italic, or Underlined, Etc.)

There are many different kinds of character formatting:

Bold	*Italic*	~~Strikethrough~~
<u>Underline</u>	Word <u>Underline</u>	<u>Double Underline</u>
Initial Caps	SMALL CAPS	UPPER CASE
script	Super^{script}	Sub_{script}

For extra emphasis, you can "combine" any of these formats to create words that are (for example) **bold and underlined**, or *italic and double-underlined*. Ami Pro supports only one kind of underline per character, however, so you can't have such combinations as double-word underline.

Mouseketeers: How to Change Character Formatting

Because there are so many ways to select the character format you want, I thought it would be helpful to include the details in separate sections for keyboard and mouse. First, the mouse ways.

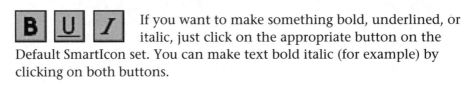 If you want to make something bold, underlined, or italic, just click on the appropriate button on the Default SmartIcon set. You can make text bold italic (for example) by clicking on both buttons.

If you want to make text anything else (such as strikethrough or double underline), you need to access the Text menu. The Text menu is covered in the keyboard section that follows. If you use certain effects often, such as word underline, strikethrough, or initial caps, add those buttons to one of the SmartIcon sets. See Chapter 4 for details.

Keyboarders: How to Change Character Formatting

In addition to using the keyboard method for certain types of character formatting, I also use it when I'm changing one or two words in a sentence and don't want to take my fingers off the keyboard. Here are the key combinations for all the character formats:

To make characters	Press
Bold	**Ctrl+B**
Italic	**Ctrl+I**
Underline	**Ctrl+U**
Word Underline	**Ctrl+W**

To change the capitalization of some text, select it by pressing **Shift** and using the arrow keys. Open the Text menu by pressing Alt+T, and then choose Caps by pressing **C**. Select a capitalization option by pressing its selection letter (shown here in bold): **U**pper Case, **L**ower Case, **I**nitial Caps, or **S**mall Caps.

To apply other text formatting, open the Text menu and select Special Effects by pressing **Alt+T** and E. In the dialog box that appears, select an option by pressing **Alt** plus the selection letter of the option you want. Press **Enter** to close the dialog box.

Remember that these key combinations let you select text first and *then* change it if you want to. If you use the keyboard commands as you type, remember to press the same keys again to turn that character formatting off. Also, to apply combination character formats (such as bold italic), press **Ctrl+B** and then **Ctrl+I**.

Sorry Keyboarders, you must have a mouse to copy formatting with Fast Format.

It's a Bird, It's a Plane, No It's Fast Format!

 You can copy multiple formats from one piece of text to another with the Fast Format button on the Default, Editing, and Tables SmartIcon sets. First, select the text you want to copy. Then click on the **Fast Format** button. Double-click on a word (or drag over a section of text) to which you want to copy the formatting. Continue dragging or double-clicking your way to a beautifully formatted document. When you're done, press **Esc**, or click on the **Fast Format** button again.

The Least You Need to Know

All words and no character formatting make a document a pretty dull thing. Your words will sparkle with these tips:

- ☛ You can change character formatting either before you type or after you type (by selecting it).

- ☛ Use the status bar to change the font and point size quickly.

- ☛ **B** **U** **I** If you use a mouse, change text to bold, italic, or single underline by clicking on the appropriate button on the Default SmartIcon set.

- ☛ To change text with the keyboard, use the proper key combination—usually Ctrl plus some other letter, such as B for Bold.

- ☛ Copy formatting with Fast Format. Select the text with the formatting you want to copy, click on the **Fast Format** button, and drag over text to copy formatting.

Chapter 12
Beauty and the Paragraph

In This Chapter

- The true meaning of the word "paragraph"
- Aligning paragraphs with the margins
- Centering a paragraph or a heading
- Changing a paragraph's indents
- Creating a hanging indent
- Adjusting the amount of line spacing within paragraphs

You'll want to change the way paragraphs look for many reasons: to create centered headings, indented paragraphs, a right-aligned address, and bulleted or numbered lists. In this chapter, you'll learn how to turn your "beasts" into "beauties."

Webster's Gonna Get a Bit Confused by This

This is the meaning of the word "paragraph" according to Webster's:

A subdivision of a written composition that consists of one or more sentences, deals with one point, or gives the words of one speaker.

You'll know paragraph marks are there when you delete one accidentally and a paragraph takes on the formatting of the paragraph above it. Turning on paragraph marks so you can see them makes this less likely to happen. You'll find out how to display paragraph marks in the next section.

Okay, now forget that definition. In Ami Pro, a *paragraph* is any collection of text or graphics that ends in a carriage return (that is, a pressing of Enter). This includes normal paragraphs, as well as single-line paragraphs, such as chapter titles, section headings, and captions for charts or other figures. When you press Enter in Ami Pro, you are marking the end of a paragraph.

So How Can I Tell Where Paragraphs Begin and End?

At the end of each paragraph, Ami Pro inserts a *paragraph return mark* that is normally invisible, but that you can display if you want to. Why would you want to see these little paragraph "pests" all over your screen? To understand why, you need to know a bit about paragraph formatting.

Just as you can select characters and format them in a particular way, you can also format paragraphs. For example, you can center a paragraph between the margins, change the indentation for the first line, or change the spacing between paragraphs, to list a few. Paragraph formatting is stored in those paragraph returns that you don't see.

Also, when you press Enter to create a new paragraph, the formatting of the current paragraph continues to the next one. This is kind of like character formatting. For example, if you turned bold on but never turned it off, all subsequent text would be bold. Once you make changes to a paragraph (such as changing its margin settings), those changes are effective forever until you change them again.

So to display these little creatures, click on the **View Preferences** button on the Proofing SmartIcon set, or press **Alt+V** and **P** to open the **View** menu and select View Preferences. Click on Tabs & **returns**, or press **Alt+R**. Press **Enter** or click **OK** to close the dialog box.

View Preferences button

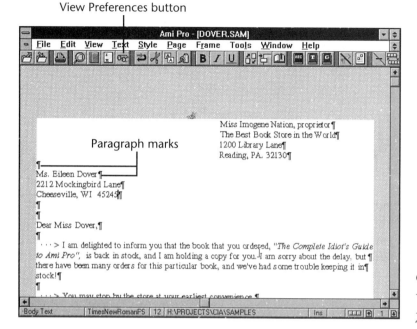

Gee, you never know what's out there 'til you display it.

Warning: Paragraph Styles Ahead

When you type a paragraph, it is assigned a *style*. The style of a paragraph defines certain parameters (such as the paragraph's margins, first line indentation, and alignment). A style controls how a paragraph looks. When a style is assigned to a paragraph, that paragraph changes to fit the definition of the style. For example, if you had a style called Heading that was defined as a center-aligned paragraph, and you assigned the Heading style to a line of text, that line would become center aligned.

Some aspects of a paragraph can be changed without changing the style definition (which would, in turn, affect all the paragraphs with that style). You'll learn how to make these types of changes in this chapter. In Chapters 14 and 15, you'll learn how to make global changes that affect the world economy and all the paragraphs with a particular style. More about this in a minute.

If you need to remove a paragraph's manual formatting (the stuff that you'll learn how to do in this chapter), select the paragraph and press **Ctrl+N**. When you press Ctrl+N, you return a paragraph to its default or normal formatting, which is determined by the style that has been assigned to it.

Some Things to Know About Formatting Paragraphs

As I mentioned earlier, you can make only some types of changes to an individual paragraph. All other changes are made to a *paragraph style*, thereby affecting all the paragraphs with that style. If this becomes a problem, you can always create a new paragraph style with the paragraph settings you want, and assign that style to one paragraph only. (Skip ahead to Chapter 15 if this is your style.)

Anyway, here are the types of changes you can make to an individual paragraph. (Not to get confusing, but you can also make these same changes to a paragraph style, if you want to affect several paragraphs at once.) These commands are found together on the **Text** menu:

Alignment   The placement of text in a paragraph between the left and right margins. For example, you might have left-aligned or centered paragraphs.

Indentation   The amount of distance from the page margins to the edges of your paragraph. It's common for the first line of a paragraph to include an indent, for example.

Spacing   The spacing between lines in a paragraph, such as single or double line spacing.

There are some types of changes that can be applied only to a paragraph's style. These commands are found together in the Modify Style dialog box (you'll learn how to make these adjustments in Chapter 15):

Line spacing before and after a paragraph   This controls white space between paragraphs. For example, by changing a paragraph's style to add a line after a paragraph, you don't need to press Enter twice when you begin a new paragraph.

The amount of hyphenation   When words in a paragraph bump into the right margin, Ami Pro can break a word with a hyphen and make the right margin look more even.

Lines before and/or after a paragraph   You can add a black (or colored) line before and/or after a paragraph to set it off from the rest of the text.

Page or column breaks   This controls whether a page or column break is allowed within a paragraph, or if a page or column break should be forced just before or after a paragraph to avoid splitting up the paragraph.

Creating a numbered or bulleted list   Numbered and bulleted lists summarize important points, list important steps to follow, or display a list of items.

If you need to move to the next line without creating a new paragraph (and adding a blank line, if the paragraph's style includes a blank line following each paragraph), press **Ctrl+Enter**. This inserts a "soft return" (the opposite of a "hard return," which marks the end of a paragraph).

For example, you might have a style called Address, which is left aligned and includes a blank line following. You type the first line of the address and press **Ctrl+Enter** to move to the next line of the address. When you're through with the entire address, press **Enter** to close the paragraph, and a blank line will be inserted because it's part of the Address style.

Making Those Darn Changes

The rules for character formatting apply here as well: you can format paragraphs as you type, or you can select them later and format them. If you change paragraph formatting as you type (to create a heading, for example), you have to change it back later. (Remember to think of it as a light switch: if you turn it on, you have to turn it off.) If you select already-typed paragraphs, only the selected paragraphs are changed.

In addition, you can use either the mouse or the keyboard to change paragraph formatting. Again, I use a combination of both, depending on what I'm doing at the time.

If you want the formatting to apply to a specific paragraph, select the paragraph first. Press the **Ctrl** key and double-click on the paragraph to select it. Drag the mouse to select additional paragraphs. If you prefer the keyboard, move the insertion point to the beginning of a paragraph, and then press **Shift+Ctrl+↓** until the paragraphs you want are selected. Then select the paragraph format. (We'll get to this in a minute.)

If you are formatting existing paragraphs that you've selected, you're done. If you are formatting text as you type, you'll need to turn off the formatting when you no longer want the text to have this formatting. This is done by turning off the formatting attributes you just turned on. For example, if you wanted to insert a heading, and you selected bold format and then typed the heading, you'd need to "turn off" bold formatting before typing the next paragraph. So click on the **Bold** button again to turn bold formatting off. Then continue typing.

Hey, That Paragraph Is Out of Alignment!

Paragraph alignment controls how the text in a paragraph is placed between the left and right margins. There are four types of alignment:

Left alignment causes all the text in a paragraph to line up evenly on the left-hand margin. Text along the right-hand margin is "ragged," which means that it doesn't form an even line down the page. This is the default paragraph alignment style.

Right alignment causes all the text in a paragraph to line up evenly along the right-hand margin, leaving text on the left-hand margin "ragged." This is the opposite of left alignment. I use this type of alignment to put a date or a return address in the upper right corner of my letters.

Center alignment causes all the text in a paragraph to remain an even distance between the left and right margins. I rarely use this for normal paragraphs, but I use it often for headings.

Justified alignment causes all the text in a paragraph to be evenly spaced out, so that both the left and right margins maintain an even edge. Depending on the size of the words within a single line, this can cause unequal spacing between words. This type of alignment is good for newspaper-style columns.

Changing Alignment

Here's what you do to change a paragraph's alignment. First, select the paragraph(s) you want to affect. Then if you have a mouse, click on one of these buttons from the Default SmartIcon set:

 Left-Aligned Text button

 Centered Text button

You'll find the Justify button on the Editing SmartIcon set:

 Justified Text button

By the Way . . .

The Right-Aligned Text button is not located on any SmartIcon set by default (big-time bummer), but you can add it to any set if you like. See Chapter 4 for details. However, you can also right-align paragraphs with the keyboard.

If you prefer to use the keyboard, use one of these key combinations:

Ctrl+L Left-aligned text

Ctrl+R Right-aligned text

Ctrl+E Centered text

Ctrl+J Justified text

Making a Dent with Indents

An indent is like a margin's first cousin because the two are so closely related (as a matter of fact, it's really easy to get the two mixed up). An *indent* is the amount of distance from the page margin to the edge of your paragraph. A *margin* is an invisible boundary that runs down both edges of the page. Normally, a paragraph flows between the margins. But an indent allows you to move the edges of individual paragraphs an extra distance away from (or toward) the margin. You can set these types of indents in the Indent dialog box:

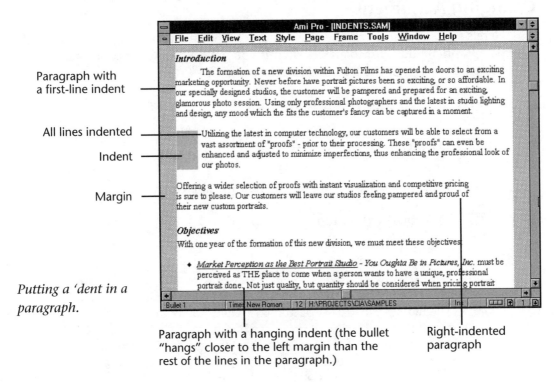

Putting a 'dent in a paragraph.

All   Indents all the lines of a paragraph the indicated distance from the left margin.

From right   Indents all the lines of a paragraph the indicated distance from the right margin.

First   Indents the first line of a paragraph the indicated distance from the left margin. The number you enter here is added to the number under All.

Rest   Indents every line *except* the first line of a paragraph. The number you enter here is added to the number under All. You can create a *hanging indent* by entering a number here, and nowhere else.

Putting 'Dents in Your Paragraphs

To change the indents of a paragraph, move the insertion point to the paragraph. If you want to indent several paragraphs at once, select them first.

Hanging indent describes a paragraph in which the first line of the paragraph hangs closer to the left margin than the rest of the lines in the paragraph. Numbered and bulleted paragraphs use a hanging indent, which allows the number or bullet to "hang" closer to the left margin than the rest of the paragraph text.

Open the Text menu and select Indention (press **Alt+T** and **D**). Select the type of indentation you want by clicking on it or pressing **Alt** plus the selection letter. Enter an amount and click **OK** or press **Enter**. (To move to another indentation area before you close the dialog box, click on it or press **Tab**, and then type a number.) You can change the paragraph back to its original indentation by selecting Revert to style.

You can also change the indention of a paragraph (or paragraphs) with the Ruler. The Ruler is a great way to indent a paragraph by more than one tab stop, or to a point which is an unusual distance from the margin. (You'll need a mouse to do this.) See Chapter 13 for the "rules" of using the Ruler.

These settings will give you some common effects:

- ☞ To format a paragraph with a 1/2 inch indent on the first line only, enter .05 under First.
- ☞ To create a hanging indent, enter .05 under Rest.
- ☞ To format a paragraph with all lines indented from the left, enter .05 under All.
- ☞ To indent a paragraph 1 inch from both margins, enter 1 under All and also under From right.

> ## By the Way . . .
>
> There are three buttons for changing the indentation of paragraphs, but none of them are located on any of the existing SmartIcon sets. Don't frown; you can easily add them yourself—see Chapter 4.

TECHNO NERD TEACHES

When dealing with indents and line spacing, you can choose the system of measurement. By default, Ami Pro displays measurements in inches, because that's what everyone in the civilized world uses. However, you can change the system of measurement to centimeters, picas, or points.

A centimeter is used by the uncivilized parts of the world to measure things smaller than an inch. A pica is a typesetting term used to measure the width of characters; there are six picas in an inch. A point is used to measure the height of characters; there are 72 points in an inch.

Spaced-Out Paragraphs

You can adjust the line spacing within individual paragraphs (for example, making them double-spaced). A double-spaced printout is great for a reader who is editing; it gives her space to write comments (okay, maybe that's not such a good idea . . .). By the way, you can also adjust the number of lines (if any) that precede or follow a paragraph. See Chapter 15.

To adjust the line spacing, open the Text menu and select **Spacing** (press **Alt+T** and **S**). Then click on the option you want, or press **Alt** plus the selection letter. If you don't like **Single**, **Double**, or **1 1/2** spacing, select **Custom** and enter your own number. You can convert the paragraph back to it's original line spacing style by choosing **Revert to style**. Click **OK** or press **Enter**, and you're through.

The Least You Need to Know

Conjure up terrific paragraphs with this bag of tricks:

- ☞ A paragraph is created when you press Enter.

- ☞ You can display paragraph marks by opening the View menu, selecting View **P**references, and then selecting Tabs & **r**eturns.

- ☞ Some elements of a paragraph can be changed individually, while others can only be changed by changing the paragraph's style.

- ☞ Press **Shift+Ctrl+↓** at the front of a paragraph to select it.

- ☞ To remove manual formatting, press **Ctrl+N**.

- ☞ Click on the appropriate button (shown below) to align a paragraph, or press **Ctrl+L**, **Ctrl+R**, **Ctrl+E**, or **Ctrl+J**.

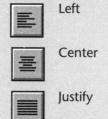 Left

Center

Justify

- ☞ To change a paragraph's indents, open the Text menu and select In**d**ention. Enter the amount of indentation you want and press **Enter**.

- ☞ To change the spacing within paragraphs, open the **T**ext menu and select **S**pacing. Then click on the option you want and click **OK**.

Okay people, move along; nothing to see here.

Chapter 13
Tools of the Trade: That Handy, Dandy Ruler

In This Chapter

- ☞ Displaying the ruler
- ☞ Understanding the different types of rulers
- ☞ Setting tabs
- ☞ Adding tab leaders
- ☞ Changing indents with the ruler

What is there to say about rulers? Rulers aren't nearly as interesting or as important a subject as global warming, the economy, Amy Fisher, or the clear version of Pepsi. I'm glad I don't have to write a whole book on rulers (and I'll bet you're glad you don't have to read one). Oh, well, let's get on with it: to paraphrase the Latin poets of old (who never concerned themselves with rulers, skin cancer, or Madonna's next album)—"Carpe Diem!" Or more to the point, "Carpe Rulum!"

The Role of a Ruler

The ruler is used to change tab settings, indentations, margins, and column widths. In every Ami Pro document, there is one big ruler that keeps track of all this stuff and applies it to every paragraph in a document.

You can change these settings for individual paragraphs by changing the paragraph's *style ruler*, or by selecting an individual paragraph and inserting your own ruler. You "rule" over the settings in your document in whatever manner you think is best.

Viewing Rulers

The *current* ruler is the one that governs whatever is happening to a paragraph. It's settings are based on the page layout (document) ruler, unless they've been overridden by the style ruler or the paragraph ruler.

To see the current ruler, click the **Ruler** button on the Default and Editing SmartIcon sets. Or, if you have time to waste, you can open the View menu and select Show **Ruler** (press **Alt+V**, and then **R**). As you move the insertion point from paragraph to paragraph, you may see the settings on the current ruler change, which indicates that a style or paragraph ruler is present.

In this chapter, you'll learn how to establish and modify the settings for the paragraph ruler. This type of ruler changes the settings for selected paragraphs, overriding the settings within the paragraph's style, or within the page layout (document) ruler. When you insert a paragraph ruler into a document (which you'll learn how to do in a moment), you won't be able to tell unless you watch the settings on the current ruler change as you move from paragraph to paragraph. However, if you think this is a real bother, you do have one option. Ami Pro provides you with a convenient way to detect the presence of this overpowering paragraph ruler if you want to. Just open the View menu and select View **Preferences** (press **Alt+V**, and then **P**). Select **Marks** (press **Alt+M**), and then click **OK** or press **Enter** to close the dialog box. Paragraph ruler marks appear along the left edge of text to show you which paragraphs have a paragraph ruler applied.

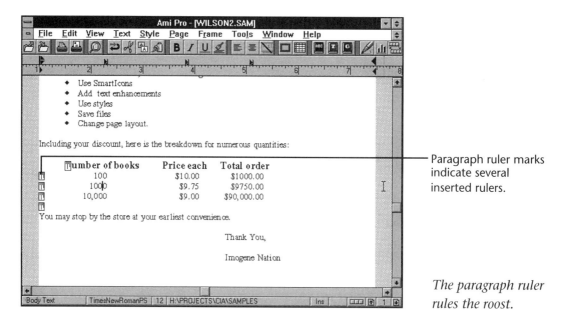

Paragraph ruler marks indicate several inserted rulers.

The paragraph ruler rules the roost.

Inserting a Paragraph Ruler

To insert a paragraph ruler, first select the paragraph you want to affect. Then click on the ruler at the top of the screen, and change the paragraph's margins, tab settings, or indentations. You could open the Page menu, select ruler, and then select Insert to change the inserted ruler, but by that time your coffee's cold, so why bother?

If you want to delete an inserted ruler, make sure that Marks is selected in the View Preferences dialog box. Now that you can see the suckers, move to the paragraph whose ruler you want to delete. Open the **Page** menu and select **Ruler** (press **Alt+P**, and **R**). Then select **Delete** (press **D**).

Picking Up the Tab

The Tab key in a word processor is like the Tab key on a typewriter. When you press it, the cursor jumps to the next tab stop (but it does not pass Go or collect $200). Tabs are great for creating short lists like this one:

Department	Department Number
Accounting	100
Sales	200
Marketing	210
Client Services	300

A **tab** is used to align columns of text, such as a short two-column list. Tabs are set on the ruler.

If you need more than a few columns or rows, you should probably create a table. A *table* makes it easier for you to enter large amounts of information, adjust column widths, and add borders and shading. You'll learn how to make tables in Chapter 17.

Treatise on Tab Types

There are four different types of tabs, each one perfect for some suitable occasion:

- **Left**   The default tab type, this type of tab aligns characters on the left, for example:

  Jane   Salesperson

  Scott   Client Service Representative

  Beth   Corporate Trainer

- **Right**   This type of tab aligns characters on the right, for example:

  Description:

  Syntax:

  Example:

- **Numeric**   This type of tab is great for working with numbers. It aligns numbers by the decimal point:

  100.21

  10.927

  3515.65

  .5586

☛ **Center**   This type of tab is great for centering headings above your columns of data:

Stock	Buy/Sell
TM Technologies	Buy this one!
GSA	Sell right away!
American Paper	Buy this one soon!
Paramount Comm.	Buy lots of this!

Follow the Leader

Normally the space between tabbed columns is empty, like all the examples I've shown you so far. As an option, you can have Ami Pro fill the space with a *leader*. A leader is often used in a Table of Contents:

Leaders are dots or dashes that fill the spaces between tab positions in a columnar list.

Introduction..1

Sales Analysis..5

Market Share...11

Fiscal Plan..13

The idea behind a leader is that it "leads the eye" across the page to the next item in the list. In this example, the leaders help you see that the Sales Analysis starts on page 5 of the report. There are three types of leaders: underline, dash, and period.

Take Me to Your Ruler: Setting Tab Stops

It's pretty easy to set tabs with the ruler. Here's what you do. First, select the paragraph(s) for which you want to set tabs. Or you can pre-set tabs before you type if you want; just move the insertion point to the place where you want to change the tab settings. (Remember: if you want to change the tabs for an entire document, you're in the wrong theater. The page layout ruler is now playing at a theater near you—Chapter 16.)

If the ruler is not displayed, open the View menu and select Show **Ruler**. After selecting your paragraph(s), click on the ruler to activate it. Then click on the appropriate button to select the type of tab you want:

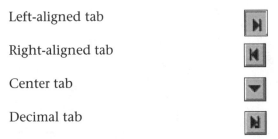

Left-aligned tab

Right-aligned tab

Center tab

Decimal tab

If you want to add a tab leader, click on the **Leader Character** button until the appropriate character appears. Then click on the ruler to set the position of the tab. Tab marks appear on the ruler, in a shape that matches the type of alignment you choose.

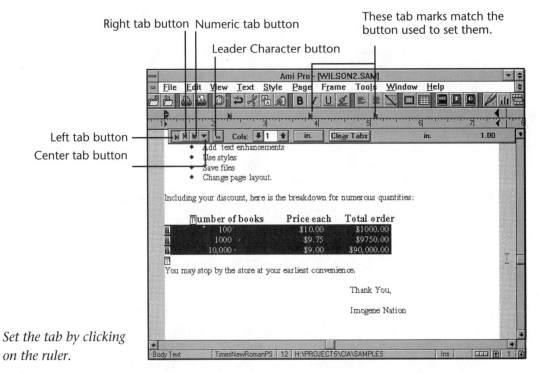

Right tab button   Numeric tab button

Leader Character button

These tab marks match the button used to set them.

Left tab button

Center tab button

Set the tab by clicking on the ruler.

Nuking a Tab

If you need to remove a tab, just drag the tab off the ruler with the mouse. If you prefer to do this the hard way (with the keyboard), open the Edit menu, select **Go** To, select **Ruler** under Next item, and then press **Enter** to move the cursor to the ruler. Whew! Now use the arrow keys to move to the tab you want to get rid of, and press **Delete**.

Changing Indents with the Ruler

In Chapter 12 (unless you skipped it—bad, bad) you learned how to change the indentation of a paragraph using the **Text Indention** command, but you can also change the indention of a paragraph (or paragraphs) with the ruler. The ruler is a great way to indent a paragraph more than a single tab stop, or to a point that is an unusual distance from the margin. (You'll need a mouse to try this one.)

If the ruler is not displayed, open the **View** menu and select Show **Ruler** to display it.

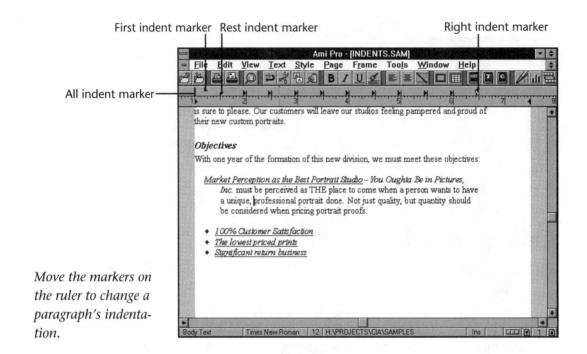

First indent marker   Rest indent marker   Right indent marker

All indent marker

Move the markers on the ruler to change a paragraph's indentation.

There are four types of indents: All (indents all the lines of a paragraph the same distance from the left margin), Right (indents all lines of a paragraph the same distance from the right margin), First (indents only the first line of a paragraph), and Rest (indents all lines *except* the first line an equal distance from the left margin). In addition, you can also create a *hanging indent*, in which the first line of a paragraph is indented closer to the left margin than the rest of the paragraph. With the ruler, you drag little markers around (each representing a type of indent) to change the indentation of a paragraph.

To change indentation with the ruler, select the paragraph(s) you want to affect. Then just drag the All, Right, First, or Rest indent markers on the ruler. To create a hanging indent, hold down **Ctrl** as you drag the Rest indent marker to the right of the First indent marker.

The Least You Need to Know

I'll put my cards on the table: here's what I feel were the most important points of this chapter.

- ☛ The page layout (document) ruler determines the settings for each paragraph, unless it is overridden by settings in a paragraph's style. Settings on the style ruler, in turn, can be overridden by settings in the paragraph ruler.

- ☛ To display the ruler, click on the **Show/Hide Ruler** button on the Default SmartIcon set, or use the **View Show Ruler** command.

- ☛ You can organize small amounts of information in columns by using tabs.

- ☛ There are four different tabs you can use: left-aligned, centered, right-aligned, and numeric.

- ☛ To set tabs, select the paragraph, and select the appropriate tab button. Then click on the ruler to set the tab's position.

- ☛ You can add a tab leader, which puts dots or dashes in the empty space normally taken up by a tab. Select a leader with the Leader Character button on the ruler.

- ☛ Indents (All, Right, First, or Rest) can also be set by dragging the appropriate marker on the ruler. Create a hanging indent by pressing **Ctrl** and dragging the Rest marker to the right.

Geez, another @*!# blank page!?

Chapter 14
The Essence of Style

In This Chapter

- ☛ What is a style?
- ☛ How to tell what style is applied to a paragraph
- ☛ Applying a style to a paragraph
- ☛ Copying a style from paragraph to paragraph

Styles are the greatest inventions since pantyhose, instant pudding, and VCRs. Okay, maybe they're not that exciting, but they do save you lots of hassle in typing letters, memos, and such. Once you understand how styles work, they will significantly change your life!

Okay, this chapter opening has degraded to the level of a cheap promo for the sleazy TV movie of the week. But styles really are important, which is why I talk about them here and in the next chapter. So, on with the show!

Getting a Sense of Style

So what exactly is a style? A *style* is a collection of both character and paragraph formatting that defines a particular element within a document. For example, you can create a style for each different heading level within your document. The major heading style could be defined as bold, 24-point, Arial font, while the minor heading style could be defined as italic, 18-point, Arial font. Styles make it easy for you to make changes to a document. For example, if you decide to change to Palatino font for major headings, you simply change the style. Ami Pro would then automatically change all the major headings within the document (all the paragraphs with that style) to Palatino font.

Styles box

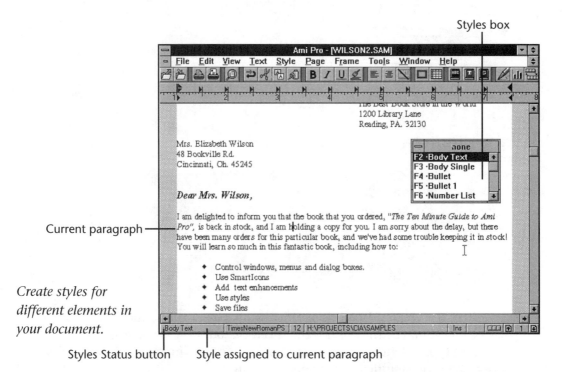

Current paragraph

Create styles for different elements in your document.

Styles Status button   Style assigned to current paragraph

Now don't get too depressed; you don't have to create a style for every little thing. Anytime you begin typing and don't specify a style, Ami Pro assigns the paragraph the Body Text style, which is a generic style. If a paragraph is unique, don't bother to create a unique style, just use the Body Text style and make individual changes. But remember that styles save you the trouble of making the same character and paragraph formatting changes over and over again as you create your document.

Up until now, every paragraph you've typed has started its life in the Body Text style: Times New Roman 12-point font, in a left-aligned paragraph. You can change an individual paragraph by overriding the style; jump back to Chapter 12 for the exciting details. Or you can modify the style (and affect all the paragraphs that have been assigned that style). Modifying (and creating your own) styles is what the next chapter is all about, so stay tuned.

How Can I Tell What Style Is Applied to a Paragraph?

When the insertion point is placed in a paragraph, the name of the style you are currently using appears in the Style Status button on the status bar at the bottom of the screen.

Selecting a Style to Use

The styles that are available for your document come from the style sheet you selected when you created the document. If you don't remember selecting a style sheet, you probably accepted the Default style sheet. Ami Pro provides customized style sheets for special purposes, such as creating a letter or a memo, so remember to choose the best style sheet for the job you want to perform. (See Chapter 8 for details on selecting a style sheet when you create a new document.)

TECHNO NERD TEACHES

In some cases, you may have to modify a style (or create a new one) whether you want to or not. That's because some aspects of a paragraph can't be changed any other way (bummer). You can change a paragraph's font, indents, alignment, spacing, and tabs without changing the style. But to change anything else, you're going to have to change the style. And by some strange coincidence, you'll learn how to do some of that later in this chapter.

TECHNO NERD TEACHES

Ami Pro stores its styles in a *style sheet*. You select the style sheet you want to work with when you create a new document (see Chapter 8). If you make changes to a style, you're making changes that are effective for that document only, unless you save the changes to the style sheet. (You'll learn how to do this in Chapter 15.)

Let's start with simple things first. Suppose you wanted to section off text by preceding it with a heading. Well, you're in luck: Ami Pro has quite a few styles (including several heading styles) already defined for you. Once a style has been created, all you need to do is apply one of the styles to a paragraph and make modifications if necessary.

Here's how to apply a sense of style. First, place the insertion point where you want the style applied. This can be an existing paragraph or some place within the document where you want the style to start. Select several paragraphs if you want to format multiple paragraphs at one time.

Next, click on the **Styles Status** button on the status bar and click on an existing style. (You can create your own styles; instructions are in the next chapter.) If you want to use the keyboard, just press the function key assigned to the style. Here are the function key assignments for the Default style sheet (read the Techno Nerd tip for details on changing to a different style sheet):

Style	Function Key
Body Text	F2
Body Single	F3
Bullet	F4
Bullet 1	F5
Number List	F6
Subhead	F7
Title	F8
Header	F9
Footer	F11

Repeating the Same Ol' Style

 To repeat a style you've applied to one paragraph for another paragraph in your document, select the style again from the status bar. You can also copy styles from one paragraph to the other with Fast Format. To copy a paragraph's style to a single paragraph, select the paragraph whose style you want to copy and click the **Fast Format** button. Select Only **p**aragraph style from the dialog box, and then drag over the paragraph to which you want to copy formatting.

To copy formatting to several paragraphs, simply drag the little paintbrush over as many paragraphs as you want. You can also double-click within the paragraphs to which you want to apply the captured format. Press **Esc** to end Fast Format.

You can also select styles from the Styles box. To get it to come out of hiding, open the **V**iew menu and select Show Styles **B**ox. Then click on a style to select it. (Displaying the Styles box also helps if you are using the keyboard, because it displays all those function keys—so you don't have to remember which function key assigns what style.)

If you want to copy the formatting of a paragraph (and not just the style), select Only **t**ext font and attributes from the dialog box, then drag over the paragraph(s) to copy the formatting.

The Least You Need to Know

The reason for using styles is to save time in formatting paragraphs. This list will save you time reading this chapter:

- ☞ You can tell what style is applied to each paragraph by placing the insertion point within the paragraph and looking at the Styles Status button on the status bar.

- ☞ To apply a style to a paragraph, select it from the Styles Status button on the status bar, or press the function key associated with the style, or select the style from the Styles box.

continues

continued

☛ To display the Styles box, open the **View** menu and select Show Styles **Box**.

☛ To copy a paragraph's style to another paragraph, select the paragraph whose style you want to copy, click on the **Fast Format** button located on the Default SmartIcon set, and then drag over or double-click within the paragraph to which you want to copy the style.

Chapter 15
Setting Your Own Style

In This Chapter

- ☞ Redefining a style
- ☞ Changing to a different style sheet
- ☞ Adjusting the amount of hyphenation in a paragraph
- ☞ Adding lines before or after paragraphs
- ☞ Creating numbered and bulleted lists
- ☞ Creating your own style
- ☞ Adding a style to a document style sheet

After you've spent a long time getting a *sidebar* (for notes to the reader) or a heading just right (with special indentation, character formatting, or unique fonts), the last thing you want to do is repeat all those steps the next time you want to add a note or a heading to your document. So what do you do?

You create two styles (one to remember each set of formatting selections), and you use those styles to create similar text in other parts of your document. And (surprise, surprise) in this chapter you'll learn how.

There's one important thing you should know about the Modify Style dialog box: If you intend to use a keyboard to select items, *don't*. Although I'll provide the keyboard steps (don't I always?), you'll find it tough going because this dialog box is so complex that you may have to press certain keys several times before they work. (Yuck.) So give yourself a break and use the mouse.

Although I always tell you to open the Modify Style dialog box through the Style menu, you can simply click your right mouse button to open it instead (and it's much quicker).

 You can also display the Modify Style dialog box by clicking on the **Modify Paragraph Style** button on the Editing SmartIcons set. Both of these methods are faster than using the menus, so use whichever you prefer.

Redefining an Existing Style

Sometimes it's just time to change your style (you could start with that polka dot bow tie your Aunt Millie gave you). Keep in mind that when you change a style, you automatically change all the paragraphs with that style. If you want to change just one paragraph, follow the directions in Chapter 12. However, some aspects of a paragraph (such as the number of lines that follow it) can only be changed by modifying its style—so don't jump back to Chapter 12 just yet.

Changing the Sheets

The styles that are available to you come from the style sheet you selected when you first created your document. If you need a new style, chances are it might be in another style sheet. To change to a different style sheet, just open the **Style** menu and select **Use Another Style Sheet** (press **Alt+S** and then **U**). Select a style sheet from the list, and click **OK** or press **Enter**. It's best to choose a style sheet that's suited to the task at hand; for example, select a memo sheet if you're creating a memo. If you've already selected a style from your current style sheet, and then you switch to another style sheet, that's okay. Any styles being used are stored with the document, and are always available, regardless of whether or not the current style sheet has that same style.

About Face: Changing a Style's Font

You can change the font of selected text with the Face button on the status bar. To change the font associated with a particular style, you use the

Modify Style dialog box. Don't get too hyper—the process is remarkably similar to selecting a font for text.

Open the **S**tyle menu and select **M**odify Style (with the keyboard, just press **Ctrl+A**). If necessary, select a style to modify from the Style list (press **Alt+Y**). Select Font from the Modify list (press **Alt+F** and then **Spacebar**). Select a font (here it's called a *face*) and a point size if you like. (Press **Alt+F** and then **Alt+I**). When you're finished, click **OK** or press **Enter**. In all the paragraphs with that style, the font is automatically changed to reflect your choice.

Don't Go Breaking My Heart (or My Paragraph)

You can control what happens to paragraphs when they reach the end of a page. By default, they are sawed in two like a magician's assistant, with the second half placed at the top of the next page. If you want to ensure that a paragraph is not split over two pages or columns, modify the paragraph's style (or create a new one if you don't want to affect all the paragraphs of that style).

Open the **S**tyle menu and select **M**odify Style (with the keyboard, just press **Ctrl+A**). If necessary, select a style to modify from the Style list (press **Alt+Y**). Select **B**reaks from the Modify list (press **Alt+B** and then **Spacebar**). Select a break option:

Option	Press
Page break **b**efore paragraph	**Alt+B**
Page break **a**fter paragraph	**Alt+A**
Column break before paragraph	**Alt+C**
Column **b**reak after paragraph	**Alt+B**
Allow page/column break **w**ithin (This is the way it normally works.)	**Alt+W**

You can also control whether two paragraphs stay with each other on the same page by selecting Previous paragraph or Next paragraph under Keep With. When you're through, click **OK** or press **Enter**.

Line, Line, Everywhere a Line

You can add a dark line before or after a paragraph to set it off from other text. You can even adjust the thickness of the line to really make a bold statement. For example, you can place a thick line under all your major headings.

Totally separate, and yet equally important, you can place a blank line before or after a paragraph. You'll probably want to include a single blank line after most paragraph styles. This reduces keying time by providing a blank line between paragraphs for you.

To add a *dark* line above or below a paragraph, open the **Style** menu and select Modify Style (with the keyboard, just press **Ctrl+A**). If necessary, select a style to modify from the Style list (press **Alt+Y**). Select Lines from the Modify list (press **Alt+L** and then **Spacebar**). Select either Line above or Line below, or both if you like. (Press **Alt+B** one or two times.) Select a line thickness by clicking on it or using the arrow keys. Adjust the length of the line by choosing Text, Margins, or Other. You can even change the color of the line (if you have a color printer), with the color bar. Display additional colors by clicking on the down arrow. When you're through, click **OK** or press **Enter**. A line will appear either above or below all the paragraphs with that style.

To add a *blank* line after a paragraph style, open the **Style** menu and select Modify Style (with the keyboard, just press **Ctrl+A**). If necessary, select a style to modify from the Style list (press **Alt+Y**). Select Spacing from the Modify list (press **Alt+P** and then **Spacebar**). Select Above or Below. (Press **Alt+A** or **Alt+B**). Enter the height of the blank line. You'll see a sample to guide you. If you want this blank line to be added regardless of whether the neighboring paragraph has a blank line too, select Always. Otherwise, select **When** not at break. When you're through, click **OK** or press **Enter**. A blank line will be inserted either above or below all the paragraphs with that style.

Getting Hyper Over Hyphenation

To hyphen, or not to hyphen, that is the question. Whether 'tis nobler in the mind to suffer the slings and arrows of excessive hyphenation, or take arms against a sea of dashes, and by opposing, end them.

Well, Hamlet may not have known what to do, but you will. If you want to control whether or not *hyphenation* occurs within paragraphs of a particular style, simply open the Style menu and select Modify Style (with the keyboard, just press **Ctrl+A**). If necessary, select a style to modify from the Style list (press **Alt+Y**). Select Hyphenation from the Modify list (press **Alt+H** and then **Spacebar**). Click **OK** or press **Enter**.

When a word in a paragraph of the selected style enters into the *hyphenation hot-zone*, it is broken with a hyphen. No more than two consecutive lines will be hyphenated, however. You can control the size of this "hot-zone" by opening the Tools menu, selecting User Setup, and selecting Options (press **Alt+L**, then U, then **Alt+O**). Select **Hyphenation hot-zone**, and enter the number of characters from the right margin where the hot-zone should begin. For example, if you entered 3, a word would be hyphenated if it entered a region three characters from the right margin. You can also permit hyphenation within the last word of a paragraph, column, or page by selecting the appropriate option. When you're done, click **OK** or press **Enter** to return to the User Setup dialog box. Then click **OK** or press **Enter** again to return to your document.

The **hyphenation** feature allows Ami Pro to break words with a hyphen and place the remainder on the next line.

There is a region along the right margin called the **hyphenation hot-zone**; if a word enters this area, it will be hyphenated. For example, if the hot-zone is set to 5 characters, and a word is located less than 5 characters from the right margin, it will be hyphenated.

You can easily override hyphenation on a selected word without changing the paragraph style. Just select the word, open the **E**dit menu, select **M**ark Text, and then select **N**o Hyphenation. (With the keyboard, press **Alt+E**, then **M**, then **N**.)

Shoot! I Almost Forgot to Tell You About Bulleted (and Numbered) Lists!

In the previous chapters, you learned about indents and about *hanging indents*, where the first line of a paragraph "hangs out" from the rest of the paragraph to the left. A special kind of hanging indent is a *numbered* or *bulleted* list. I've used bulleted lists throughout these chapters to:

☛ Create snazzy lists like this one.

☛ Highlight what's coming up.

☛ Summarize the important points that were covered. Notice that the first line of a paragraph with a hanging indent is further out into the left margin than the rest of the lines. That's why a hanging indent is so great for bulleted and numbered lists.

A **numbered list** or **bulleted list** is a special kind of paragraph with a hanging indent, in which the number or bullet is placed to the left of all the other lines in the paragraph.

I usually use numbered lists when I want to explain actions that need to be carried out in a certain order, such as step 1, step 2, and so on. Ready to number or bullet? Here's what to do.

Press **F4** or **F5** for a bulleted list, or **F6** for a numbered list, and then start typing. The bullet or number is inserted automatically! If you want different bullets or numbering, you can modify the style.

Changing the Size of Your Bullets

You can modify the bulleted or numbered list styles to suit your fancy. Open the Style menu and select Modify Style (with the keyboard, just press **Ctrl+A**). Select one of the bulleted or numbered styles from the Style list (press **Alt+Y**). Select Bullets & Numbers from the Modify list (press **Alt+E** and then **Spacebar**).

Now select your options; if you choose more than one, select them in the order in which you want them to appear. If you want to change the bullet style, select Bullet (press **Alt+L**) and choose one from the list. To change the number style, select **N**umber (press **Alt+N**) and select one from the drop-down list. If you want a period after the number, enter it in the Text box. If you want the numbers to line up at the ones place, select **R**ight Align. The Text option is cool for stuff like *Note:* or *Warning:*. You can add bold, italics, and so on by selecting the appropriate option. Click **OK** or press **Enter**.

Remember to turn off bulleted or numbered lists when you're through. Pressing Enter to create a new paragraph only continues the list. To turn the list off, select a different style. For example, press **F2** to change to Body Text style.

Creating Your Own Style

Let's create a style for the sidebar paragraph I mentioned earlier. Suppose you were going to use the sidebar paragraph for special instructions to the reader, and you'd like to add indentation, italicized text, and a different font to set it off from the rest of the document.

The easiest way to create a style is to format a paragraph first, and then use its formatting to define a style. So start by typing a paragraph that we can use as a sample. Then follow along with me to create your first style.

First, change the indentation of the sample paragraph to right-aligned by pressing **Ctrl+R**. Then select the text for the paragraph.

TECHNO NERD TEACHES

When you create a style, it's available for that document only. If you want to make a style available for more documents, you must add that style to a style sheet (which you'll learn how to do later in this chapter). A *style sheet* defines the working environment for a document, such as its margin settings, page orientation, and so on.

As you learned in Chapter 6, Ami Pro comes with additional style sheets you can use to create specialized documents, or you can create your own style sheets.

I Make the text italic by clicking on the **Italic** button on the Default SmartIcon set. Select a cool font using the **Face** button on the status bar.

When you have the paragraph looking the way you want it to, define a style based on it. With the paragraph selected, open the **Style** menu and select Create Style. (Press **Alt+S** and then **C**.) Enter a style name using up to 13 characters, including spaces. Choose Selected **t**ext (press **Alt+T**), and then click on Create (press **Alt+C**). If there is a function key available, it is assigned the new style. You can then use this function key to apply the new style to the selected paragraph, or to other paragraphs. If no function key is assigned, just click on the **Styles Status** button on the status bar, or use the Styles box to assign the style to later paragraphs.

If you want to create a style that's close to another style, you can select Style under Based On in the Create Style dialog box. Then you can make simple changes to the new style with the Modify Style dialog box, as explained earlier in this chapter.

Saving Styles So You Can Use 'Em in Other Documents

When you buy a VCR, chances are good that the remote you use with your TV won't work with the VCR. After playing juggle-the-remotes for several years, I finally bought one of those universal remote things that works with both my TV and my VCR. Creating a style is like using the remote that comes with your TV: having the style is great, but you can only use it on that one document, unless. . . .

SPEAK LIKE A GEEK

A **style sheet** defines the working environment for a document, such as its margin settings, page orientation, and so on. It also contains predefined styles that you can use in any document based on that particular style sheet.

Unless of course, you save your style to a *style sheet*. Ami Pro has many style sheets already customized for creating common documents, such as memos, reports, and sales proposals. So before you save your styles to a style sheet, you'll want to see which style you're currently using by selecting the Doc Info command on the File menu.

Whew! If I haven't lost you, and you're still interested in adding a style to the current style sheet, here's how: start by opening the **Style** menu and selecting Style Management. The styles listed on the left are either modified versions of the styles originally contained in the style sheet, or they are new styles—but it really doesn't matter. From the list on the left, click on whatever style you want to add, and then click on **Move** or press **Alt+M**. Select additional styles and repeat the move process if you want. When you're through, click on **OK** or press **Enter**.

The Least You Need to Know

If Ami Pro's predefined styles don't fit your mood, just change them or create your own with these tips:

☞ To modify a style, display the Modify Style dialog box by clicking the right mouse button or by clicking on the **Modify Paragraph Style** button (located on the Editing SmartIcon set).

☞ To change style sheets, open the **S**tyle menu and select **U**se Another Style Sheet. Select a style sheet from the list, and click **OK** or press **Enter**.

☞ To change a style's font, open the **S**tyle menu and select **M**odify Style. If necessary, select a style to modify from the Style list. Select **F**ont from the Modify list. Select a font (here it's called a *face*) and a point size.

☞ To select the break point for a paragraph style, open the **S**tyle menu and select **M**odify Style. If necessary, select a style to modify from the Style list. Select **B**reaks from the Modify list, and select a break option. Click **OK** or press **Enter**.

☞ To add a line above or below a paragraph style, open the **S**tyle menu and select **M**odify Style. Select a style to modify from the Style list. Select **L**ines from the Modify list. Select either Line **a**bove or Line **b**elow, or both if you like. Select a line thickness. Adjust the length of the line by choosing **T**ext, **M**argins, or **O**ther. Click **OK** or press **Enter**.

continues

continued

☞ To add a *blank* line after a paragraph style, open the **S**tyle menu and select **M**odify Style. Select a style to modify from the Style list. Select S**p**acing from the Modify list. Select **A**bove or **B**elow. Enter the height of the blank line. Select Al**w**ays or **W**hen not at break. Click **OK** or press **Enter**.

☞ To control hyphenation within a paragraph, open the **S**tyle menu and select **M**odify Style. Select a style to modify from the Style list. Select **H**yphenation from the Modify list. Click **OK** or press **Enter**.

☞ Press either **F4** or **F5** to create a bulleted list, or **F6** for a numbered list. The change the style of the list, open the **S**tyle menu and select **M**odify Style. Select a bulleted or numbered style from the Style list. Select Bull**e**ts & Numbers from the Modify list, select your options, and then click **OK** or press **Enter**.

☞ To create a style, format a paragraph and then select it. Open the **S**tyle menu and select **C**reate Style. Enter a style name. Choose Selected **t**ext, and then click on **C**reate.

☞ To save a style to the current template, open the **S**tyle menu and select Style Mana**g**ement. From the list on the left, select the style you want to add, and then click on **M**ove. Select additional styles and repeat the move process if you want. When you're through, click on **OK** or press **Enter**.

Chapter 16

Front Page News: Changing Page Layout

In This Chapter

- Setting margins
- Adding a header or a footer
- Adding a border around a page
- Changing page size and orientation
- Changing page layout on selected pages within a document

At last you're ready for the big time: formatting an entire document or sections of it. Formatting a document or a section is not as common as formatting characters or paragraphs—but the stuff you'll learn in this chapter will have a global, worldwide effect.

In Chapter 13 (which I know you read and memorized just for this moment), you learned that Ami Pro has three levels of rulers which contain the settings for a document. The first level, the *page layout* or document ruler, governs the entire document unless it is overridden by one of the other rulers. The second level is the *style ruler* which holds the settings for a paragraph's style. The style ruler overrides settings on the page layout ruler. Lastly, there may be an *inserted ruler* which overrides whatever settings are currently in effect—changing both the paragraph and/or the page settings at a particular point within a document.

The *current ruler* displays whatever settings are currently in effect at the insertion point, so use it to decipher what's really going on. To display the current ruler, open the **View** menu and select Show **R**uler. By moving the insertion point to different places within the document, you can verify settings (and even change them if you want to).

So, now you're through with minor league stuff. In this chapter, you get to play with the big boy: the page layout ruler. I'll start by showing you how to make changes that affect an entire document; then I'll show you how to make these same kinds of changes for only part of your document.

A Marginal Review

In Chapter 13, you learned how to use the ruler to change a paragraph's tab settings and indentations. Here, I'll show you how to use the ruler to change margins. (If you want to change the margins later in the document, see the instructions towards the end of this chapter.)

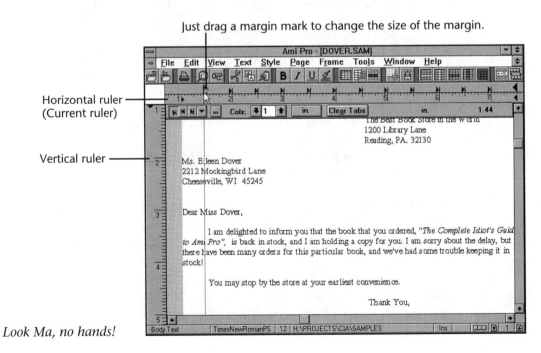

Just drag a margin mark to change the size of the margin.

Horizontal ruler (Current ruler)

Vertical ruler

Look Ma, no hands!

It's all fairly simple: just drag the Left or Right Margin mark to wherever you want it. If you'd rather use the keyboard, open the **Page** menu and select **Modify Page Layout** (press **Alt+P** and then **M**). Select **Margins & columns** from the Modify list (press **Alt+M**). Enter the **Left**, **Right**, **Top**, or **Bottom** margin settings (press **Alt+** the selection letter). Press **Enter**.

Click the right mouse button to display the Modify Page Layout dialog box.

 To change the top or bottom margins, follow the keyboard steps, or display the vertical ruler by opening the View menu, selecting View Preferences, and then selecting Vertical ruler. You can also click the **View Preferences** button (located on the Proofing

You can also click the **Page Layout** button on the Editing SmartIcon set to display the Modify Page Layout dialog box.

SmartIcon set) to display the View Preferences dialog box. Once it's displayed, drag the Top or Bottom Margin mark to change the top or bottom margins.

Time for a Tab (Again)

In Chapter 13, you learned how to set the tabs for selected paragraphs with the *current ruler*. You can set the tabs for the entire document by changing them on the Page Layout ruler, which is accessed through the Modify Page Layout dialog box. To set the tabs for the whole document, open the **Page** menu and select **Modify Page Layout** (press **Alt+P** and then **M**). Select **Margins & columns** from the Modify list (press **Alt+M**). Then click on the appropriate button to select the type of tab you want:

Left-aligned tab

Right-aligned tab

Center tab

Decimal tab

If you want to add a tab leader, click on the **Leader Character** button until the appropriate character appears. Then click on the ruler to set the position of the tab.

Want to clear out the party? Click Clear Tabs, and all tabs will be removed. Then you can start with a clean slate, adding only the tabs you want. When you're done, click **OK** or press **Enter**.

TECHNO NERD TEACHES

If you need to override the settings on the Page Layout ruler later in your document, just follow the directions at the end of this chapter. If you want to override the settings for a few paragraphs, go back to Chapter 13.

SPEAK LIKE A GEEK

When you select **portrait orientation**, your document is printed so that it is longer than it is wide, as in 8½ by 11 inches. This is the normal orientation of most documents.

When you use **landscape orientation**, your document is printed so that it is wider than it is long, as in 11 by 8½ inches.

This Page Is Just Your Size!

Sometimes getting something to fit is impossible. Not so with Ami Pro, which allows you to change the page size of your document as easily as you change lanes on the highway.

Open the **Page** menu and select **M**odify Page Layout (press **Alt+P** and then **M**). Select **Page** settings from the Modify list (press **Alt+S**). Select a page size by clicking on it, or by pressing **Alt+** the selection letter of the option you want and pressing the **Spacebar**. To create a custom size for that hard-to-fit page, click Custom or press **Alt+C**, and then enter the page dimensions. Click **OK** or press **Enter**.

The Page Orient Express

As you learned in Chapter 10, you can print your document in *Portrait* mode or *Landscape* mode. Just open the **Page** menu and choose the Modify Page Layout command. (Press **Alt+P** and then **M**.) Then click on **Page** settings (press **Alt+P**).

Click on either the Portrait or the Landscape option button. If you're using the keyboard, press **Alt+P** or **Alt+L**. When you're finished, choose **OK** or press **Enter**.

Line Up Your Pages

Want a page that really stands out? Just surround it with a thin border or add a line to any combination of the four sides. Open the Page menu and select Modify Page Layout (press **Alt+P** and then **M**). Select Lines from the Modify list (press **Alt+L**). Then click on the location you want for the line(s); for example, click on All. (Keyboarders: press **Alt+** the selection letter of the option you want.)

Select a Style for the border (press **Alt+S**). Finally, select a position for the line, relative to the margins. For example, you could place the line in the Middle of the margin. If you have a color printer, click on the color bar to select a color for your line. Click **OK** or press **Enter**.

You can change the page orientation midway through a document if you like. For example, if you're trying to print a report (in portrait mode), and you have a chart at the end that you want to print in landscape mode, just insert a new page layout within your document on the page with the chart. Don't fret; you'll find out how to insert page layouts at the end of this chapter.

Headers Don't Have to Give You a Headache

A *header* is text (such as a title) that can be printed at the top of every page in a document, and a *footer* is text (such as page numbers, chapter numbers, and so on) that can be printed at the bottom of every page.

To create a header or a footer, place the insertion point in the top or bottom margin of the first page on which you want a header or footer. Type some text if you like; for example, type **Page #**. Press **Tab** one time to center text, and twice to right-align text. Add character formatting, such as bold and italic, by clicking on the appropriate buttons on the Default SmartIcon set (or by pressing the key combinations you learned in Chapter 11).

To insert a page number, open the **Page** menu and select Page **Num**-bering (press **Alt+P** and then **N**). You can also click the **Page Number** button on the Long Documents SmartIcon set. Click on a numbering **Style** (or select one by pressing **Alt+S**, and then using the arrow keys). If you want the page numbering to begin with something other than 1, select Start with **n**umber (press **Alt+N**), and then enter a new number. Don't bother entering text in this dialog box; it's much easier to simply type it in the margin. Click **OK** or press **Enter**.

To insert a date, place the cursor where you want the date to appear. Then open the Edit menu, select Insert, and select **Date/Time** (press **Alt+E**, then **I**, and then **D**). Select a date option and style from those listed. Click **OK** or press **Enter**.

Inserted date

Inserted field for total pages

Inserted page number

Header

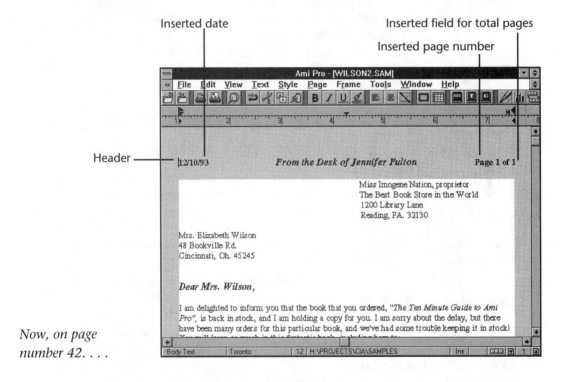

Now, on page number 42. . . .

If you want to get fancy, you can add more than just the date and time to your headers or footers by using *fields*. Fields are codes that instruct Ami Pro to insert current data into the document at a particular place. For example, you can insert the total number of pages, the total number of words, or other information into the header or footer using fields. Position the cursor within the header or footer, open the Edit menu, select Power Fields, and select Insert. (Press **Alt+E**, then **F**, and then **I**.) Choose a field from the Fields list, and click on **OK**.

When you're done creating your header or footer, press **Esc**, and you'll be returned to your regularly scheduled document page.

Left Foot(er), Right Foot(er)

You can change the header or footer later in your document—for example, you could have unique headers and footers for each section of your document. Simply insert a "floating" header or footer at any point within your document. To do so, open the **Page** menu and select Header/Footer (press **Alt+P**, and then **H**). Or you can click the **Floating Header/Footer** button on the Long Documents SmartIcon set to display the Headers/Footers dialog box.

Select Floating Header/Footer. Under Insert, select Floating **h**eader or Floating footer. Under Apply to, select the pages to which you want this new header to apply (the floating header/footer applies to pages from the current insertion point to the end of the document). Click **OK** or press **Enter**.

> **TECHNO NERD TEACHES**
>
> If you want to create a header or footer that's repeated only on the even (right-hand) or odd (left-hand) pages, follow the normal header or footer instructions to insert the header or footer on page one. Then open the **Page** menu and select **Modify Page Layout**. Under Pages, select **Right**, and then click on **OK**. Move to page two of your document and change the header or footer by clicking inside the margins and making your changes. Press **Esc** when you're through.

Type the text for your new header/footer, or insert page numbers, the date, etc. When you're done, press **Esc** to return to the document.

So, You Only Want This on Some Pages?

In this chapter, you've learned how to change a document's margins, tab settings, page size and orientation, borders, headers, and footers. But what if you want your changes to affect only some of the pages in a document? I mean, what's a person to do?

Well, whenever you modify the page layout, Ami Pro offers you a choice as to which pages you want to affect. Follow any of the instructions given earlier for making a formatting change (for example, if you want to change the page orientation, follow the instructions in that section). But, before you click **OK** to close the Modify Page Layout dialog box, choose one of these options under Pages:

All   The page layout settings affect all the pages in the document, unless the settings are overridden by an inserted page layout (which I'll show you how to do in just a sec).

Right   The page layout settings affect only the right (even-numbered) pages in the document.

Left   The page layout settings affect only the left (odd-numbered) pages in the document.

Mirror   The page layout settings affect all the pages in the document, but certain settings are reversed for odd and even pages. For example, if you select Left pages and Mirror and set a 1" left margin and a 1/2" right margin, those settings will be reversed on right-hand pages. That means that right-hand pages will have a 1/2" margin on the left and a 1" margin on the right (like the facing pages of a book).

If you select **Mirror**, choose **Facing Pages** from the **View** menu to see both the left-hand and right-hand pages at once.

If you want the original page layout to affect all the pages of your document except for a select few, insert a new page layout in those places instead of using the Pages section of the Modify Page Layout dialog box. To insert a page layout, move to the top of the page where you want to change page settings. Open the **Page** menu, select Insert Page Layout, and then select Insert (press **Alt+P**, then **I**, and then **I** again). Make your changes. They will override the original page layout settings for the remainder of the document. To remove the inserted page layout (and revert back to the original settings) at some later point, open the **Page** menu, select Insert Page Layout, and then select Revert (press **Alt+P**, then **I**, and then **R**).

The Least You Need to Know

I hope that the last three chapters have left you with a feeling of total control: control over text, paragraphs, and your entire document. (Now if I could only gain control over my waistline, I'd be a happy gal.) Here's what you learned in this chapter:

☞ You can change margins, tabs, page borders, paper size and page orientation, headers, footers, and page numbers for individual portions of your document by creating sections.

☞ To make changes to the entire document, change the page layout ruler by accessing the Modify Page Layout dialog box. To change selected pages, insert additional page layout rulers later in the document with the **Page** **I**nsert Page Layout command.

☞ To quickly access the Modify Page Layout dialog box, click the right mouse button within a margin, or click the **Page Layout** button on the Editing SmartIcon set.

☞ To change the margins, simply drag the Left or Right Margin marker on the ruler.

☞ To change the top or bottom margins, display the vertical ruler with the **V**iew View **P**references command and, once again, drag the margin marker.

☞ To change tab settings for the entire document, open the **Page** menu, select **M**odify Page Layout, and select **M**argins & columns. Click on the appropriate button to select the type of tab you want, and then click on the ruler.

continues

continued

☞ Change the page size and orientation by opening the **P**age menu and selecting **M**odify Page Layout. Select **P**age settings, and choose a page size. To create a custom size for that hard-to-fit page, click **C**ustom and then enter the page dimensions. To change the page orientation, select either **P**ortrait or **L**andscape. Click **OK** or press **Enter**.

☞ To add a border on one or all sides of the page, open the **P**age menu and select **M**odify Page Layout. Select **L**ines from the Modify list and click on the location of the line(s). Select a line style and a line position relative to the margins. Click **OK** or press **Enter**.

☞ To insert a header or footer, click inside the top or bottom margin of the first page. Enter text, or insert a date or page number. To insert a date, use the **E**dit **I**nsert **D**ate/Time command. To insert a page number, use the **P**age **P**age Numbering command, or click the **Page Number** button on the Long Documents SmartIcon set. Press **Esc** to return to the document.

Part III
Other Stuff You Paid for But Never Learned How to Use

Yes, I am one of the millions of Americans who own one of those new handi-cams (that's a video camera that was left in the dryer too long). Anyway, it comes "full-featured," which is a nice way of saying that there are entirely too many buttons on it. I've had the camera for a year, and I only know what the ON button is for.

Maybe you've been using Ami Pro like I use my handi-cam: just point and shoot—never mind the fine-tuning. There's nothing wrong with that; I've got a shelf full of videos to prove it. But when you're ready to know what "all those other buttons are for," come back and read this section.

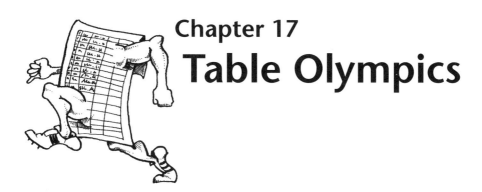

Chapter 17
Table Olympics

In This Chapter

☞ When to use tabs, and when to use a table

☞ Creating tables and adding text to them

☞ Adding rows and columns to a table

☞ Creating a table heading

☞ Adding a formula to a table

In life, a table makes it easy for you to keep food off your lap. In Ami Pro, *tables* make it easy to enter and organize large amounts of information; tables are much easier to use in this case than tabs are. (In life, tabs are convenient when you don't have any money; in Ami Pro, tabs are appropriate for two-column lists such as a phone list.)

Tables are made up of *rows* (the horizontal axis) and *columns* (the vertical axis). The intersection of a row and a column is called a *cell*. If that sounds like the definition of a spreadsheet, you're right—tables are very much like simple spreadsheets.

By the Way . . .

You can use a table for more than just tabular data; tables are great for creating side-by-side text (such as résumés) and/or graphics.

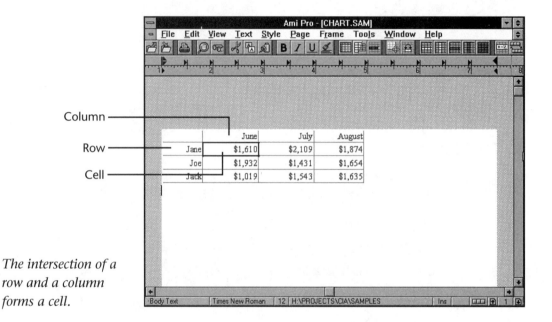

Column ———

Row ———

Cell ———

	June	July	August
Jane	$1,610	$2,109	$1,874
Joe	$1,932	$1,431	$1,654
Jack	$1,019	$1,543	$1,635

The intersection of a row and a column forms a cell.

Tabs are used to align columns of text, such as a short two-column list. Tabs are set on the ruler.

A **table** is used to organize large amounts of columnar data. Tables consist of **rows** (the horizontal axis) and **columns** (the vertical axis.) The intersection of a row and a column is called a **cell**.

Get the knives and forks ready: here's how you "set" a table into your document. Start by placing the insertion point where you want to set the table.

Click on the **Create Table** button on the Tables SmartIcon set, or open the Tools menu and select Tables. Enter the number of rows and columns, and then click **OK** or press **Enter**. An empty table with the number of rows and columns you specified will appear at the insertion point.

The gridlines that you see help you enter data into the cells, but they don't print. If they bother you, remove them from your screen by opening the View menu and selecting View **Preferences** or by clicking on the **View Preferences** button on the Proofing SmartIcon set. Deselect **Table** gridlines, and press **Enter** or click **OK**.

TECHNO NERD TEACHES

You can insert a table into a *frame* (a box) to make it moveable. That way, you can place the table exactly where you want it within your document. See Chapter 21 for more on frames.

The Three T's: Typing Text in a Table

Enter text into a table by starting with the first cell. (If necessary, click in it to move the insertion point there.) To move to the next cell, press **Tab**. Press **Shift+Tab** to move to a previous cell. When you get to the end of a row, pressing **Tab** will move you to the first cell in the next row. Alternatively, you can click on a cell to move there.

Here are some tips for entering data into a table:

E-Z

Instead of typing data, you can have Ami Pro create a table automatically by copying information from a spreadsheet program (such as Lotus 1-2-3 for Windows or Microsoft Excel). Use the old "cut and paste" method, with the **C**opy and **P**aste commands on the Edit menu of each program. For example, you could select cells in an Excel spreadsheet, select **C**opy, move to Ami Pro, and select **P**aste.

- ☞ If you want to type several paragraphs in the cell, press **Enter** at the end of each paragraph (just as you would any other time). The height of the table will grow to accommodate the amount of text you enter.

- ☞ Press **Ctrl** plus any arrow key to move to the next cell in that direction.

- ☞ Press **Home** to move to the beginning of the text in the current cell. Press **Home+Home** to move to the first cell in the current row.

☞ Press **End** to move to the end of the text in the current cell. Press **End+End** to move to the last cell in the current row.

☞ When you're done entering data and you want to return to the document, press **Esc** or click in the document.

☞ If you want to change the width of a column, move the pointer to the column's right edge (the pointer will change to a four-headed arrow). Drag the column's edge to any location to make the column bigger or smaller. (You won't be able to make a column bigger if the resulting table won't fit on the page.)

Editing Your Data

To correct a typo, press the **Backspace** key to delete one character at a time. To replace the contents of a cell with something else, select the cell (oops—wait a minute—you'll learn how to do that next), and then type the new entry.

Selecting the Cells You Want to Change

You can select entire rows or columns in order to format them in one step. For example, you can select a row of column headings and format them as bold so they stand out. To select a cell, click and drag over it. To select a row, click to the left of it. To select a column, click at the top of it. To select an entire table, open the Table menu and choose Select Entire Table. (Press **Alt+B** and then **B**.)

To select a single cell with the keyboard, simply press **Tab** or **Shift+Tab** to move to that cell, and then press and hold the **Shift** key as you use the arrow keys to select the contents of the cell. To select multiple cells with the keyboard, press **Shift+Ctrl** as you press an arrow key. You can select an entire row or column by opening the Table menu (press **Alt+B**) and choosing either Select Row or Select Column (press either **R** or **O**).

Formatting Cells

After selecting the cell or cells you want to format, follow the normal steps to apply character formatting. For example, if you want to make the selected cells bold, click on the **Bold** button on the Default SmartIcon set. If you want to change the font, select a new one from the **Face** button on the status bar. If you want to change the alignment, click the appropriate button on the Default SmartIcon set or use the Text Alignment command. See Chapters 11 and 12 for more tips on changing formatting.

If you don't like the format of numbers (you don't want any decimal places, for example), change the Table Text style. Open the Style menu and select Modify Style (press **Ctrl+A** or click the right mouse button). Select **Table Text** from the Style list, and Table format from the Modify list. Choose a Cell format. For example, choose **Currency** if you want to display dollar signs in front of each number. Select the No. of decimal places, and enter a number. For example, if you don't want decimals, enter **0**. If you don't want a comma between the thousands place and the hundreds place, deselect Thousands separator. You can also change the format of negative numbers, and the symbol used to represent currency. For example, instead of the $, you could type ¥, £, or if you're having a bad day, ☺.

A Line Here, a Line There

Adding borders (dark lines around cells) is an especially effective type of formatting with tables—as is shading (adding a bit of gray to darken a particular cell and call attention to it). To add a border, first open the Table menu and select Lines & Color (press **Alt+B** and then **N**). Or you can click the **Table Lines** button on the Tables SmartIcon set. Select a Line position and a Line style. If you want to fill the cells with a color, choose a color from the color bar. Click **OK** or press **Enter**.

Why do you have to add borders when they're already there? Well, the "borders" you're seeing are the *gridlines*, which help you enter text into a table but don't print. To have borders on your final printout, you must add them.

Changing Your Mind: Copying, Moving, and Deleting Cells

When you copy or move a cell's contents to another cell, you wipe out (replace) anything currently in the cell to which you're copying (or moving) data—so be careful! You copy or move the contents of cells by selecting the cells, and then clicking on the appropriate button on any SmartIcon set:

Click	To
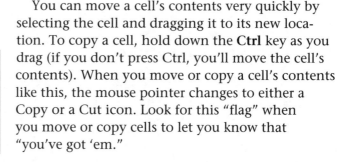 Copy	Copy a cell's data.
Cut and then Paste	Move a cell's data

I find it easiest to grab a cell if I position the pointer in the middle of the cell I want to copy or move, and then drag the mouse.

You can move a cell's contents very quickly by selecting the cell and dragging it to its new location. To copy a cell, hold down the **Ctrl** key as you drag (if you don't press Ctrl, you'll move the cell's contents). When you move or copy a cell's contents like this, the mouse pointer changes to either a Copy or a Cut icon. Look for this "flag" when you move or copy cells to let you know that "you've got 'em."

To delete the contents of a cell, select the cell and press **Delete**.

To delete the current row, press **Ctrl+-** (the minus on the numeric keypad). To delete more than one row, select the rows and press **Ctrl+-**.

Making Your Table Bigger

Want a bigger table? Just add more rows or columns. To add more rows or columns, move to the place in the table where you want to add them.

Then open the Table menu and select Insert Column/Row (press **Alt+B** and then **I**). Select Columns or Rows (press **Alt+C** or **Alt+R**) and enter the number of rows or columns to insert (press **Alt+I**, and then type a number). Select the position: **B**efore or **A**fter the current row (press **Alt+B** or **Alt+A**).

  You can insert a single row or column after the current row or column by clicking the **Insert Row** or **Insert Column** button on the Tables SmartIcon set.

The Incredible Shrinking Table

Okay, so you know how to make your table big and strong, but how do you shrink a fat table? To delete rows or columns, move to the row or column you want to delete (select multiple rows or columns if you like). Then open the Table menu and select Delete Column/Row (press **Alt+B** and then **D**). Select Delete **c**olumn or Delete **r**ow (press **Alt+C** or **Alt+R**), and then click **OK** or press **Enter**. Click on **Y**es or press **Y**.

  You can delete a single row or column after the current row or column by clicking the **Delete Row** or **Delete Column** button on the Tables SmartIcon set. Click on **Y**es or press **Y** to delete the rows or columns.

 To add a single row below the current row, press **Ctrl++** (the plus on the numeric keypad). To add more than one row, select that number of rows above where you want to add additional rows (for example, to add two rows, select two rows), and then press **Ctrl++**.

 You can't add a column to a table if the resulting table will be wider than the page. If you have that problem, adjust the width of your columns and try again. You may want to change to landscape page orientation instead—see Chapter 16.

To delete an entire table, click the **Delete Table** button, or open the Table menu and select Delete Entire Table (press **Alt+B** and then **T**).

 To make it easy on yourself, display the row and column labels by opening the **View** menu and selecting View Preferences (press **Alt+V** and then **P**). Select Table row/column headings, and click **OK** or press **Enter**.

Math 101

You can perform simple arithmetic on the contents of cells. But before we get into any of that, let me explain how cells are referenced. First, columns are identified with a letter, with the first column being column A. Rows are identified with numbers. Cells are addressed by their column and then their row. For example, the second cell in the second row is cell B2.

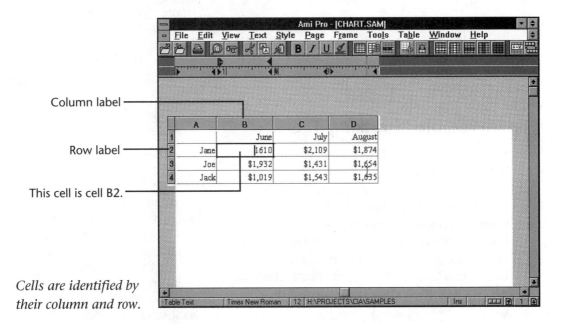

Column label ———

Row label ———

This cell is cell B2. ———

Cells are identified by their column and row.

Once you can identify two cells by their addresses, you can add or subtract (multiply or divide) their contents. Here's a list of math symbols and what they mean that you can use in your formulas.

Function	Symbol
Addition	+
Subtraction	–
Multiplication	*
Division	/
Percent	%

For example, to subtract cell B4 from B3, use the formula B3–B4. (I'll show you exactly how to enter the formula in a cell in just a minute.)

To specify a *range* of cells, insert a colon. For example, to specify the cells C2, C3, and C4, just type C2:C4. With ranges, you can get pretty complicated; for example, the formula (C2:C4)s–C5 means to add the cells C2, C3, and C4, and then subtract C5.

> **SPEAK LIKE A GEEK**
>
> A **range** is a group of adjacent cells in a table that form a rectangle. A range is addressed by listing the upper left cell, followed by the lower right cell of the range. For example, the range C2:D3 includes the cells C2, C3, D2, and D3.

Entering a Formula

 After you enter a formula, the result of that formula is displayed in the current cell. So before you enter the formula, move to the cell where you want the result displayed. To enter a formula into a cell, click the **Edit Formula** button on the Tables SmartIcon set, or open the Table menu and select Edit Formula. Enter your formula, and click **OK** or press **Enter**.

Just so you know, if you go back to one of the cells referenced in a formula and change its value, the formula result will automatically be recalculated—no sweat. For example, if cell B5 contains the formula B3+B4, and you change the value in cell B3, cell B5 will automatically be changed to reflect the new sum.

> **TECHNO NERD TEACHES**
>
> You can copy formulas to save time. Simply select a cell, click on the **Copy** button, move to another cell, and click on **Paste**. When you copy a formula, the cells in the formula change to fit the location to which you're copying. Sound strange? Well, it works like this: let's say you entered the formula B2+B3 into cell B4. Then you copied cell B4 to cell C4. The formula in C4 would change to the formula C2+C3, because it wouldn't make any sense to add the two cells in column B, when we're in column C. See?

This formula could also be written: B2+B3+B4.

Cell where result of formula will be displayed.

Enter your formula in this dialog box.

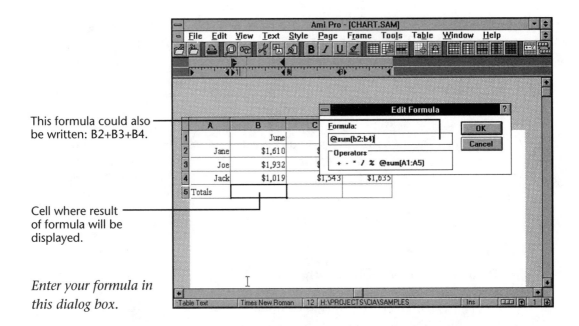

If you see "Ref" in a cell instead of the result of your formula, you've got a problem. Either the cells you referenced in the formula don't exist, or they contain text instead of numbers. Be sure not to include spaces after numbers you type, because that will turn the data into "text" as far as Ami Pro is concerned. For example, if you typed 123 followed by a space, and then pressed **Tab** to go to the next cell, Ami Pro wouldn't see this as a number to add or subtract; it would be considered text. Retype the number without the space, and everything will be fine.

By the Way . . .

If addition's your game, there's a simpler way to go about it. If you wanted to add the cells B2, B3, and B4, you might type: B2+B3+B4. Instead, you could use the @SUM *function.* Just type @SUM(B2:B4) instead.

If you want to add a whole row or column (and not just selected cells), use the Quick Add feature. Move to the cell where you want to place the total, and then open the **Table** menu and select Quick **Add.** (Press **Alt+B** and then **A.**) Select **R**ow or **C**olumn, and the appropriate cells will be totalled up for you!

The Least You Need to Know

I'll put my cards on the table—here's what I feel were the most important points of this chapter:

- ☞ Tables are made up of *rows* (the horizontal axis) and *columns* (the vertical axis). The intersection of a row and a column is called a *cell.*

- ☞ It's better to use tables than to use tabs if you have large amounts of data to organize. To create a table, click on the **Table** button on the Default SmartIcon set, and drag over the grid to select the number of columns and rows.

- ☞ When entering data into the various cells in a table, move from cell to cell by pressing **Tab** and **Shift+Tab**.

- ☞ To change the width of a column, drag the column's right edge to its new location.

- ☞ To select a row or column, click at the beginning of it.

- ☞ Add borders or shading to a cell with the Lines & Color command on the Table menu, or click the **Table Lines** button on the Tables SmartIcon set.

- ☞ If you need to move a cell's contents, select the cell's contents by clicking in the middle of the cell. Then drag the cell to its new location. To copy a cell, hold down the **Ctrl** key as you drag.

- ☞ To add more rows or columns, click the **Insert Row** or **Insert Column** button on the Tables SmartIcon set.

continues

continued

☞ You can delete a single row or column after the current row or column by clicking the **Delete Row** or **Delete Column** button on the Tables SmartIcon set. Click on **Yes** or press **Y** to delete the rows or columns.

☞ A cell is referenced in a formula by its column (a letter) and row (a number). For example, the second cell in the third row is cell B3.

☞ You can insert a formula into a cell by clicking the **Edit Formula** button on the Tables SmartIcon set.

☞ Display the row and column markers in a table by clicking the **View Preferences** button on the Proofing SmartIcon set and selecting Table row and column headings.

Chapter 18

Getting It Right: Checking Your Document for Errors

In This Chapter

- 👉 Checking your document for spelling errors
- 👉 Looking up an alternative for a word
- 👉 Finding grammatical errors
- 👉 Searching and replacing words within a document

I am not the world's best speller. Poor Miss Dingerham, she tried so hard, but I just never got it: "I before E . . . except in the 2,000 other words where it's E before I." Thank goodness for spell checkers, grammar checkers, and all those nifty programs built into Ami Pro that help me focus on what I'm trying to say, rather than how I'm saying it.

Spelling Bee

When Ami Pro checks a document for spelling errors, it searches for mistakes everywhere (it reminds me of ol' Miss Dingerham). Ami Pro checks headers, footers, footnotes, and even the text in boxes (*frames*). Spell checking a document is simple—just click on the **Spelling** button on the Default SmartIcon set. For you keyboard users out there, press **Alt+L** to open the Tools menu, and then press **S** to select Spell Check.

Click here to search the —— entire document, including headers and footers.

Click here if you want Ami Pro to search from the beginning of the document.

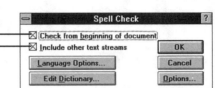

Looking for errors in all the right places.

TECHNO NERD TEACHES

You can enter text into various areas of a document: the main document, a fixed or floating frame (box), a header or footer, or a footnote. Each of these areas is called a *text stream.* When you use the spell checker, the search begins at the insertion point (unless you specify that the search should start at the beginning of the document), and continues to all *lower text streams.* Spell Check checks the spelling of each text stream in the following order:

Main document
Fixed frame text
Footnotes
Floating frame text
Floating headers or footers
Fixed headers or footers

So be careful of where you place your insertion point; you could cause Ami Pro to overlook certain parts of your document in the spelling check.

When Ami Pro checks your document for spelling errors, it begins its search at the insertion point and runs to the end of the document, unless you direct it to start at the beginning of the document. (You remember the *insertion point*; it's that blinking vertical line that marks your place in your document.) So select Check from **b**eginning of document (press **Alt+B**) if you want Ami Pro to search from the top of page one. Select Include other text streams (press **Alt+I**) if you want Ami Pro to search your entire document. (Read the Techno Nerd tip if you want to know everything there is to know about text streams. Don't worry—if you fall asleep, this book will wake you up in ten minutes.) Click **OK** or press **Enter**, and Ami Pro immediately starts checking for spelling errors. Also, if you've repeated a word accidentally, or mis-capitalized one, Ami Pro will tell you.

You can quickly spell check a single paragraph or section of your document by selecting it first, and then clicking on the **Spelling** button on the Default SmartIcon set (or by pressing **Alt+L** and then **S**). Only the highlighted text will be checked for spelling errors.

By the Way . . .

You can customize the way Ami Pro spell-checks your document by clicking on the **Options** button (or pressing **Alt+O**) in the Spell Check dialog box. For example, Ami Pro can be instructed to ignore the capitalization of words that are all uppercase, or to ignore words with text and numbers. To select an option, click on it (or press **Alt+** the selection letter). Then click **OK** or press **Enter** to return to the Spell Check dialog. Finally, click **OK** or press **Enter** to start the spell check.

SPEAK LIKE A GEEK

Any separate text area within an Ami Pro document is called a **text stream**. For example, the main document text and the headers and footers are two different text streams.

What to Do If Ami Pro Finds a Mistake

If Ami Pro finds a misspelled or repeated word, a box with more buttons than an airplane cockpit appears, giving you lots of options.

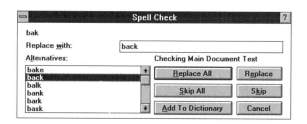

All these buttons in this dialog box, and they still forgot one: Panic.

Select the appropriate button to perform one of the following actions:

☞ **Correct the spelling of the word.** If you agree with the suggestion in the Replace with box, click on the Replace button (press **Alt+E**). If you want to correct this word throughout the document, click on Replace All instead (press **Alt+R**). If you want, you can type your own correction (press **Alt+W** or click on the Replace with text box and type the correction), and then choose Replace or Replace All. You can also select an alternative from the Alternatives list box (click on it, or press **Alt+L** and use the arrow keys to select a word).

☞ **Ignore the correction.** If you want to skip just this occurrence of the unrecognized word, click on the Skip button (press **Alt+K**). To skip all occurrences of the unrecognized word, click on the Skip All button (press **Alt+S**).

☞ **Add this word to the dictionary.** If you choose this option, the specified word won't be considered misspelled ever again. Just click on the Add To Dictionary button or press **Alt+A**. Choose this option for specialized words that you use in your job, such as "cardiopulmonary," "electrolyte," "anthropomorphic," "Nanotechnology," or "SmartIcon set."

☞ **Delete the repeated word.** If a word is repeated (such as the the), you'll see a message telling you so. If it shouldn't be repeated and you want to delete the extra word, press **Backspace** and click on the Replace button (press **Alt+E**). Otherwise, click on Skip (press **Alt+K**).

You continue this process until the spell check is finished.

Handling the Informant

I was going to use the title "Using the Thesaurus" for this section. But then I decided to see what synonyms the Thesaurus would offer to spice up my title. "Handling the Informant" is what it came up with. I guess that illustrates one of my reservations about using a thesaurus: it can make your writing sound stilted and fake. I mean, how often does someone say, "Our sales for the fourth quarter were consequential" instead of simply, "Our sales for the fourth quarter were great."

To use the Thesaurus, just follow these *consequential*, great, important, considerable, critical steps. First, select the word you want to look up, or move the insertion point to the word. Then click the **Thesaurus** button on the Default SmartIcon set, or open the Tools menu and select the Thesaurus command (press **Alt+L** and then **T**). A box "full of meaning" will appear. The word you selected in the document appears under Word looked up.

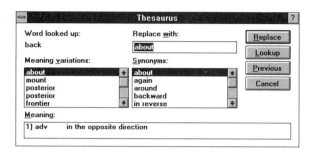

You can replace your boring prose with one of the colorful alternatives listed in the Thesaurus box.

In the Thesaurus dialog box, you can select from several options:

☞ Replace your word with the one listed under Replace with. Click on **Replace**, or press **Alt+R**. To return to the document without replacing your word, press **Esc**.

☞ Choose from the synonyms listed in the **Synonyms** list box. Click on a replacement word, and then click on **Replace**. With the keyboard press **Alt+S**, use the arrow keys to select a word, and then press **Alt+R**.

☞ Change the synonyms listed. Choose from general variations of the selected word that appear in the Meaning variations box. (Press **Alt+V** and use the arrow keys to select a variation.)

☞ Look up additional meanings for a word displayed in the **Syn**onyms box. Highlight a word in the Synonyms list and click on Lookup. (Press **Alt+S**, use the arrow keys to highlight a word, and then press **Alt+L**.) To return to the previous word, click on **Previ**ous or press **Alt+P**.

I Doesn't Need No Grammar Checker!

The Grammar Check command checks your document for problems of a grammatical nature and suggests ways to improve your writing and clarify your meaning.

The **G**rammar Check command works just like the spelling checker; it starts checking your document at the insertion point, unless you specify that you want it to start at the beginning of your document. Also, **G**rammar Check will check the current text stream, and all lower text streams. In short, this means that Grammar Check (like Spell Check) will check your document in a certain order; for example, it will check the main document text before it checks the text in headers and footers. If you want the nitty gritty on text streams, read the Techno Nerd tip at the beginning of this chapter.

Be sure to use **S**pell Check to verify your spelling. **G**rammar Check does not check for spelling errors, only errors in grammar.

To check the grammar in your document, click on the **Grammar Check** button on the Default SmartIcon set, or open the Tools menu and choose Grammar Check (press **Alt+L** and then **G**). Select a grammar style to check your document against. By default, business writing is the style that's used, but you can choose casual writing (among others) if you prefer. Indicate your additional preferences by clicking on them or by pressing **Alt+** the selection letter:

Show readability **s**tatistics   Displays the total number of words, the percentage of sentences that use *passive voice*, and the readability index.

Show **e**xplanations   Displays brief explanations of the problem, and an example.

Check from **b**eginning of document   Starts the grammar check at page one.

Include other text streams   Includes other text streams than the one in which the insertion point is located.

Check in **d**raft mode   Displays sentences that go past the end of a column or page.

If you want to get real fancy, you can click on the **Options** button and choose the various grammatical rules you wish to apply to your document. Click on a rule or press **Alt+** the selection letter to select it. Then click on **OK** or press **Enter** to return to the Grammar Check dialog box.

When you're ready to start, click **OK** or press **Enter**. If Ami Pro finds something questionable, you see a box offering some suggestions.

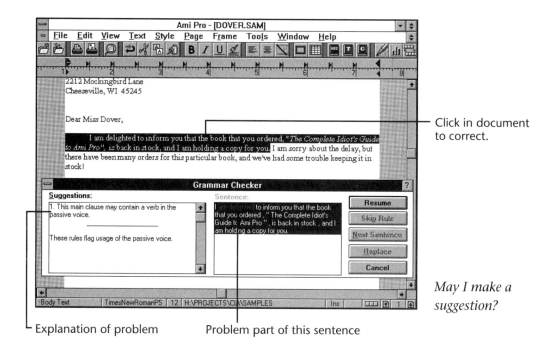

Click in document
to correct.

May I make a
suggestion?

Explanation of problem   Problem part of this sentence

From here, you have these options:

☞ Accept a suggestion by selecting one of those listed in the Re-
placements options box and clicking on **R**eplace.

☞ If the Replacement options box is not displayed or if you want to
make your own correction, click inside the document window (or
press **Alt+F6**) and change your text. To check the grammar in the
rest of the document, click on **Resume** or press **Alt+F6** again, and
then press **Enter**.

☞ Get more information about what's wrong by scrolling through
the explanation within the Suggestions box.

☞ Bypass the suggestion by clicking on the **Skip** button. You can
bypass the entire sentence by clicking on the Next Sentence
button instead. You can tell Ami Pro to ignore this "grammatical
faux pas" for the rest of the document by clicking on Ski**p** Rule.

At the end of the grammar check, Ami Pro displays something it calls Readability Statistics (if you selected that option at the beginning of the grammar check). The readability statistics tell you the total number of words, sentences, and so on; the average number of words per sentence; the percentage of sentences that use *passive voice*; and the *readability indexes*. For an average reader, look for a Gunning Fog index of about 10 or 11, a Flesch-Kincaid score of about 8 or 9, Flesch Reading Ease of about 65, and a Flesch Reading Ease Grade Level of about 7 or 8. Numbers above these indicate some rather difficult material. (Translation: "Instead of two sleeping pills, try reading this.") Lower numbers than these indicate easier material. (Translation: "This text makes a perfect accompaniment to Saturday morning cartoons.")

Indiana Fulton and the Hunt for the Great Lost Word

Suppose you just finished a big report, only to find out that your client's real name is *Pets Are Us Incorporated* and not *Bill's Pet Shop*. You can use Ami Pro's Find and Replace feature to replace all occurrences of the incorrect name right before the meeting with the Top Dog. You can also search for a word without replacing it, which is helpful when locating the correct section within a document.

The Hunt Is On!

To find a word or a phrase in your document, open the Edit menu and select the Find & Replace command, or press **Ctrl+F**. Or you can click the **Find & Replace** button on the Editing SmartIcon set. Type the word (or phrase) you're looking for in the Find text box. Click **Find** or press **Enter** to begin the search for the lost word. But before you do, there are some handy options you can choose from:

☞ If you want to locate only the complete word you typed, and not words that include it as a part (for example, you want to find "search" but not "searching"), click on **Options** or press **Alt+O**, and then select **W**hole word only. Click **OK** or press **Enter** to return to the Find & Replace dialog box.

☞ If you want to match upper- or lowercase (for example, "Word" but not "word"), click on **Options** or press **Alt+O**, and then select Exact case. Click **OK** or press **Enter** to return to the Find & Replace dialog box.

☞ If you want to search from the beginning of the document, click on **Options** or press **Alt+O**, and then select Beginning of document. To search backwards through a document, select Find backwards. To search all text streams, select Include other text streams. Click **OK** or press **Enter** to return to the Find & Replace dialog box.

☞ If you want to search for a word with particular formatting, click on **Attributes** or press **Alt+A**, select the formatting attributes you want, and then click **OK** or press **Enter** to return to the Find & Replace dialog box.

When you have selected all the options you want, click on **Find**. Ami Pro will look for the first occurrence of the selected word. If you want it to continue looking, click on the Find Next button, or press **Alt+N**. To return to your document, click on **Cancel** or press **Esc**. To continue the search (search for the same text or formatting) at a later time or in another document, press **Ctrl+F** and then **Enter**.

The Great Switcheroo: Finding a Word and Replacing It with Something Else

To search for a word or phrase and replace it with other text, start by opening the Edit menu and selecting the Find & Replace command (or by pressing **Ctrl+F**). Or you can click the **Find & Replace** button on the Editing SmartIcon set. Type the word (or phrase) you're looking for in the Find text box, and type the word (or phrase) you want to replace it with in the Replace with box. Click **Find** or press **Enter** to start the search; but before you do, here are some handy options you can choose from:

☞ If you want to locate only the complete word you typed, and not words that include it as a part (for example, you want to find "search" but not "searching"), click on Options or press **Alt+O**, and then select Whole word only. Click **OK** or press **Enter** to return to the Find & Replace dialog box.

☞ If you want to match upper- or lowercase (for example "Word" but not "word"), click on Options or press **Alt+O**, and then select Exact case. Click **OK** or press **Enter** to return to the Find & Replace dialog box.

☞ If you want to search from the beginning of the document, click on Options or press **Alt+O**, and then select Beginning of document. To search backwards through a document, select Find backwards. To search all text streams, select Include other text streams. Click **OK** or press **Enter** to return to the Find & Replace dialog box.

☞ If you want to search for a word with particular formatting, click on Attributes or press **Alt+A**, select the formatting attributes you want, and then click **OK** or press **Enter** to return to the Find & Replace dialog box.

When you're ready to start, click on either **Find** (to confirm changes before replacing) or **Replace All** (to replace without confirmation). Ami Pro will look for the first occurrence of the selected word. If you chose Find, confirm the replacement by clicking on Replace & Find Next, or continue searching by clicking on Find Next. If you want to replace all occurrences of the word without looking at them any more, click Replace Remaining. Click **Cancel** or press **Esc** to return to your document and quit the find and replace operation.

Getting Fancy with Find and Replace

You can find a paragraph style and/or replace it with another paragraph style by entering the style name(s) in the appropriate boxes in the Find & Replace dialog box. Click on Options or press **Alt+O**, and then select **S**tyle under Find & replace type. Click **OK** or press **Enter** to return to the Find & Replace dialog box, and then follow the instructions given earlier to either find or replace your paragraph style throughout your document.

The Least You Need to Know

Let's see if I can help you "find" the important points in this chapter:

- To spell-check a document, click on the **Spelling** button on the Default SmartIcon set.

- To look up an alternative for a word, select it, and then click the **Thesaurus** button on the Default SmartIcon set.

- To check your document for grammatical errors, click the **Grammar Check** button on the Default SmartIcon set.

- To search for words in a document, use the Find & **R**eplace command on the **E**dit menu or click the **Find & Replace** button on the Editing SmartIcon set. Enter a word to search for, and then press **Enter**.

- To replace words in a document, again use the Find & **R**eplace command on the **E**dit menu or click the **Find & Replace** button on the Editing SmartIcon set. Enter a word to search for, enter a word to replace it with, and click either **Find** or **R**eplace All.

Here's another page about nothing at all.

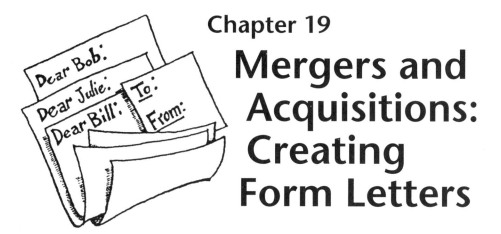

Chapter 19
Mergers and Acquisitions: Creating Form Letters

In This Chapter

- The magical world of merging
- Creating a merge data file
- Writing your dummy letter
- Merging to create form letters
- Creating mailing labels and matching envelopes

About six months ago, I was reading one of the magazines I subscribe to when I spotted an ad with my name in it. The ad read, "If you've been thinking of buying a computer, Jennifer Fulton, now is the time." I stared at that for a few minutes before it hit me—it was just another variation of the old form letter. You would've thought I was over the thrill of seeing my name in a *personalized* letter. I mean, who really believes that "you may have already won!"?

But there's no denying that form letters and mailing labels are two of the best reasons for typing your letters on a computer. So let's see how this computer magic is done.

Look Before You Merge

First of all, let me warn you that this very boring topic produces some real cool results: for example, print 200 personalized letters when you only type one. So before you continue, get a caffeine equivalent (coffee, cola, chocolate, or a large mallet), some aspirin, and a ton of letterhead, and then prop this book up someplace where you can see it as you work. Believe me, this is not a process you'll want to memorize. All set? Okay, let's go!

In order to create form letters or mailing labels in Ami Pro, you need two files:

- ☞ Your *main document file* contains the generic text and formatting (such as margin settings, paper size, and the like) that you want to appear in every copy of the final document.

- ☞ Your *merge data file* contains the variable information (such as the individual names and addresses).

The process of taking the names and addresses from the merge data file and mixing them into the main document to create multiple form letters (or mailing labels) is called *merging*.

Still awake? Well, you're almost past the worst of the boring background stuff. Just one more section to go before you get to do something.

That's One for the Record

The merge data file contains the stuff that changes with each form letter or each mailing label. For example, if you wanted to send a letter to each of your customers, the merge data file would contain each customer's name, address, and maybe even a customer number.

In your customer merge data file, each individual client would represent a data record. A *data record* is a collection of the related information about (in this example) a specific client: name, address, phone number, and client account number. Each client would have a corresponding record in the merge data file.

The individual pieces that make up a data record are called *fields*. For example, the client's name would be one field, and the address would be another. Each field has its own name; for example, the client name field could be called NAME, and the account number field could be called ACCOUNT (clever, eh?). The names for each field are stored in the *header record*, which is usually just the first line in the merge data file.

After you create a merge data file, you'll enter the field names into your dummy letter so Ami Pro will know where to place the real information from each record. For example, you'll enter a field called First Name in your dummy letter, and Ami Pro will replace it with real data, such as the name *George*.

Giving Birth to a Merge Data File

Before you create your merge data file, think about how you are going to use the individual fields. In a typical business letter, for example, you usually include the client's full name and address:

Mr. George Blabberton
Chief Cook and Bottle Washer
Universal Foods, Incorporated
210 W. 86th Street
Piggstown, Vt. 31209

But in the greeting, you can get more friendly:

Dear George,

However, if you create a NAME field which contains the client's *entire name*, you'll be stuck with a greeting like this:

Dear Mr. George Blabberton,

I have to think that with this greeting, even Mr. George Blabberton will be able to figure out he's just received a form letter. So instead, break the client's name into several parts: Mr/Mrs/Ms, First Name, and Last Name.

There's something else to think about: will you want to sort the merge data file's records in any particular order before creating your form letters or mailing labels? Even though it may make sense to have one field for a client's entire address, you can't sort by town or ZIP code unless each of these is its own field. (You can't sort on something that's *part* of a field.) In this case, you will want to create separate fields for the parts of an address: Address, City, State, and ZIP.

Creating a Merge Data File

Well, I've given you enough to think about; let's get down to business! As step one in the process of creating form letters, we'll create a merge data file. After we create our merge data file, we'll create a dummy letter and insert the field names. Then we'll merge the two to create beautiful form letters that would fool even your mother.

Your merge forms control center.

To create a merge data file, just follow these steps. (If you want hands-on practice rather than some generic steps, skip ahead to the "Put It to Work" exercise. When you're ready to create your own real merge data file, come back to this section.) First, open the File menu and select Merge. With the keyboard, press **Alt+F** and then **G**. Choose option 1 by pressing **Enter**. Click on New or press **Alt+W**. The Create Data File dialog box will be displayed.

Made it this far? Great! Now you're ready to select the field names for your merge data file. Here's what to do:

Your first field acts as the *key field*, which means that it's kind of like the tab on a folder, helping you identify a particular record within the database. For that reason, you may want to make the first field of your database something important, such as Last Name, or Client ID Number.

1. Add fields for your database. Type a field name (with spaces if you want) in the Field Name box, and then click on **Add** or press **Enter**. For example, type **Last Name** and press **Enter**.

2. Repeat for all the fields you want to add. Add another field by typing its name and pressing **Enter**. Keep doing this until you've added all the fields you need.

3. Change the order of the fields (if necessary). In order to make data entry as smooth as possible, you might want to change the order of some of the fields to match the records you'll be typing from. Select a field in the **Fields in data file** list and click on the big up or down arrows to move it.

4. Remove fields you don't want to use. Select a field from the **Fields in data file** list, and click on **Remove** or press **Alt+R**. For example, if you typed a name for a field incorrectly, just remove that field and add it again.

5. When you're satisfied, click on **OK**. Ami Pro creates a data file (which looks and smells like an ordinary document), and then displays the Data File dialog box. Here's where you'll actually enter the individual records (client's names and addresses for example) in the data file.

Well, you made it this far. Skip to the next section to learn how to enter your data.

Put It to Work

Creating a Sample Merge Data File

For practice let's create a small data merge file. First, open the **File** menu and select Merge. Select option 1 by pressing **Enter**, and then select New.

Under Field **Name**, type **Mr/Ms/Mrs** and press **Enter**. Type **Last Name** and press **Enter** to add it. Continue this process to add **First Name**, **Job Title**, **Company**, **Address**, **City**, **State**, and **ZIP**, pressing **Enter** to add each one separately.

Oops! We forgot to allow for a second address line. Type **Address 2** and press **Enter**. To move the field up to where it should be (just after the Address field and before City), select it and then click on the big up arrow a few times.

We're done adding fields, so click on **OK**. Congrats! Your merge data file is created, and is waiting for you to enter some data (which you'll do as soon as you learn how).

Filling In the Blanks

Entering information into the merge data file is fairly simple:

- ☛ It's okay if the data is bigger than one of the text boxes; it won't affect how that data appears in your document.

- ☛ Press **Tab** or **Enter** to move to the next field; press **Shift+Tab** to move backward. If you get down to the bottom of the dialog box, and there are still more fields to enter, that's okay—just press **Tab** or **Enter** and you'll move on to the next field.

Instead of clicking on **Add** when you've entered data in the last field of a record, just press **Enter** to automatically start a new record.

- ☛ If a field does not apply for a particular record (for example, you don't know a client's title), leave it blank by pressing **Tab** or **Enter** to bypass it.

- ☛ When you're through entering the data for a single record, click on Add or press **Alt+A**.

☞ When you're through entering data, click on the **Close** button to save the merge data file, and then enter a name for it. For example, type **CLIENTS** and press **Enter**.

You'll be returned to the Welcome to Merge dialog box. Now you're all set to create the dummy letter.

Put It to Work

Entering Our Sample Data File's Variable Information
Starting with the first field of our test merge data file, enter these client records. If a field doesn't apply, press **Tab** or **Enter** to move to the next field. When you're through adding a record, click on **Add** or press **Enter** to move on to the next record.

Mr/Ms/Mrs	Last Name	First Name	Job Title
Ms.	Smitt	Eileen	Comptroller
Mr.	Axe	John	
Mr.	Cooper	Scott	Field Manager

Company	Address	Address 2
Bobco	12 North St.	
PI Electric	One Fire Pl.	Suite #312
Allied Limited	5218 N. 118th	

City	State	Zip
Olmo	OK	73521
Guston	NJ	07401
Spud	ID	83318

When you are finished adding records, click on **Close**. Enter the name **DUMMYDB** for the file. We'll create the dummy letter for our sample in the next section.

Maintaining Your Records

If you need to add new records or change data in your database, the procedure is fairly simple. If your database file is not currently displayed, open the File menu and select Merge. Click on **option 1**. Select your database from the list and click on Edit or press **Alt+E**.

To add a new record, click on New Record or press **Alt+N**, enter the new data, and then click on Add (or press **Alt+A**).

To locate a particular record so you can change its data (for example, to change an address), click on the appropriate tab, or click on the left or right arrows and page through the database. The double arrows take you to the first or last record in the database. You can also click on Go To (or press **Alt+G**), select a field from the drop-down list box (such as Last Name), and then enter the data for which to search (for example, Fulton). Click on **Go To** or press **Enter** to begin the search. Once you've made changes to a record, click on Update or press **Alt+P**.

Click **Close** when you're done updating your database.

At Long Last: Creating the Dummy Letter

Now we get to have fun. First, let me tell you the steps for creating a form letter, and then we'll do one together.

You left off just after entering data into the merge data file. When you clicked on **OK**, you were returned to the Welcome to Merge dialog box. Here's what you do now.

Select option 2 by pressing **Enter**. If you want to use the current document as your dummy letter, click Yes or press **Alt+Y**. Otherwise, click on No (or press **Alt+N**) and go through ten bazillion dialog boxes to create a new document: select New (or press N), select a style sheet for the new document (or just press **Enter**), and Ami Pro will open a new file for your letter. (Did you get all that? Sometimes it's easier to just "say Yes to documents.") Now select the data file you just created from the list. Click on a file from the Files list, or press **Alt+F** and use the arrow keys to select a file. Click **OK** or press **Enter**.

Here's where you start entering the form letter's text. It's fairly easy; click inside the document (or press **Alt+F6**) and just type! When you get to the place where you need to insert a field from the merge data file (for example, you get to a place where you want to insert a first name), choose the field you want to insert from the Insert Merge Field dialog box, and then click on **Insert**. (Ami Pro keeps the dialog box handy for you in the corner of the document screen.) If you're using a keyboard, you're definitely doing this the hard way: press **Alt+F6** to move to the dialog box, use the arrow keys to select a field, and then press **Enter**. In your document, you'll see something like <First Name>, which represents the inserted field.

 Keep entering text and inserting field codes until the letter is done. When you're done with your form letter, click on the **Close** button within the Insert Merge Field dialog box to clear the dialog box away, and then save your form letter by clicking on the **Save** button on the Default SmartIcon set. Enter a name for the letter, and press **Enter** or click **OK**.

You can format the merge field codes if you want. Then when you merge the actual data into your letter, the formatting will already be done!

For example, you could insert the Title field and then italicize it by selecting it and clicking on the **Italics** button on the Default SmartIcon set. When you merge your data file with the dummy letter, you'll get something like:

Mr. John Spencer
Marketing Supervisor
The Big Company
1212 West 87th
Ratchokin, MN 89078

You can even change the fonts and/or point size of the merge filed codes to affect the data that will later be inserted at that point.

By the Way . . .

Remember to add spaces between field codes when necessary. When I was setting up the sample that you're about to do, I got in a hurry and forgot to insert a space between the field codes for the first and last names. When I merged the merge data file with my dummy letter, I got names like:

Ms.JoleneSmitt

So check your form letter carefully **before** you perform the actual merge (and have hundreds of them to correct).

Put It to Work

Creating Our Form Letter

Let's create a simple form letter for practice:

Select option 2 in the Welcome to Merge dialog box by pressing **Enter**. Select **New** in the Merge Document dialog box, and then press **Enter** to select _DEFAULT.STY. Highlight the **DUMMYDB** file and click **OK**.

Select the **Mr/Ms/Mrs** field from the Field names list and click on **Insert**. Press the **Spacebar**, insert the **First Name** field, press the **Spacebar** again, and insert the **Last Name** field. Press **Enter**.

Insert the **Title** field and press **Enter**. Insert **Company** and press **Enter**. Insert the rest of the address fields, each on its own line (except for the City, State, and ZIP fields).

Your letter looks like this:

<Mr/Ms/Mrs> <First Name> <Last Name>
<Title>
<Company>
<Address>
<Address 2>
<City>, <State> <Zip>

Now press **Enter** four times to insert some space between the address and the greeting. Type **Dearest**, press the **Spacebar**, and insert the **First Name** field. Add a comma and then press **Enter** twice.

Type the body of your letter:

You may have already won 1 million dollars! To obtain a complete list of winners, send $100 in small unmarked bills to me. Thank you for your cooperation.

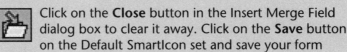 Click on the **Close** button in the Insert Merge Field dialog box to clear it away. Click on the **Save** button on the Default SmartIcon set and save your form letter. Call it PHONEY or something equally clever.

Sorting Your Database

You can sort your database before you merge it with your dummy letter. That way, you'll end up with presorted letters or mailing labels. To sort a database, display it by opening the File menu and selecting Merge. Click on **option 1**. Select your database from the list and click on Edit or press **Alt+E**.

Bummer. You can only sort on one field, so you can't sort by Last Name and First Name. Yech.

To sort the database, click on **S**ort or press **Alt+S**. Select the field to sort on from the drop-down list. For example, select Last Name. Select a sort type: **A**lphanumeric (where numbers come before letters) or **N**umeric (where numbers are sorted on their value, before letters). Select a sort order: **A**scending (A–Z) or **D**escending (Z–A). Click **OK** or press **Enter**. The field you selected to sort on will be used as the key field, so it will appear on the little tabs. Select **Close** and save the changes.

Friendly Merger

Finally! Congratulations on making it to our final act: merging the merge data file with the dummy letter to create form letters. This part is really easy, as you'll soon see.

Open the File menu and select Merge (press **Alt+F** and then G). Select **option 3** by clicking on it or pressing **Enter**. You have three choices at this point:

- ☞ **Merge & print**   Merge the data source and dummy letter together and print the form letters *now*.

- ☞ **Merge, view & print**   View the merged letters one at a time, make changes if necessary, and then print them if you want.

- ☞ **Merge & save as**   Merge the merge data file and dummy letter to create one big file that you can print later (each form letter will appear in the file on its own page).

Select one of these options and click **OK**. If you want to print more than one copy of each letter, click on **Print Opts** (or press **Alt+P**) and enter the number of copies you want. You can also change other print options.

If you selected Merge, **view** & print, you'll see a dialog box asking you what to do. If you want to make corrections to the current document, just click inside the document and make your changes. When you're ready to print, click **Print** and View Next or Print **All**. If you don't want to print this document but you want to look at the next one, click **Skip** and View Next. Click **Cancel** if you don't want to print anything.

If you want to specify only certain records for the merge (for example, you want only active employees, and you have a field in your database that indicates an employee's status), see the next section. If you want to create mailing labels, see the section at the end of this chapter for instructions.

Put It to Work

Merging Our Sample Files
Inside the Merge dialog box, click on Merge, view & print. View each document and print if you like by clicking **Print** and View Next. To view without printing, click **Skip** and View Next. It's as simple as that!

Merging with the Right People

If you want to merge only certain records from your database (such as only the active employees), it's a bit complicated, but with some help, you'll be able to do it just fine. You start from the Merge dialog box (just before you print), and click on Conditions.

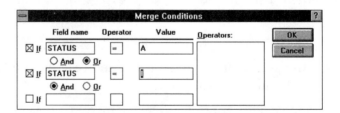

Just look at what condition my condition is in!

Now don't let this dialog box throw you; it looks like a tiger, but it's more like a pussycat. Click on the first **If**, or press **Alt+I** and the **Spacebar**. Click inside the Field name box or press **Tab**. Enter a field name to compare to; for example, if you had a field called Status, you could enter it and compare the values in that field to select the people you want to merge (only the people with an "A" in Status).

Move to the Operator field by clicking in it or pressing **Tab**. Enter an operator:

=	Equal to
<	Less than
>	Greater than
!=	Not equal to
<=	Less than or equal to
>=	Greater than or equal to

For example, you might enter = to find values that were equal to a given value. Next, move to the Value field by clicking in it or pressing **Tab**. Enter a value from the database to look for. For example, if you wanted to look for all your active employees, and you knew that they all had an "A" in the Status field, you'd enter this:

Field name	*Operator*	*Value*
Status	=	A

You can enter additional merge conditions by continuing to the next **If** statement. For example, if you wanted to merge active and inactive employees (say those that were on temporary leave of absence), but not the terminated ones, you might enter this:

Field name	*Operator*	*Value*
Status	=	A
Or		
Field name	*Operator*	*Value*
Status	=	I

You select the **Or** indicator between the two **If** statements because you want to find "employees who are either active OR inactive." Suppose you wanted to select all the sales reps in Ohio. You might use these conditions:

Field name	*Operator*	*Value*
Title	=	Sales Rep

And

Field name	*Operator*	*Value*
State	=	OH

Just remember these tips for getting good criteria:

☛ If one person (or record) must be several things in order to qualify, use **And** between the **If** statements.

☛ If you're trying to select more than one group, such as Indiana and Ohio residents, use **Or** between the **If** statements.

☛ Be sure that the value you use is correct. It must match something that's in the data file, or you'll get no results. For example, don't type "Sales Representative" if you really have something like "Sales Rep" in the Title field.

☛ To select a range of records, use **And**. For example if you wanted to find everyone with a ZIP code between 46220 and 46230, you would enter:

Field name	*Operator*	*Value*
Zip	>=	46220

And

Field name	*Operator*	*Value*
Zip	<=	46230

Once you're done entering conditions, click **OK**. You'll return to the Merge dialog box. Select a print option (may I suggest Merge, view & print?), and then click **OK**.

Final Steps: Creating Mailing Labels and Envelopes

The process of creating mailing labels and envelopes from your merge data file is remarkably similar to the one you used to create your form letter. This will seem a bit like déjà vu, but read on. . . .

Look Fo-or the Ma-a-il-ing La-a-bel

To create mailing labels with your merge data file, open the File menu and select New (press **Alt+F** and then **N**). Select **_LABEL.STY** as your style sheet. Make sure that Run **m**acro is selected (press **Alt+M**), and then click **OK** or press **Enter**.

Choose the type of labels you use from those listed, or click on Custom and enter the custom dimensions of your labels. Click on **Merge**. Here's where it starts looking familiar (it's about time!).

Select your database file from those listed, and click **OK** or press **Enter**. Insert the fields you want into the sample label. For example, click on **First Name** in the Insert Merge Field dialog box and then click on **Insert**. When you're done inserting fields, click on Continue Merge.

You should now be at the Welcome to Merge dialog box (have we seen this somewhere before?). Select **option 3** by clicking on **OK** or pressing **Enter**. There's that ol' Print dialog box. If you want to print your labels now, select Merge & print. If you want to save them in a file to print later, select Merge & **s**ave as.

If you want to change the number of times each label is printed, or the location of the first line of print, click on Labels and make your adjustments. Click on **OK** to return to the Merge dialog box.

Click on **OK** to print the mailing labels. Whew!

I've learned from experience that the best envelopes are produced when you check them yourself. So select Merge, view, & print, and then adjust the location of the address by dragging the margin markers (those black triangle things) on the horizontal and vertical rulers. Change the font and size of the addresses if you want. Any changes you make to that first envelope automatically affect the others. Once you're satisfied, print 'em!

Printing Envelopes for Your Form Letters

 Again, this may seem a bit like déjà vu. Be sure that your form letter is displayed on-screen. Then open the File menu and select Print Envelope, or click on the **Envelope** button on the Default SmartIcon set. You'll see a message asking you if you want to use your merge data file. Of course you do, so click **Yes** or press **Y**.

Now this begins to look like the same steps we took to print an envelope for a simple letter way back in Chapter 10. I won't make you go all the way back there; here are the basic steps you need to know (you will need to return to Chapter 10 if you want all the gory details).

Select an envelope size. If you've got an odd-sized envelope, click on **More envelope sizes** and select a size, or enter the dimensions of the envelope yourself.

To print your return address, click on **Print return address**. If necessary, select your address from previously saved addresses in the Return address **n**ames list box. Click **OK** or press **Enter.**

Back to the ol' Merge dialog box. By now, you know your way around this one. Select a print option and click **OK**.

The Least You Need to Know

Congratulations! You have won several million dollars' worth of wonderful tips on merging files:

- ☛ A *record* is a collection of related information about a single person or thing, such as a client or product. The individual pieces that make up a record are called *fields*.

☞ To create a merge data file, open **File** menu and select Merge. Choose **option 1**. Click on New. Add fields by typing a name and clicking on **Add**. When you're done, click **OK**.

☞ To enter data into the merge data file, press **Tab** or **Enter** to move from field to field. Press **Tab** to skip over a field that doesn't apply. When you're through entering data for a single record, click on **Add**. When you're through entering data, click on **Close**, enter a name for the data file and press **Enter**.

☞ To create a form letter, start at the Welcome to Merge dialog box. (If necessary, open the **File** menu and select Merge.) Select **option 2**. Select your data file from the list and click **OK**. Type the text of the letter. When you need to insert a field into the letter, select it and click on **Insert**.

☞ To merge the merge data file with the form letter, open the **File** menu and select Merge. Select **option 3**. Select a print option and click **OK**.

☞ To create mailing labels, open the **File** menu and select **New**. Select **_LABEL.STY** as the style sheet. Select Run **macro** and click **OK**. Select your label type and click on **Merge**. Insert fields into the sample label by selecting them and clicking on **Insert**. Click on **Continue** Merge. Select **option 3**, choose a print option, and click **OK**.

☞ To create matching envelopes, open the form letter. Open the **File** menu and select Print Envelope or click on the **Envelope** button on the Default SmartIcon set. Click **Yes** to merge data from data merge file. Select an envelope size, click on **Print** return address (if you want), and click **OK**. Select a print option and click **OK**.

**Blank (this) Subliminal (book) message
(is) page (GREAT!)**

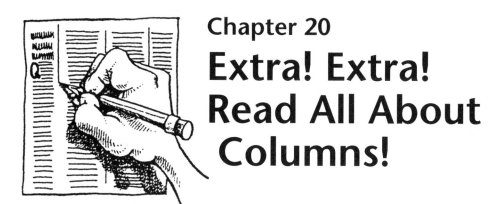

Chapter 20
Extra! Extra! Read All About Columns!

In This Chapter

- ☛ The difference between a table and a column
- ☛ How to add newspaper-style columns to a document
- ☛ Deciding which view mode to use when working with columns
- ☛ Making columns fatter (or thinner)
- ☛ Adding vertical lines between columns
- ☛ Keeping text and graphics together

I'll let you in on a little secret: columns are not just for newsletters anymore. This may shock those of you who thought you would just skip this chapter because you don't write the company newsletter, but columns are found in some of the better documents the world over. For example, you might add interest to a report by splitting the document into two columns—a skinny one on the left for short summaries of major points, and a fatter one on the right for your actual report. And what better way to format an index than to use two columns?

Newspaper-style columns are columns similar to those found in newspapers, in which text flows between invisible boundaries down one part of the page. At the end of the page, the text continues at the top of the first column on the next page.

A different type of column is the *parallel column*, which is just a fancy way of saying "table." With a table, you read across several columns of text and numbers (instead of down). If you want to "set a table" into your document instead of creating newspaper-style columns, see Chapter 17.

This Just In: What You Should Know About Using Columns

Newspaper-style columns are like those you find in your hometown newspaper, the ones that snake back and forth, from the bottom of the page to the top and back again. Columns can be "interrupted" by graphics (pictures or charts) that illustrate the story being told. (You'll learn how to insert graphics and other objects into a document in Chapter 21.)

When you start a new document, you are really typing text into a single column that stretches the width of the margins. At any point in your document, you can change the number of columns by creating a *section*.

When you add columns to a document, the column width is adjusted automatically so they fit equally between the margins. For instance, if you add three columns, the width of your paper is divided into three equal parts. You can elect to create column widths that are uneven (to achieve an interesting effect) if you want.

Reading the Fine Print: Viewing Column Layout

Each viewing mode displays columns a little differently, with each mode offering its own advantages. For example, in Draft mode, you can enter text faster than in other viewing modes, but your columns won't appear as columns, and you'll think you're hallucinating or something. Although you may have four columns set up, Draft mode will display the text in regular-looking paragraphs, seemingly oblivious to the presence of columns. To switch to Draft mode, open the View menu and choose the **Draft Mode command** (press **Alt+V** and then **D**), or click on the **Draft/Layout** button on the Long Documents SmartIcon set.

Switch to Layout mode to see how your columns will really look when printed. Use this view to make final adjustments to text and column widths (entering large amounts of text into columns may be a bit confusing and slow with this viewing mode). To switch to Layout mode, open the View menu and choose the Layout Mode command (press **Ctrl+M**), or click on the **Draft/Layout** button on the Long Documents SmartIcon set.

SPEAK LIKE A GEEK

A **section** is any part of a document that has different settings from the main document for things like the number of columns, as well as margins, paper size, headers, footers, and page numbering. A section can be any length: from several pages to several paragraphs—or even a single line (such as a masthead for your newsletter).

In Draft mode, columns appear as regular paragraphs.

In Layout mode, columns appear as they do when printed.

The same columns look different in different viewing modes.

When using Layout mode, you may want to zoom in (to get a closer look at text) or zoom out (to get an overview of the page layout). To see a close-up of a column, open the View menu and select Enlarged (press **Alt+V** and then **E**). To "back up" and look at the layout of an entire page, open the View menu and select either Full Page (press **Ctrl+D**) or Facing Pages (press **Alt+V** and then **A**).

When you modify the page layout to create columns, you change the entire document. To change the number of columns for a particular section of your document, insert a new page layout by opening the Page menu, selecting Insert Page Layout, and then selecting Insert. Once you've inserted a new page layout, use the Modify Page Layout dialog box (as explained here) to change the number of columns from that point forward. To change back to the original number of columns later in the document, open the Page menu, select Insert Page Layout, and select Revert.

Our Gossip Columnist Explains How to Insert Columns

Here's Miss Mayflower (our gossip columnist) with the latest on inserting columns into your document. (Stay tuned for an update on a recent Elvis spotting.)

To create columns, open the **Page** menu and select Modify Page Layout (press **Alt+P** and then **M**), or click on the **Modify Page Layout** button on the Editing SmartIcon set. Select **Margins & columns** from the Modify list (press **Alt+M** and press the **Spacebar**). Click on the number of columns desired, or press **Alt+** the underlined number. The sample will change to display the number of columns selected.

Adjust the *gutter width* (the width of the space between columns) if desired. With the keyboard, press **Alt+G** and then enter a number.

Ami Pro can automatically adjust the text on a partially filled page so that each column ends at the same point going across (this makes the bottom of your last page look more even). To do this, select Column balance (press **Alt+C**). Click on **OK**.

Making Columns Fatter

You can change the width of columns with the ruler. To change the width of a column, just drag the column marker on the horizontal ruler to wherever you'd like. (You can also drag the column margin indicators to the desired position on the ruler at the top of the Modify Page Layout dialog box.)

Drag a column margin marker to change the gutter width between columns.

Drag in the gutter to adjust the size of a single column.

Drag between markers to adjust the column width.

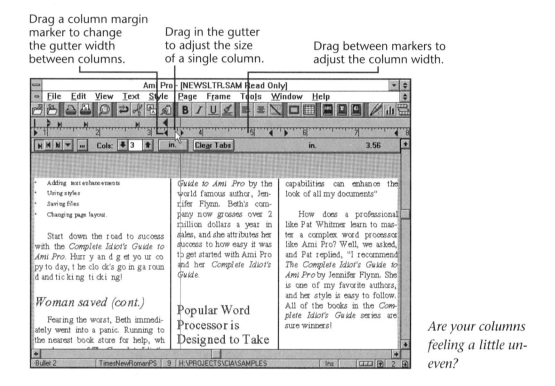

Are your columns feeling a little uneven?

Here are some pointers on adjusting the widths of columns:

- ☞ To adjust the gutter width between two columns without changing the actual width of the columns, click on the ruler between the left and right margin markers for one of the columns, and then drag.

- ☞ To adjust the width of a column without adjusting the gutter width (spacing) between it and the next column, click on the ruler in the gutter between the two columns, and then drag.

☛ To adjust the width of a column manually, click on either the left or right margin marker, and drag. This method adjusts both the width of a column, and the distance between it and the next column (gutter width).

Miss Mayflower Discusses How to Enter Text

Miss Mayflower says that if you want to enter text in a column, you just type. When you reach the bottom of a column, text will flow into the next column automatically (even if that column is on the next page). Here are some other things to consider:

The bottom edge of each column on the last page will appear uneven unless you select Column balance in the Modify Page Layout dialog box.

You can insert frames for text or graphics, and the text in the columns will flow around the frame. (*Frames* are boxes that can be placed anywhere on a page, and which hold text or pictures.)

You can set text attributes (such as alignment) within a column. So if you choose centered alignment, text is centered within the column. If you want the edges of your columns to look even, use justified alignment.

Each column has its own margins, which can be changed with the ruler or the Modify Page Layout dialog box. Review the instructions for changing column widths in the previous section.

If you want to force a paragraph to start at the top of the next column before you reach the bottom of a page, you can insert a *column break*. For example, perhaps you have a heading that you want to start at the top of the next column. To insert a column break, just place the insertion point where you want to start a new column (on the first letter of the column heading, for example), open the **Page** menu, select **Breaks**, and then select Insert column break.

Pinstriping Your Columns

You can add a vertical line (I think of it as a pinstripe) between columns; but when you do, don't be surprised if it doesn't show up in Draft mode. Switch to Layout mode to see the actual columns and their "pinstripes."

Here's what you do to pinstripe your columns. First, move to the section where you want to add lines. Open the **Page** menu and select Modify Page Layout (press **Alt+P** and then **M**), or click on the **Modify Page Layout** button on the Editing SmartIcon set. Select Lines from the Modify list (press **Alt+L** and then press the **Spacebar**). Click in the Line between columns check box, or press **Alt+L**. Click on a line style (or press **Alt+S** twice and use the arrow keys). The sample changes to show the lines. If you want colored lines (either for viewing or for printing if you have a color printer), select a color from the color bar. Click **OK** or press **Enter**.

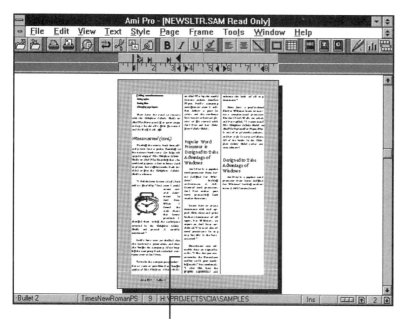

Vertical lines give your columns that pinstriped look.

Vertical lines added between columns

By the Way . . .

The **Line** between columns option will place lines between all the columns in that section. There is no way, for example, to place a line between two of the columns in a three-column section using this option. However, if you're desperate to do something like that, you can draw a line and place it between just two of the columns on a page if you want. (You'll learn more about Drawing in Chapter 23.)

You can also add interest to a newsletter (as I did) by placing borders or shading (or both) around paragraphs. You do that by placing text in *frames*, which I'll show you how to do in the next chapter . . . so hang around.

Keeping It All Together

When you insert a picture or graphic into your newsletter or brochure (something you will learn to do in Chapter 21), you may want to position that picture in a particular spot. For example, you may want a starburst SALE sign at the bottom of the first page, regardless of the surrounding text changes you make (either adding or deleting). Or you may want the chart you've imported to stay with the paragraph that explains it. In either case, here's what you do.

First, import the graphic, following the instructions in Chapter 21. I know that not including the instructions here sounds like cheating, but there are just too many choices to cover them all in this chapter. Just keep your thumb here, read the first few pages of Chapter 21, and come back. I'll wait.

Select the graphic by clicking on it. Open the Frame menu and select Modify Frame Layout, or click on the **Modify Frame Layout** button on the Graphics SmartIcon set. With the keyboard, press **Alt+R** and then **M**. To force the graphic to stay with a particular paragraph, click on either With **para** above (to anchor the frame to the text immediately preceding it), or **Flow** with text (to anchor the frame to the text surrounding it). To force the graphic to remain in the same spot on a page, regardless of what happens to the surrounding text, click on **Where placed**. To repeat the same frame throughout a document, click on either **Repeat all pages** or **Repeat right/left** (to repeat the frame on only the right or left page). Click **OK** or press **Enter**. (You'll learn more about the Modify Frame Layout dialog box in—yes, you guessed it—Chapter 21.)

The Least You Need to Know

Probably the very least you need to know is that Ami Pro is *not* a desktop publishing program (although it does a fine imitation of one). Still, with just a little skill, you can turn out a fine report or a church newsletter. Just remember these things:

- In newspaper-style columns, text flows from the bottom of one column to the top of the next when it reaches the bottom of a page. In a table, text is read across.

- You can insert text into columns faster using Draft mode, although the text will not be displayed in actual columns as you enter it. Switch to Layout mode to see your text in columns.

- To create columns, open the **Page** menu and select Modify Page Layout, or click on the **Modify Page Layout** button on the Editing SmartIcon set. Select Margins & columns from the Modify list, and click on the number of columns desired. Click **OK** or press **Enter**.

- To vary the number of columns within a document, create a new section by opening the **Page** menu, selecting Insert Page Layout, and then selecting Insert. Change the number of columns for this section using the Modify Page Layout dialog box.

continues

continued

To change back to the original number of columns later in the document, open the **Page** menu, select Insert Page Layout, and select **Revert**.

☞ Columns within a section are of equal width. To create columns of uneven width, move the column margin markers on the ruler.

☞ You can add vertical lines between all the columns in a section by opening the **Page** menu and selecting Modify Page Layout or clicking on the **Modify Page Layout** button on the Editing SmartIcon set. Select Lines from the Modify list. Click in the Line between columns check box, and select a line style. Click **OK** or press **Enter**.

☞ To force a graphic to stay in a particular spot on a page, click on it and choose the Frame Modify Frame Layout command, or click on the **Modify Frame Layout** button on the Graphics SmartIcon set. Select Where placed. To allow the graphic to move in order to stay near a particular paragraph, select either With **para** above or **Flow** with text.

Part IV

Why I Always Stick Around for the Credits

You've seen them: those people who are still in their seats when the movie is over and the credits are rolling. You'll be halfway home while they're still waiting for the movie to end. Well, I'm one of those people. Because when I watch the credits, I find out all sorts of interesting things I wouldn't have known otherwise: like who the "best boy" is and where the movie was made. This section is like movie credits; it's full of all those interesting things I wanted to tell you about Ami Pro, but ran out of room for earlier.

Chapter 21

But Officer, My Text Was Framed!

In This Chapter

- ☞ Adding borders and shading
- ☞ Importing graphics, text, charts, tables, and other objects
- ☞ Resizing a graphic
- ☞ Placing a frame around text or a graphic
- ☞ Moving or resizing a frame
- ☞ Controlling how text flows around a frame

My mother always told me "a house is not a home until you decorate it." The same is true of documents; adding a chart here or a picture there really dresses things up and makes the document yours.

Of course, you should avoid "over-decorating" your document. If you dress your document up with too much shading or too many borders and frames, your reader won't be able to see your point through all that glitter.

On the other hand, you shouldn't choose just one technique (such as shading) and use it everywhere in your document. I once baby-sat for a lady who loved owls and had them all over her house: little owls, big owls, owl wallpaper, owl salt and pepper shakers, and even owl toilet paper. (I'll never know where she found that!) Every time I sat for her kids, I had that creepy feeling that I was being watched—but whooo? Whoooo?

To avoid giving your documents that owlish look, vary your decorating with several techniques (shading, borders, text frames, and graphics), so you won't overload your reader with any one type of formatting.

A **frame** is a small box in which you place text or graphics so you can maneuver them easily within your document.

Get Ready for the Great Frame-Up

Frames are boxes into which you can place text or graphics. "Cool, but why would I want to do that?" you ask. Since frames are treated separately from the main document, you can format the text that's in 'em differently than the main document text. Also, you can put frames anywhere you want. The main document will either flow around the frame (like a river around a rock), stop at its edges, or flow behind the frame. Your choice.

Frames are versatile fellows that can be resized, can be made to appear transparent (so what's behind them shows through), can be made to appear opaque (covering what is behind them), or can have a line or shadow around or behind them.

Graphic frame with no border

Frame for title has no border.

Frame for heading has top and bottom borders.

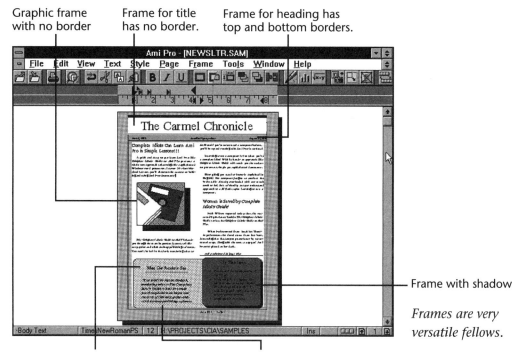

Frame with shadow

Frames are very versatile fellows.

Frame for title is transparent, so the color of the bottom frame shows through.

Frame for quotation is filled with color.

But First, a Word from Our Sponsor

Before we get down to the business of creating frames, there's some stuff you ought to know, especially if you're planning on inserting some graphics (pictures) into your document. Normally, you can't just plunk down a graphic in the middle of a column of text and expect the text to avoid the graphic like some party

Actually, you have no choice. Ami Pro places all its imported graphics into frames automatically. However, instead of leaving the fate of your pretty picture to the whims of some distant programmer, you should create the frame yourself, the way you want it, and then import the graphic. This saves lots of hassle over letting Ami Pro create the frame for you.

crasher. If you want to place a graphic in the middle of a column or two (or three) of text, and you want your text to wrap around it neatly (without leaving gaping holes to the left or right), you should create a frame first. Text wraps easily around a frame. You can then place the graphic within the frame, which will shield the graphic from the text, and the text will never know it's there.

You also use the frame to gain better control of where a graphic is placed in your document. For example, if you want to place your graphic in a margin (or alongside a particular paragraph), you can do that by moving the frame that surrounds the graphic. If your document is going to be professionally printed, you can use frames as empty "placeholders" for pictures and other artwork that will be inserted at the print shop. You can use frames to position other objects, such as tables, charts, or even text (a quote, for example, or a summary of an important point) anywhere within your document (you can even place a frame in the margins if you want).

By the Way . . .

When you work with frames, you should use Layout mode, because in Draft mode you won't be able to see where graphics are located within your document. As a matter of fact, it'll look as if they aren't really there at all.

At Last: Creating a Frame

Well, you've hung in this far, so I guess you're ready for the nitty-gritty on inserting frames into a document.

First, if you're in Draft or Outline mode, switch to Layout mode by pressing **Ctrl+M**. Then move to the spot where you'd like to place a frame.

Click on the **Add a Frame** button on the Default SmartIcon set. When you click on the Add a Frame button, the mouse pointer changes to a tiny box. Move the box-pointer to the place where you want to locate the upper left corner of the frame-to-be. Click and drag towards the imaginary lower right corner of the frame-to-be. When you've got the size you want, release the mouse button, and you've got yourself a brand-new baby frame!

You can create a frame with the keyboard, but it's a hassle because you have to enter the exact dimensions and the on-screen location where you want the frame placed. Best you use a mouse and avoid the headache.

Getting Rid of a Frame

If you want to get rid of your frame (and its contents), click on the frame to select it, and then press **Delete**. Adios, framo!

If you want the frame to be invisible (to not print), select it by clicking on it. Then click on the **Modify Frame Layout** button on the Graphics SmartIcon set, or open the Frame menu and select Modify Frame Layout (press **Alt+R** and then **M**). Select Lines & shadows from the Frame list (press **Alt+L**, and then press the **Spacebar**). Under Lines, deselect All (press **Alt+A**). Under Shadow, select None (press **Alt+N**). Click **OK** or press **Enter**.

By the Way . . .

When you create a frame, it's formatted in the manner currently set as the default. If you haven't changed the default, your new frame has a thin border surrounding it and a small shadow behind it. You can change these characteristics if you wish—in fact, I'll show you how in a minute.

Also, if you are going to place text in the frame, don't worry that you'll have to learn something really new (although I will give you some pointers later on). All the rules for formatting, alignment, and indentation are the same as before; just treat the text like any other text in your document. The difference is that because the text has a frame around it, you can move that text anywhere you want.

Getting a Handle on Frames

Okay, you've got a frame, but what can you do with it? Well, you can resize it, move it, copy it, and even color it in—but first, you have to select it. To select a frame, simply click on it. Whenever you select a frame, *handles* (little boxes) appear on the outer edges.

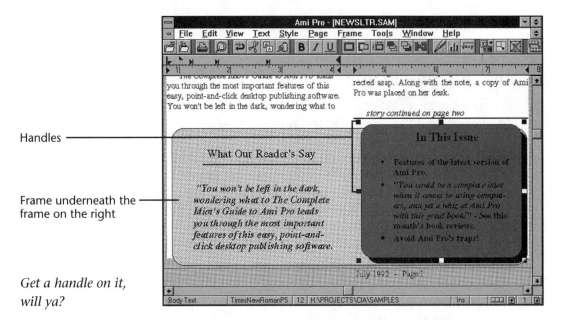

Handles ———

Frame underneath the frame on the right ———

Get a handle on it, will ya?

Markers that appear along the edge of an object when it is selected are called **handles**. They are used to "grab" an object for resizing.

Objects include items that are considered separate from the main document and are, therefore, manipulated independently from the main document. Common objects include frames, tables, charts, graphics, and drawings.

You can also select a group of frames, and move or copy them together as though they were one. Just click on the first frame, press and hold **Shift**, and click on additional frames one at a time.

If a frame you want is playing hide-and-seek under another frame, click on the top frame to select it. Then press **Ctrl** and click to select the bottom frame.

A Frame Support Group

If two or more frames need to work together on a page, they should join a frame support group and receive therapy once a week. Once frames are *grouped*, they are treated as a unit—when you move/copy one, you automatically move/copy the other. Select the frames you want to group by holding down the **Shift** key as you click on each one. Once you've selected the frames you want to group, click on the **Group/Ungroup Frames** button on the Graphics SmartIcon set, or open the Frame menu and select Group (press **Alt+R** and then **G**).

To ungroup the frames later (so you can change their position or size), click the **Group/Ungroup Frames** button again, or select the Group command again from the Frame menu.

But It's Not the Right Size!

Resizing a frame is easy, once you know how. First, click on the frame to select it. Then drag a corner handle until the frame is the size you want. Dragging a corner handle assures you that the frame will stay in proportion; if you want to change the proportions of a frame, drag it by one of its sides.

 If you want help judging the new size of your frame, use the horizontal and vertical rulers as guides when you drag. To display the horizontal ruler, click on the **Show/Hide Ruler** button on the Default SmartIcon set, or open the View menu and select Show Ruler (press **Alt+V** and then **R**). To display the vertical ruler, click the **View Preferences** button on the Proofing SmartIcon set, or open the View menu and select View Preferences (press **Alt+V** and then **P**). Select Vertical ruler (press **Alt+V**). Click **OK** or press **Enter**.

 If you need a frame of an exact size, select it by clicking on it. Then click on the **Modify Frame Layout** button on the Graphics SmartIcon set, or open the Frame menu and select **M**odify Frame Layout (press **Alt+R** and then **M**). Select Size & position from the Frame list (press **Alt+S**, and then press the **Spacebar**). Select a different unit of measurement (inches, centimeters, picas, or points) by clicking on the **Unit of Measurement** button in the Margins area of the dialog box (it's the button marked in., cm., picas, or pt.). Enter the **W**idth and **H**eight of the frame. Click **OK** or press **Enter**.

Across the Border

Using borders and shading are two of my favorite ways to emphasize important text. *Borders* (Ami Pro simply calls these lines) can be placed on any or all of the four sides of a text paragraph, the cells in a table, or a graphic (a picture or a chart). *Shading* (Ami Pro calls this the background or the fill color of a frame) is a box of gray (or color, if you use a color printer) that forms a background for the text or cells in a table.

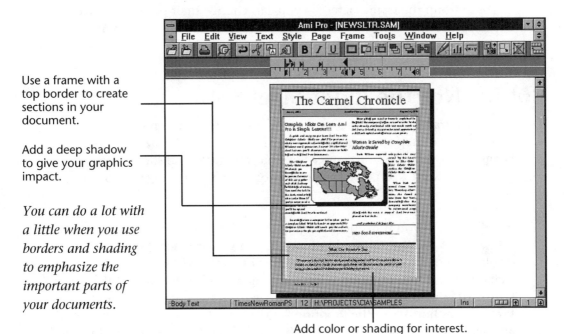

Use a frame with a top border to create sections in your document.

Add a deep shadow to give your graphics impact.

You can do a lot with a little when you use borders and shading to emphasize the important parts of your documents.

Add color or shading for interest.

Placing a border around a frame is fairly easy: first, click on the frame to select it. Then click on the **Modify Frame Layout** button on the Graphics SmartIcon set, or open the Frame menu and select Modify Frame Layout (press **Alt+R** and then **M**). Select Lines & shadows from the Frame list (press **Alt+L**, and then press the **Spacebar**). Select a line position (either one or more sides, or all sides) and a line style. You get a colored border by selecting a color from the Line color bar. To adjust the position of the border between the margins and the edges of the frame, select an option under **Position**. For example, Middle places the border halfway between the frame margin and its edge. Outside places the border on the outer edges of the frame.

If, later on, you want to remove a border completely, select the same frame, open the Frame menu, and select **M**odify Frame Layout. Select Lines & shadows from the Frame list, and deselect all the check boxes under Lines. Click on **OK** or press **Enter**.

Sporting Some Cool Shades

Fill your frame with color with the Modify Frame Layout dialog box. Simply select a color from the **B**ackground color bar. To select a slightly different shade of a listed color, click on the down arrow and select a color from this larger selection.

You can't add shading or color to the background of a graphic (picture) with Ami Pro. To do that, you would need to access the program that was used to create the graphic, and change it there. There is a technique you can use with some success, however. Look for the techno nerd tip in the "Sporting Some Cool Shades" section.

Casting a Shadow over Your Frame

Cast a shadow over your frame by selecting a shadow option in the Modify Frame Layout dialog box: **N**one (for no shadow at all), **S**hallow (for a thin shadow), **N**ormal (for a medium-sized shadow), or **D**eep (for a thick shadow). Change the side upon which the shadow falls by clicking on one of the arrows. Change the color of the shadow with the **S**hadow color bar.

As you make your selections, the sample will change to show how your frame will look. When you're satisfied, click **OK** or press **Enter**.

Moving and Copying Frames

To move a frame, click inside it and hold down the mouse button. Drag the frame to its new location, and then let go of the mouse button. (You'll see a ghostly outline of the frame to guide you as you move it.) When you move a frame, whatever's in it moves too.

You don't have to be able to see a location on-screen to drag a frame to it. Just drag the frame to an edge of the window, and Ami Pro will adjust the screen view to allow you to keep moving. However, if the new location for the frame is on another page, you will need to use the **E**dit Cut and **E**dit Paste commands (press **Ctrl+X** and **Ctrl+V**) to move it.

 If you want to place your frame in an exact spot relative to the edges of the page, click on the frame to select it. Then click on the **Modify Frame Layout** button on the Graphics SmartIcon set, or open the Frame menu and select Modify Frame Layout (press **Alt+R** and then **M**). Select **S**ize & position from the Frame list (press **Alt+S**, and then press the **Spacebar**). Enter the position for the frame: so much **D**own from top, and so much **I**n from left. Click **OK** or press **Enter**.

 To copy a frame (frame and contents—the whole kit and kaboodle), click on the frame to select it. Then click on the **Copy** button on the Default SmartIcon set or open the Edit menu and select Copy (press **Ctrl+C**). Click on the **Paste** button, or press **Ctrl+V**. A twin frame will appear. Click on it and drag it wherever you like.

Other Ways to Arrange Frames

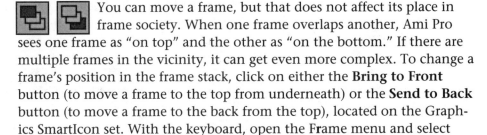 You can move a frame, but that does not affect its place in frame society. When one frame overlaps another, Ami Pro sees one frame as "on top" and the other as "on the bottom." If there are multiple frames in the vicinity, it can get even more complex. To change a frame's position in the frame stack, click on either the **Bring to Front** button (to move a frame to the top from underneath) or the **Send to Back** button (to move a frame to the back from the top), located on the Graphics SmartIcon set. With the keyboard, open the Frame menu and select either Bring to Front or Send to Back.

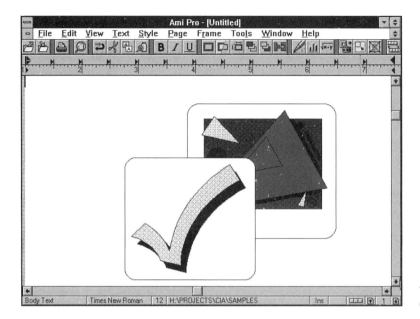

Now come on out, don't be shy!

Getting at What's Underneath

If you have frames stacked on top of one another, generally, the one on top covers up whatever's underneath. This may be great, but if you want the top frame to be clear so parts of the underneath frame show through, you can make it that way — and it's pretty easy.

First, click on the top frame to select it. Then click on the **Modify Frame Layout** button on the Graphics SmartIcon set, or open the Frame menu and select Modify Frame Layout (press **Alt+R** and then **M**). Select **T**ype from the Frame list (press **Alt+T**, and then press the **Spacebar**). Select **T**ransparent to get a see-through frame (press **Alt+T**). Select **O**paque to get a frame that covers what's under it (press **Alt+O**). Click **OK** or press **Enter**.

Keep That Text A-Flowin'

When you first insert a frame, it's set up so that the text in your document will flow (wrap) around the edges of the frame. If you want to be sure your text does not appear next to the frame (only above or below it) or if you want the text to flow through the frame as if it weren't there, you can change this arrangement.

If you want to place your frame in an exact spot relative to the edges of the page, click on it to select it. Then click on the **Modify Frame Layout** button on the Graphics SmartIcon set, or open the Frame menu and select Modify Frame Layout (press **Alt+R** and then **M**). Select Type from the Frame list (press **Alt+T**, and then press the **Spacebar**). Select a text wrapping option:

- ☞ To wrap text around all sides of a frame, select **Wrap around** (press **Alt+W**).

- ☞ To flow text behind a frame, select No wrap **around** (press **Alt+A**).

- ☞ To wrap text at the top and bottom of the frame (but not along the sides), select No wrap **beside** (press **Alt+B**).

When you've made your selection, click **OK** or press **Enter**.

Your Text Is Surrounded (By a Frame)!

If you want to import a graphic into the frame, see the section on importing graphics later in this chapter. If you want to place existing text in a new frame, select the text and click the **Cut** button on the Default SmartIcon set or press **Ctrl+X**. Click on the frame to select it, and then click on the **Paste** button on the Default SmartIcon set or press **Ctrl+V**. Now that your text is surrounded by a frame, you can move it anywhere you like, including into the margins if that suits your fancy.

If you want to type new text into a frame, double-click on the frame and start typing. Press **Esc** or click outside the frame when you're done entering text. If you type a lot of text, Ami Pro does not increase the size of the frame automatically—so some text may be hidden. Drag the sides of the frame to increase its size, and the hidden text will be displayed. Change anything about the text that you don't like: its font, size, or attributes. After all, it's just text. By the way, if you want to change the margins for the text paragraph in a frame, change them the same way you would any main document text: by dragging the appropriate markers on the ruler. See Chapter 13 for help.

Welcome to the Import Business

They say that nothing says it better than a picture (except maybe some words). Anyway, if you want to dress up your document with a graphic (nerd word for picture) or a chart, you've got several options:

☛ You can create your own picture with Drawing, a program that comes with Ami Pro. You'll learn how to use Drawing in Chapter 23.

☛ You can create a picture in some other program, such as PC Paintbrush, DrawPerfect, or CorelDRAW!.

☛ You can take it easy, and simply buy and import some artwork drawn by someone else (called *clip art*). Ami Pro comes with a limited selection of clip art, but there are thousands of other clip-art disks you can buy from various sources. Ask your computer dealer to help you find a nice selection.

☛ You can create a chart with Ami Pro, or import one from your *spreadsheet* program.

When you bring a graphic into your document, you *import* it—bet you didn't know you'd be getting into the import business! (You can also link or embed a graphic instead of importing it. These options allow you easy methods for changing or updating the graphic later on. If you're interested, skip ahead to the next section for a quickie lesson.)

When you import a graphic, Ami Pro places it in a frame. For better results, you'll want to create the frame yourself first, and then import the graphic into it. After you've created your frame, click on the

SPEAK LIKE A GEEK

A **spreadsheet** program organizes information in columns and rows, and performs calculations. If you want to balance a checkbook or analyze last year's budget, use a spreadsheet program. Common spreadsheets include Lotus 1-2-3 for Windows, Microsoft Excel, and Quattro Pro.

Import Picture button on the Graphics SmartIcon set, or open the File menu and select Import Picture (press **Alt+F** and then **I**). Select the File type (press **Alt+T** and use the arrow keys to highlight a file). Change to a different directory or drive if needed. Select a file from those listed.

If you want Ami Pro to import a copy of the file (and not the original), select Copy image (press **Alt+C**). If you import a copy of the file, the imported copy will not be updated in Ami Pro when you make changes to the original. However, if you import the original file, it will be changed automatically in Ami Pro whenever the original is changed. The only drawback is that this type of graphic (the original) takes longer to display on-screen. Click **OK** or press **Enter**.

If you mess up and want to restore the graphic to its original size and shape, open the **F**rame menu and select the Graphics **S**caling command (press **Alt+R** and then **S**). Click on **O**riginal size (press **Alt+O**), and then click **OK** or press **Enter** to restore the graphic.

Just a Trim, Please

When you import a graphic into a frame, it's automatically sized to fit in it. If your graphic is the size of a small elephant, you can either adjust its size (this is called *scaling* a graphic) or cut parts away or trim (this is called *cropping*).

To scale a graphic—or change its size and keep its proportions—select it by clicking on it, and then drag one of the corner handles until the graphic is the size you want. (As you drag, you'll see a ghostly outline—but don't let that spook you!) If you drag the graphic by a side handle, it will be the size you want but you'll get a kind of "squashed" look, which you may not like. So it's best to use one of the corner handles.

To crop (trim) a graphic, double-click on it. Move the mouse pointer over the graphic, and it will change to a hand. Drag the graphic to an edge of the frame, so only the part you want to keep is displayed. Click outside the frame when you're through giving your graphic a trim.

The Ins and Outs of Linking and Embedding

Linking an object means to create a connection between an imported object (such as a graphic) and its original application, so that any changes you make to the original object can be updated into your document.

Instead of importing a graphic, you can *link* it to the original application you used to create it. That's a handy feature to use if you think you might want to go back to that application and change the original graphic sometime. If you do, you can just update the original graphic, and the changes will be carried into the Ami Pro document. Otherwise you'd have to import it again.

To link a graphic (or other object, such as a chart or a table), start the application you used to create the graphic. Then select the graphic and use the **Edit Copy** command. Switch over to Ami Pro and use its **Edit Paste Link** command to create the link between the two applications.

If you make some changes to your graphic and want to update your document, open the **Edit** menu and select **Link Options**. Select the name of the graphic file, and then click on **Update**. The graphic in your document is updated to reflect the changes you made to it.

Okay, So What's Embedding?

You have an alternative to linking a graphic (or other object)—and that's *embedding*. The difference between linking and embedding is in where the actual object is stored. When you import a graphic and link it to its original application, the graphic is *not* stored as part of the document. Instead a link (or connection, if you prefer) is maintained between your document and the program that created the graphic. Because the graphic is not actually part of your document, when you open that other program and make changes to the graphic, those changes are not reflected within your document until you update it. The link helps your document find the changed graphic and update the linked version of it.

Embedding an object means to create a connection between an object and the application that created it, so that if changes are needed, you can access that application (by double-clicking on the object).

With embedding, on the other hand, a graphic (or other object) *is* stored as part of the document. Just as in linking, however, there is a special connection between the document and the program that created the graphic. But this time the connection takes a different form. When you want to make changes to an embedded graphic (or other object), you don't go to the program that created it, but to your Ami Pro document. Double-click on the object, and you'll be escorted to the original program, where you'll work within its program window to make your changes. Finish making your changes and exit the graphics program, and you're whisked back to your document—where the graphic already reflects your changes. Unlike a linked object, an embedded object is updated immediately as soon as any changes are made. That's because you're not making changes to an object that's stored somewhere else, but to the one that's stored within the document.

To embed a graphic (or other object) into your document, start with the graphics program. Select the graphic, open the Edit menu, and choose Copy. Switch to Ami Pro, open its Edit menu, choose Paste **S**pecial, and select **OLE Embed**. Your graphic is embedded into the document. Remember that when you want to make changes to it, just double-click on the graphic.

How Do I Import Text?

If you want to open an existing document that was created in another program (such as WordPerfect or Microsoft Word for Windows), click on the **Open** button on the Default SmartIcon set or press **Ctrl+O**. Select a file type from the List files of **t**ype drop-down list box, by clicking on the down arrow and then picking a type. Change drives or directories if you need to, and then select the file you want to open from those listed. Click on **OK** or press **Enter**.

If you want to copy the foreign document into an existing Ami Pro document, move the insertion point to the appropriate place within the

Ami Pro document. Then click on the **Open** button on the Default SmartIcon set or press **Ctrl+O**. Select a file type from the List files of type drop-down list box, by clicking on the down arrow and then picking a type. Change drives or directories if you need to, and then select the file you want to open from those listed. Instead of clicking OK, click on Insert or press **Alt+I**. This will insert the foreign document into your Ami Pro document at the insertion point.

You cannot copy and paste part of a document created in a non-Windows program. You must open the entire file, let Ami Pro convert it for use, and then delete the sections you don't want.

If you want to import just part of a document that was created in another Windows program, open that document and select your text. Open its Edit menu and select Copy. Switch to Ami Pro, open its Edit menu, and select **Paste**.

How Do I Import a Chart or Other Object?

Some charts, such as those created by Lotus 1-2-3 for Windows and Microsoft Excel, can be imported through the Edit menu. Just switch to the other program, select the chart or other object (such as a table or a graphic) you want to import, open its Edit menu, and select Copy.

Now switch back to Ami Pro, move the insertion point to the place where you want the chart, and open the Edit menu. If you want to link your chart to the application you used to create it, select Paste Link. If you want to embed the chart, select Paste **S**pecial instead. If you want to simply place the chart image in your Ami Pro document, select **P**aste. Remember, linking means that the graphic is not stored in your document, but that the graphic and the program that created the document are linked. If changes are made to the original graphic, they are reflected within your document. *Embedding* means that the graphic is stored within your document, but you can access the creating program from within your document (by double-clicking on the embedded chart), and still make changes.

By the Way . . .

You can create and embed certain objects (such as a Microsoft Excel chart) without leaving Ami Pro. Open the **E**dit menu, select **I**nsert, and then select the New **O**bject command. If your program is listed, click on it, and you'll be escorted to that program so you can create your "object." Exit that program, and the object will be embedded into your document automatically. As usual, you can double-click on an embedded object to make changes to it. If your program is not among those listed, you'll have to start the application yourself, create the object, and then use the **E**dit **C**opy and **E**dit Paste **S**pecial commands (as explained in the preceding paragraphs).

The Least You Need to Know

You're traveling into another frame of mind, a graphic dimension of linking and embedding. At the signpost up ahead is your next stop . . .the Document Zone! Submitted for your approval are these tips on frames, graphics, borders, and shading:

- To create a frame, click on the **Add a Frame** button on the Default SmartIcon set. Move the box-pointer to the place where you want to locate the upper left corner of the frame-to-be. Click and drag towards the imaginary lower right corner of the frame-to-be, and then release the mouse button.

- To modify a frame, click on the **Modify Frame Layout** button on the Graphics SmartIcon set. Select **T**ype to change text flow, placement, and opaqueness options. Select **S**ize & position to change the size and location of the frame. Select Lines & shadows to change the frame's borders, shadow, and fill color. Select **C**olumns & tabs to change how text within a frame appears. After making your changes, click **OK** or press **Enter**.

☞ Select a frame by clicking on it. Select more than one frame at a time by holding the **Shift** key as you click on frames. Group frames together as a single unit by selecting them and clicking on the **Group** button on the Graphics SmartIcon set.

☞ Change a frame's size by dragging one corner.

☞ Arrange overlapped frames by clicking on either the **Bring to Front** button (to move a frame to the top from underneath) or the **Send to Back** button (to move a frame to the back from the top), located on the Graphics SmartIcon set.

☞ To type text in a frame, double-click on it and start typing. Press **Esc** when you're through. You can also paste existing text into a frame. Select it, click on the **Copy** or **Cut** button on the Default SmartIcon set, click on the frame, and then click on the **Paste** button.

☞ To import a graphic, create a frame and then click on the **Import Picture** button on the Graphics SmartIcon set. Select the File type. Change to a different directory or drive if needed. Select a file from those listed. If you want Ami Pro to use a copy of the file (and not the original), select Copy image (press **Alt+C**). Click **OK** or press **Enter**.

☞ To link a graphic (or other object, such as a chart or a table), start the application that you used to create the graphic. Then select it and use the Edit Copy command. Switch over to Ami Pro and use its Edit Paste Link command to create the link between the two applications.

continues

continued

☞ To embed a graphic (or other object) into your document, start with the graphics program. Select the graphic, open the **Edit** menu, and choose **Copy**. Switch to Ami Pro, open its **Edit** menu, and choose Paste **S**pecial. Your graphic is embedded into the document. Remember that when you want to make changes to it, just double-click on the graphic.

☞ If you want to open an existing document that was created in another program, click on the **Open** button on the Default SmartIcon set. Select a file type from the List files of **t**ype drop-down list box. Change drives or directories if you need to, and then select the file you want to open from those listed. Click on **OK** or press **Enter**.

☞ To copy the foreign document into an existing Ami Pro document, follow the instructions above but select **I**nsert instead of OK.

Chapter 22
Charting Your Own Course

In This Chapter

- ☞ Using a table to create a chart
- ☞ Importing data for a chart
- ☞ Entering chart data from scratch
- ☞ Changing the data in your chart
- ☞ Choosing from different chart types

If there's one thing that confuses people more than anything else, it is evaluating a set of numbers. Almost everyone prefers looking at charts (graphs) to looking at columns of numbers, because a chart depicts the relationship between numbers in a way that's easy to pick up in one quick look. After all, if your department did well last month, your boss should know it, and she sure will if you show her a chart with a line that goes up and up and up.

How to Read the Map: Understanding Charts

You can create a *chart* in your Ami Pro document by entering the columns of numbers yourself, or by copying the data from a table (either an Ami

Pro table, or one imported from a spreadsheet program). You can even paste in a completed chart created in a spreadsheet program—but if that's what you want to do, go back to Chapter 21 to learn how to paste the chart into your Ami Pro document.

SPEAK LIKE A GEEK

A **chart**, sometimes known as a **graph**, is a graphical representation of columns of related numbers. For example, if one sales figure is greater than another, the column (or bar) representing it on a chart is larger. The larger sales figure could also be represented by a greater portion of a pie or by a longer line.

The **legend** tells what each part of a chart represents.

Before we get down to the nitty gritty of actually entering chart data, you should know some basics. All charts (except pie charts) have an *x-axis* and a *y-axis* along which the data is graphed. (Some of this stuff dates back to high school geometry class. So if you have a distant memory of the word "axis," that's where the echo is probably coming from.) Anyway, the x-axis runs along the horizontal side of a chart, while the y-axis runs along the vertical side. In a 3-D chart, there's an extra axis called the z-axis, which represents the depth of the chart, with the x- and y-axes representing the vertical and horizontal sides of the chart.

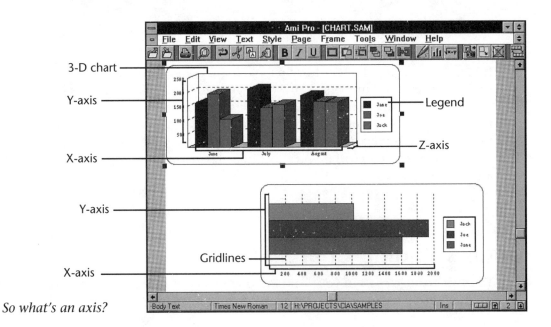

So what's an axis?

In addition to axes, some charts include *legends*, which attempt to explain what the parts of the chart represent. For example, the legend in a pie chart describes what each piece of the pie stands for.

Picking Your Piece of Pie

There are lots of different kinds of charts you can create (so it'll be easier to hide bad numbers from your boss if you need to!). Ami Pro provides more kinds of charts (it seems) than Campbell's has soups, so here are some guidelines for deciding which chart type to use:

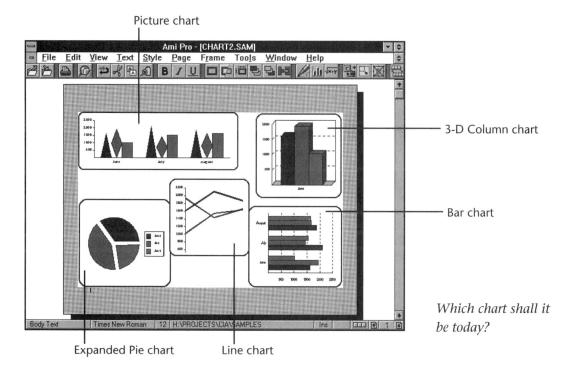

Which chart shall it be today?

Pie or Expanded Pie   Use this type of chart to show the relationship between parts of a whole. For example, a pie could represent the payroll costs of the various departments in a company. The expanded version separates one or more sections of the pie so they stand out.

Bar or Stacked Bar   Use this type of chart to compare values at a specific time. For example, the sales of various products during the month of March. The stacked version depicts the components of a single element. For example, the components of a stacked bar could break a total sales figure into the various products that it includes.

Column or Stacked Column   Use this type of chart to emphasize the difference between items. For example, two columns could be used to compare the number of people who own Toyotas with the number of people who own Fords. The stacked version depicts the components of a single element. For example, a stacked column could break total foreign car sales into manufacturers such as Nissan, Toyota, and Hyundai.

Line or Area   Use this type of chart to emphasize trends or the changes in values over time. For example, a line could depict the value changes of a certain stock. Area charts are "filled-in" line charts. Use them to compare several different trends more clearly, such as the changing values of several stocks.

Picture or Stacked Picture   These come in two varieties which are similar to column and line charts, but different shapes represent the data, such as triangles, diamonds, and squares.

This Table Will Make a Nice Chart

If you already have your data keyed into a table (whether it's an Ami Pro table or a table in a spreadsheet), it's simple to create a chart from it. First, select the table data. Open the Edit menu and select Copy (press **Ctrl+C**). If you were in some other program, switch back to Ami Pro.

Create a frame to hold your chart by clicking on the **Create Frame** button on the Default SmartIcon set. Or open the Frame menu and select Create Frame (press **Alt+R** and then **C**). Drag to create the frame.

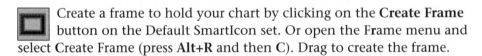

Click on the **Chart** button on the Default SmartIcon set, or open the Tools menu and select Charting (press **Alt+L** and then **C**). Now you've got lots of choices:

- ☞ Select a chart type by clicking on one of the buttons on the left. The sample chart will change to look like the type you select.

- ☞ Select your chart options. These will vary depending on the chart type you select, but you could add a legend or a grid (lines that help you determine the value of a column or bar, for example). You can even change the depth of 3-D for your chart, or add perspective.

☞ Change the colors of your chart. Colors are used in the order they appear on the color bar. To change the colors of your chart, click on the down arrow of the Color set bar to select from various color sets. Drag colors to the far left on the bar to make them available in your chart.

☞ Change the chart increments. Deselect **Automatic** by clicking on it or pressing **Alt+A**. Then change the increment amount and the minimum and/or the maximum numbers you want used in depicting the table values.

☞ Reverse yourself. To flip the values used in the x- and y-axes of the chart, click on Flip data or press **Alt+F**.

When you're done making all your choices (or none at all—it's your choice!), click **OK** or press **Enter**, and your chart will appear in its frame.

You can create your own colors by double-clicking on a colored square. Select a different color and/or fill pattern from those listed in the Fill Pattern dialog box. Click **OK** to replace the color you started with with the new color you've selected.

To change any of the chart options later on, just double-click on the chart.

But I'd Rather Create the Chart Myself!

If you don't have a table with all your data sitting around waiting to be transformed into a chart, you're going to have to enter the chart data by hand. The steps are only slightly different from those in the last section, so I'll refer you back there when necessary.

Create a frame to hold your chart by clicking on the **Create Frame** button on the Default SmartIcon set, or by opening the Frame menu and selecting Create Frame (press **Alt+R** and then C). Drag to create the frame.

 Click on the **Chart** button on the Default SmartIcon set, or open the Tools menu and select Charting (press **Alt+L** and then C). Ami Pro will ask you if you'd like to enter the data now or if you'd like to just sit there. Click **OK** or press **Enter** to show Ami Pro you mean business.

Now you're ready to enter the chart data. Just type your numbers, but remember to press the **Spacebar** between columns in order to separate them with a space. To go to the next row, press the down arrow key.

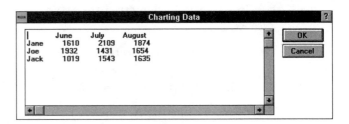

Just type your chart data and insert a space between columns.

When you're finished entering data, click **OK** or press **Enter**. Select your chart options (see the last section for details), and click **OK** or press **Enter** to create the chart.

If you need to change your data later, just double-click on the chart and select **Data** in the Charting dialog box (press **Alt+D**). Make your changes, and click **OK** or press **Enter** to return to the Charting dialog box. The sample chart will change to reflect the updated figures. Click **OK** or press **Enter** again to update the real chart in your document.

Changing Your Chart's Style

Because your chart is in a frame, you can use any of the techniques you learned in Chapter 21 to move it, copy it, resize it, or change its border or fill color.

One thing I haven't shown you yet involves picture charts, which are pretty cool once you learn how to use them. Creating a picture chart is the same as creating any other chart, so flip back a few

pages if you need to refresh your memory. Once you've made it to the
Charting dialog box, click on one of the picture charts on the left-hand
side.

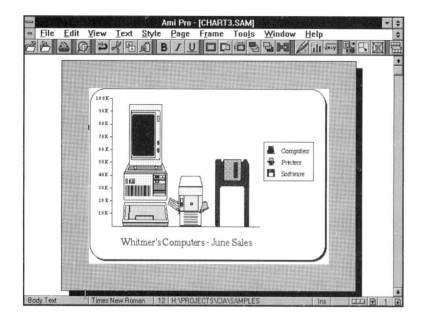

*Get your point across
with picture charts.*

You can substitute the little triangles and squares with pictures if you
want. For example, if you were showing the volume of sales for 1993 vs.
1994, you might want to use little money bags to make your chart more
interesting. You can choose from any of the drawings Ami Pro includes—
look for a listing of them in the back of your manual.

To create a picture chart from the Charting dialog box, click on **Picture**
or press **Alt+P**. Click on the first symbol (a triangle), and click on **Drawing**
or press **Alt+D**. If necessary, change to the \AMIPRO\DRAWSYM
directory, and then select a drawing from those listed. Be inventive; for
example, if you're really cutting off the competition, use the scissors
drawing, or the OK sign, or whatever. Have some fun with this! When
you're through, click on **OK** or press **Enter**. Repeat this whole business for
each data set (for example, each column of a column chart).

The Least You Need to Know

Chart an easy course across the treacherous waters of Ami Pro charting with these simple reminders:

- ☛ The *x-axis* is the horizontal side of a chart, while the *y-axis* is its vertical side. In a 3-D chart, the *z-axis* is the chart's depth plane, with the x-axis and y-axis forming the horizontal and vertical sides of the chart.

- ☛ Use a pie chart to show the relationships between parts of a whole. Use a bar chart to compare values at a specific time. Use a column chart to emphasize the differences between items. Use a line chart to emphasize trends or the change in values over time. Use a picture chart to add pizzazz to a line or column chart.

- ☛ If your chart data already exists, select it and then open the **E**dit menu and select **C**opy. Create a frame with the **Create Frame** button on the Default SmartIcon set. Click on the **Charting** button and select your chart type. Change any charting options you want and click on **OK**.

- ☛ To enter chart data from scratch, first create a frame with the **Create Frame** button on the Default SmartIcon set. Click on the **Charting** button and click on **Yes**. Enter your chart data, being careful to press the **Spacebar** between data columns. Press the down arrow to move to the next row. Press **Enter** when you're finished entering data. Select your chart type. Change any charting options you want and click on **OK**.

- ☛ To change your data later on, double-click the chart and select **Data** from the Charting dialog box. Click **OK** two times to return to your document after making changes.

☛   To create a picture chart, follow the earlier directions, and then select a picture chart from the chart types. To substitute a drawing for one of the pictures in the chart, click on **Picture** and click on the triangle within the Picture dialog box. Select a drawing and click **OK**. Repeat for each data set, and then click **OK** twice to return to your document.

This blank page stuff is really getting out of hand.

Chapter 23
Drawing Your Own Conclusions

In This Chapter

- Using the Drawing tools
- Selecting objects
- Grouping objects
- Moving, copying, and resizing objects
- Rotating and flipping objects
- Changing the color of an object

Drawing is fairly easy (even if you're not Van Gogh) and it can add pizzazz to any report. With the Drawing tools, you can create arrows pointing to important information in tables or text, add lines to create visual areas within your document, enter text at an angle, and just plain have fun.

Working with objects in a Drawing picture is like working with frames in a lot of ways, so if you read Chapter 21, you're pretty much ahead of the game. If you didn't read that chapter (or if you don't remember much about it), that's okay. I'll review the key parts here in this chapter.

But I Object!

One thing that you should know before we go any further is that the drawings you create consist of *objects*. Objects are complete unto themselves, but when they get together and party, they form *drawings*. For example, I drew a sun by creating a circle object and surrounding it with line objects that formed the sun's rays. You can place objects behind or in front of one another, or beside each other, and rearrange them at will. For example, if you wanted to create a door, you'd draw a big rectangle and then place smaller rectangles on it (for the door panels) along with a small circle for the doorknob.

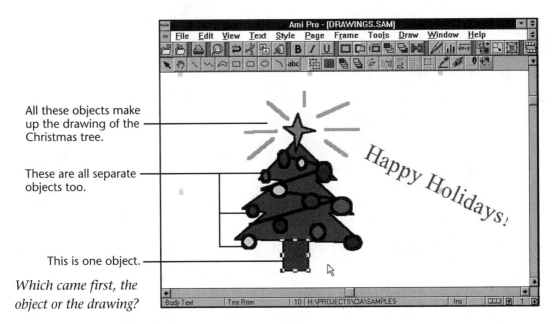

All these objects make up the drawing of the Christmas tree.

These are all separate objects too.

This is one object.

Which came first, the object or the drawing?

Your First Work of Art

When you're ready to draw something, click on the **Drawing** button on the Default SmartIcon set. Ami Pro "prepares your canvas" by creating a frame for you to work within. (Or you can create a frame of the proper size, and then click the **Drawing** button if you'd like.) Ami Pro also displays your palette: a SmartIcon set of specially designed drawing tools.

Get Out Your Drawing Tools

Four score and twenty tools ago, the Ami Pro forefathers envisioned the simplest icon for each drawing task. These icons may have made sense to them, but don't bet your life that you'll be able to guess what each one is for. Here's a listing of the Drawing tools and what each critter does.

 When you need to select an object (such as a rectangle or a circle) that makes up part of your drawing, click on this little guy (Mr. Selection Arrow button), and then click on the object you want to select. If you need to select several things at once (to move them or resize them or something), press **Shift** as you click on each object in turn, or draw a ring around them with this tool. Just click on the **Selection Arrow** button and drag from the upper left corner to the lower right corner of the area that encompasses the objects you want to select. Remember that when some-thing is selected, it shows little black *handles* (square boxes) around its edges (like the base of the Christmas tree in the figure on the previous page).

If you want to select all the objects in a drawing, click on the **Select All** button, or open the **Draw** menu and choose Select All (press **Alt+D** and then **E**). To deselect an object, just click on something else or click in an open area of the frame.

Handles appear along the edge of an **object** when it is selected. Handles are used to "grab" an object for selection and resizing.

 The Hand tool is pretty (yes, I'm going to say it) handy. Use it to select an entire drawing and move that drawing within the frame.

 Use this tool to create a line.

 Use this tool to create a series of connected lines, like a zig-zag.

 Use the Polygon tool to create a *free-form* object (something that isn't perfectly square or circular). For example, a Christmas tree or a star or even a simple triangle is a *polygon*.

Use this tool to draw a rectangle or a square.

Use this tool to draw a rectangle or a square with rounded corners.

Use this tool to draw an ellipse (oval) or a circle.

Use this tool to draw an arc. You can bend the arc in several places to get a nice curvy line if you want.

Add text to your drawing with this tool.

That's enough of an introduction for now, I think. I'll introduce you to the rest of the Drawing tools as we go along. But first, let me show you how to use some of these tools to create your first object.

Creating an Object

Creating any object with a Drawing tool follows the same pattern: click on the tool, and then drag from the upper left to the lower right to create the object. For example, to create a rectangle, click on the **Rectangle** tool and drag. Release the mouse button, and you've got yourself one fine rectangle. But just like everything in life, there's always a bit more to know. To get rid of an unwanted object, click on the object and press delete.

To create a square or a circle, click on either the **Rectangle** or the **Ellipse** tool, and then press and hold the **Shift** key as you drag. Your rectangle is filled with the current fill color, which you'll learn how to change soon.

To create a perfect line, click on the **Line** tool, and then press and hold the **Shift** key as you drag. Your line is the color of the current line color, which I'll also show you how to change real soon.

To draw a series of connected lines, click on the **Polyline** tool, and then click on the starting point. Click at the ending point for the first line. Click again to connect a new line with the ending point of the first line. Repeat to create your zig-zag.

TECHNO NERD TEACHES

You can modify the shape of a polygon later by double-clicking on it. Drag one of the handles to change its location, or drag a side of the polygon to establish a new bending point. To delete a handle (and have Ami Pro redraw the object by connecting the remaining handles), just double-click on a handle.

You can also use this same trick on circles and squares. For example, double-click in the middle of a circle, drag the top handle into the center and the bottom handle out to form a point, and you have a heart!

To draw a polygon, click on the **Polygon** tool, click to establish the first point, and then click to establish each point there after. Ami Pro draws a line between each of these points, connecting them. Double-click when you're done drawing; Ami Pro will connect the beginning and ending points for you to create a solid object. Your polygon is filled with the current fill color (which you'll learn how to change in a moment).

To draw an arc, click on the **Arc** tool, and then click at the beginning point for the arc. Drag to create an arc. Change the shape of the arc by double-clicking in the middle of the arc, and dragging one of the black handles in the direction you want the arc to bend.

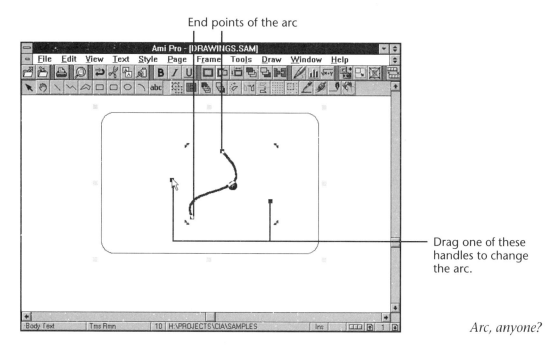

End points of the arc

Drag one of these handles to change the arc.

Arc, anyone?

To add text, click on the **Text** tool and click to establish the insertion point. Select your font and attributes (bold, italics, etc.) *before* you type, because changing them later is a bit difficult. You can change the entire text object later by selecting it and changing the font, point size, etc. But you can't select a word or a letter and change it—which is why I say it's easier to set your attributes before you type. Your text is the color of the current fill color (which you'll learn how to change in a little bit).

Grouping and Ungrouping Objects

  If two or more objects need to stay together in a drawing and not accidentally move as you work, they can be *grouped* (treated as a unit). Select the objects you want to group by holding down the **Shift** key as you click on each one, or by clicking on the **Selection Arrow** tool and dragging over them to corral them. Once you've selected the objects you want to group, click on the **Group/Ungroup Objects** button, or open the Draw menu and select Group (press **Alt+D** and then G). To ungroup the objects later (so you can change their position or size), click the **Group/Ungroup Objects** button, or select the Group command again from the Draw menu (press **Alt+D** and then G).

Moving, Copying, and Resizing an Object

Moving, copying, and resizing an object is just like working with a frame. To move an object, click inside it and hold down the mouse button. Drag the object to its new location, and then let go of the mouse button. (You'll see a ghostly outline to guide you as you move the object.)

  When you move an object, that does not affect its place in the object-order-of-things. When one object overlaps another, Ami Pro sees one object as "on top" and the other as "on the bottom." If there are multiple objects in the vicinity, it can get even more complex. To change an object's position in the object stack, click on either the **Bring to Front** button (to move an object to the top from underneath) or the **Send to Back** button (to move an object to the bottom from the top). If you're using the keyboard, open the **Draw** menu and select either Bring to Front or Send to Back.

  To copy an object, click on the object to select it. Then click on the **Copy** button on the Default SmartIcon set, or open the Edit menu and select Copy (press **Ctrl+C**). Click on the **Paste** button, or press **Ctrl+V**. Congratulations, it's twins! Click on the copy and drag it wherever you like.

To resize an object, click on it to select it, and then drag a corner handle until the object is the size you want. Dragging a corner handle assures you that the object will stay in proportion—if you want to change the proportions of an object, drag it by one of its sides.

Rotate Your Objects Every 50,000 Miles

To rotate an object, click on it and click the **Rotate** button. The object will be rotated the amount and direction indicated in the Rotate dialog box. You can change this amount or direction by opening the **Draw** menu and selecting Rotate (press **Alt+D** and then **R**). Enter a different amount (in degrees), and change the direction of the rotation from Clockwise to Counter-clockwise if you want. Click **OK** or press **Enter**.

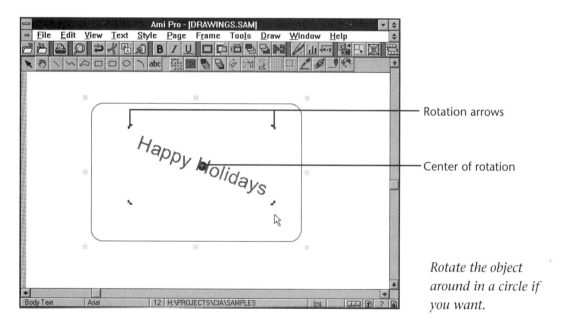

Rotation arrows

Center of rotation

Rotate the object around in a circle if you want.

You can also rotate your object manually by double-clicking in the center of it. Several *rotation arrows* will appear. Drag one of them in the direction you want to rotate the object.

You'll Flip over This

Flipping an object reverses its direction. For example, you could flip an arrow so that it points east instead of west. However, you can't flip text.

To flip an object horizontally (from east to west), click the **Flip Horizontally** button. You can also double-click on a side handle of an object to flip it. I discovered this quite by accident when I was trying to do something else. Remember it so you'll know what's going on, and you won't think your drawing is possessed. To flip an object horizontally with the keyboard, open the Draw menu (press **Alt+D**), select Flip (press **F**), and then select Horizontal (press **H**).

To flip an object vertically (turn it upside down), click the **Flip Vertically** button, or double-click a top or bottom handle. With the keyboard, open the Draw menu (press **Alt+D**), select Flip (press **F**), and select Vertical (press **V**).

Colorful Critters These Objects Are

When you create an object, the size and color of its border are determined by the Line settings. You can change these settings by selecting the object and clicking on the **Line Style** button, or by opening the Draw menu and selecting Line Style (press **Alt+D** and then L). Select a Line style and/or Color. If you're drawing an arrow or some such, change the line endings to one of those displayed. Click **OK** or press **Enter**.

The Line Setting and Fill buttons change color to reflect your current choices. When you create new objects, they will use these settings.

Fill your object with a new color by clicking the **Fill** button and selecting your favorite shade. Adjust the intensity of the color by selecting a different fill pattern. Click **OK** or press **Enter** to select your color.

Create a custom color by double-clicking on a color. Inside the Custom Color dialog box, drag the small circle to a shade you prefer, and then drag the triangle to adjust the color intensity. You can enter your own color values for **Hue**, **Sat**(uration), and **Lum**(inosity), but that get's pretty complex. Click **OK** or press **Enter** to establish the new color. Click **OK** or press **Enter** again to select the new color.

You can extract the color and line settings from an object, and use them as the new defaults or copy them to another object. First, click on an object to select it, and then click on the **Extract Line & Fill** button.

The Line and Fill default colors change to those of the object you clicked on. New objects will use these defaults. With the keyboard, open the Draw menu and select Extract Line & Fill (press **Alt+D** and then X).

To copy the current default colors to an object, click on the object to select it, and then click on the **Apply Line & Fill** button. With the keyboard, open the Draw menu and select Apply Line & Fill (press **Alt+D** and then **A**).

The Least You Need to Know

Draw your own conclusions about this chapter and what it covered:

- ☞ To create a drawing, create a frame and then click on the **Drawing** button on the Default SmartIcon set.

- ☞ Click the **Select** button to select an object.

- ☞ Move a drawing within its frame with this tool.

- ☞ To draw an object with one of these tools, click on the tool, and then drag to create the object. Press **Shift** as you drag to create a perfectly shaped object.

- ☞ With these tools, click to establish the starting point, and then click to add more lines or sides.

- ☞ Click this tool to add text in your drawing.

- ☞ Change the shape of some objects by double-clicking on the center of them and dragging one of their handles.

- ☞ Rotate an object by double-clicking on it and dragging one of the rotation handles, or by clicking on the **Rotate** button.

- ☞ To flip an object horizontally (from east to west), click the **Flip Horizontally** button. To flip it upside-down, click the **Flip Vertically** button.

continues

continued

☞   Change an object's border by changing its line settings with this tool.

☞   Change an object's color by changing its fill settings with this tool.

☞   Use an object's settings to change the default line and fill settings by clicking on the object, and then clicking on this tool.

☞   Copy the current default line and fill settings onto an object by selecting that object and clicking on the **Apply Line & Fill** tool.

Part V
What To Do When the Wolves Are at the Door

It's a quarter to three, and there's no one in the place because it's Saturday and you're stuck trying to figure out why the twenty page report that "must be on your boss' desk by Monday, 8:00 A.M. sharp—no excuses" is stuck in your printer refusing to print. You've read this wonderful book and it's helped, but let's face it—there's still something wrong.

Don't worry—this section is full of helpful information for getting you out of trouble. There's a Speak Like a Geek glossary, so when you have to talk to a computer nerd you don't look like a total idiot; a step-by-step guide for installing Ami Pro in case some jerk left that up to you; and some great troubleshooting info (of course). There's even a section on what to do with Ami Pro once you've learned the basics (just in case you have to justify the cost of the program to someone important like your boss or your wife: "But look at what all it can do!").

So, when you're feeling alone and abandoned in the Ami Pro jungle, come back here for the answers you've been looking for. You'll find stuff that'll send those wolves packing.

Installing Ami Pro

Installing Ami Pro is relatively easy—easier than using it, actually. In order to install Ami Pro, you don't really need to understand very much at all. If you've used Windows itself (even just a little), you'll be even further ahead of the game. (If you'd like a quick intro to Windows, read Chapter 3 first.) Feel free to ask a PC guru to help you if you feel at all uncomfortable.

1. Turn on your computer. Look for a switch on the front, back, or right-hand side of that big box thing. You may also have to turn on your *monitor* (it looks like a TV, but it gets lousy reception).

2. If Windows starts, great! Skip to the next step. If instead you get a rather unassuming DOS prompt that resembles C> or C:\>, type **WIN** and press **Enter**. Now you should see Windows. If you don't, or if you get an error message (such as "Bad command or file name"), Windows may not be installed, so get a PC guru to help you.

3. Insert the diskette labeled "Install—Disk 1" into drive A or B.

4. Open the Program Manager's File menu and select the **Run** command. If you're using your keyboard, press **Alt+F** and then **R**. Congratulations—it's a dialog box!

5. Type either **A:INSTALL** or **B:INSTALL** in the box that says "Command Line:" and press **Enter**.

6. Λ screen will appear, asking you to confirm the installation. Press **Enter** to continue.

If you're a former WordPerfect user, be sure to choose the option to install the SwitchKit at the end of the regular installation. SwitchKit provides additional help in the form of step-by-step instructions and support for the WordPerfect keyboard shortcuts. When you start Ami Pro, you will be asked if you want to start SwitchKit every time, or if you want to add it as a menu item. (Don't select the manual start option—that makes it too difficult to use SwitchKit.)

7. Another screen will appear. To install Ami Pro, press **Enter**. If you'd like a sneak preview of what's new in version 3.0, press **W** and **Enter**. To use the sneak preview, review the instructions for using Help in Chapter 5.

8. You'll see a screen that asks which type of installation you want to use. I'd recommend **Complete Ami Pro Install** because it's the easiest. (If you're upgrading from a previous version of Ami Pro, you must choose this option.) If you're installing Ami Pro on a laptop computer, choose the **Laptop Ami Pro Install** options. If you don't have enough room, you can choose Custom Ami Pro Install, which will install the minimum number of files needed to run Ami Pro, but you may need help to do this. Options Install is used to install Ami Pro options that were not installed from the beginning. Don't choose that option now. Click on the appropriate button to continue, or press **Enter** to choose the complete installation.

9. A message appears, asking you if you are installing Ami Pro under Windows. Of course you are, so press **Enter** to bypass this screen.

10. A new screen will appear, asking you to confirm the name of the directory in which the Ami Pro program files will be placed. You can change the name of the directory, but most people don't bother. Press **Enter** to continue.

There you go! Follow the instructions you see on-screen; you'll be told when to insert the additional installation disks. If for some reason you want to abandon the installation, you can press **Esc** or click on **Cancel**.

Ideas for Using Ami Pro at Work and at Home

If you bought Ami Pro hoping it would run itself, I have to say in its defense that it does a pretty good job. Not good enough, of course, or I'd be out of a job and you wouldn't have needed to buy this book. But that's neither here nor there; you've made an investment of time (and considerable cash, unless someone bought the program for you) to learn about how to use Ami Pro. Now let's see what all you can do with this puppy. In this section, you'll find several ideas for projects you can complete with Ami Pro. Even if you never use any of these ideas, at least it's nice to know that you didn't read all this stuff just to learn how to type a letter.

Fax Cover Letter

Ami Pro comes with several sample faxes, but you can make your own or at least dress theirs up so they're not so stuffy. After all, faxing is fun (at least more fun than the copier). Add a picture from the \DRAWSYM directory, or create a logo of your own with the drawing tools. Change the fonts if you don't like them, or bump up the point size to make certain information stand out. I used the _FAX2.STY template and added the FIREWORK.SDW drawing.

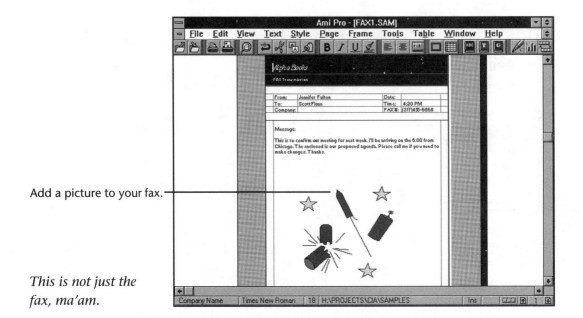

Add a picture to your fax.

This is not just the fax, ma'am.

Information Signs

Tired of everyone knocking when you're in an important meeting? Or do you just need a "time-out" from the kids? Create a sign and stick it on your door so people will know not to bother you!

Import a picture or create your own drawing and add it to your sign. Make your text big and bold so the message won't be missed!

Favorite Recipes

Got a recipe you need to share? Instead of giving your friend a tattered copy of a favorite recipe, retype it in Ami Pro. Just use one of the bulleted list styles for the ingredients list, and then use Body Text for the instructions.

If you want to go crazy and organize all your recipes, use a merge data file. Just open the File menu and select Merge. Create a merge data file with these fields: CATEGORY, RECIPE NAME, INGREDIENTS, NO. SERVED, INSTRUC-TIONS.

Input the data and then create a merge document with everything laid out nice and pretty. Then merge that document with your recipe file, and print.

You can modify the page layout settings and change the size of the paper you print on so that the result will fit into one of those large recipe boxes.

Stationery

It's easy to create great looking stationery like the one here. Start with a large frame, change its background color to a dramatic black or gray, and then enter your text: *From the Desktop of Jennifer Fulton.* (Be sure that you change the font color to white so it will show up on the black background.)

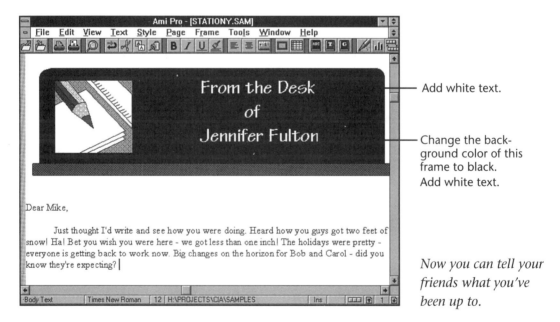

— Add white text.

— Change the background color of this frame to black. Add white text.

Now you can tell your friends what you've been up to.

Add a skinny frame that stretches from margin to margin, and change its background color to some lighter shade of gray. Place this frame at the bottom of the black frame.

If you want, import a small picture into a frame and place it in the corner. Change its background to the same color as the big frame, and be sure to use the Bring to Front command, if necessary, to place the picture frame on top of the larger frame.

Save the whole thing with some easy to remember name such as STATIONY.SAM, and then reopen it whenever you need to write a letter. (Be sure to save your letter under another name, so you won't overwrite your blank stationery file.)

Matching Envelopes

Create matching envelopes for your stationery: just start a new document with the _ENVELOP.STY style sheet and complete the dialog boxes as they appear.

When the macro is done, switch to Full Screen view and create a small frame for the picture. Change its background to black like you did for the stationery. Create another frame for your return address, and paste your address in place. Stretch the picture frame so it surrounds the address frame, creating a black border all around.

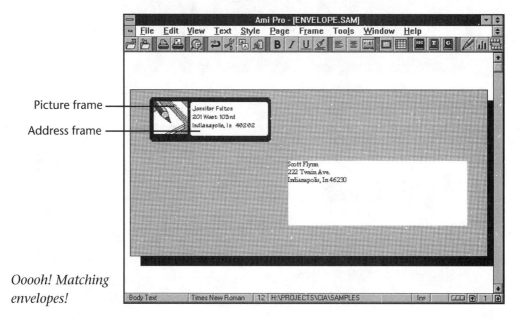

Ooooh! Matching envelopes!

Wedding Announcements

If you've got a wedding coming up, Ami Pro can really help you stay organized and get those announcements out on time! Create a data merge file for each guest. You may want to include these fields in your file: First, Last, Address1, Address2, City, State, and ZIP. Enter the guest information and continue with the Merge procedure. (Save your data merge file under the name WEDDB for Wedding Database.)

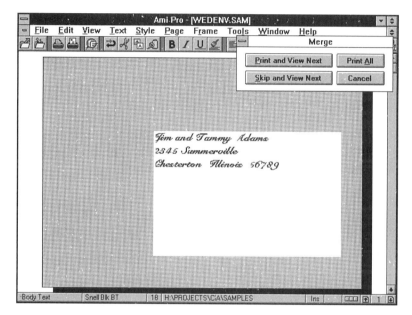

Don't elope over envelopes!

Create a merge document for the wedding invitations, or if you're using preprinted invitations, create a merge document for the envelopes. For envelopes, choose the _ENVELOP.STY but deselect the **W**ith contents and Run **m**acro options. Insert your data fields.

If you need to change the size of the envelope, open the **P**age menu and select **M**odify Page Layout. Click on **P**age settings and enter the size of the envelope. When you change the envelope size, you'll probably need to change the margin settings using the ruler.

Select the merge field names, and change the font to something fancy. Close the Merge Fields dialog box and continue with the merge.

Feed the envelopes into your laser printer one at a time and print them. They'll look like you spent hours doing the calligraphy.

Print out a copy of your WEDDB file and keep it as a list of invitees. Update it to indicate the number of expected guests so you can keep an accurate tally. (You could even add a field to the data merge file called RSVP, and use it to enter the number of people expected.)

Thank-You's and Other Greeting Cards

Create cute thank-you cards for any occasion: baby or wedding showers, birthday or Christmas gifts. Change the page layout to landscape, and insert a frame for "Happy Birthday" or some such, and a picture on the right-hand side of page one.

On page two, insert a greeting frame on the right-hand side. If you're feeling artistic, as I was, create a simple balloon with the drawing tools. Copy it and place the balloons around your greeting.

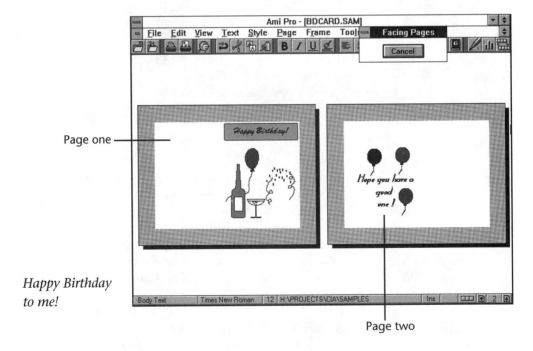

Happy Birthday to me!

Print page one of your card, flip it over, and print page two on the same piece of paper. Fold in half, and it'll be a great card!

Personalized Notepad

I'm always writing things down, so I thought, "Why not write this stuff on something fun?" With the clip art Ami Pro provides, you can quickly create some nice notepads of your own. Or, if you feel ambitious, create some simple artwork with the drawing tools.

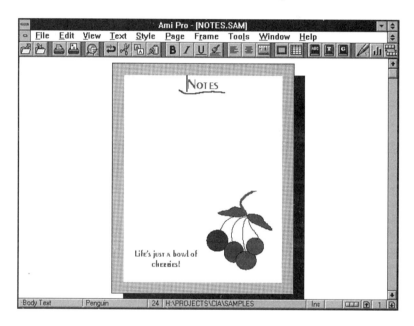

Take note of this...

I just printed out one copy and had the printers print up a bunch. Now I've got something to write all my little memos on!

Agendas

You can make a nice-looking agenda fairly quickly in Ami Pro. I used the _CALDAY.STY when I opened a new document, and simply modified it a little. You could start from scratch if you wanted: create a table of three columns and about 95 rows, adjust the column widths, fill the cells in the first column with black or light grey, and then add lines at the bottom and sides of every cell in the second and third column (use the second column for time, and the third for the actual agenda information).

But why fuss, when you can just as easily modify the _CALDAY document? In the dialog box that appears, instead of typing your name and address, enter something like "Quarterly Sales Meeting." Type over the existing date and add time and location information.

Two column table

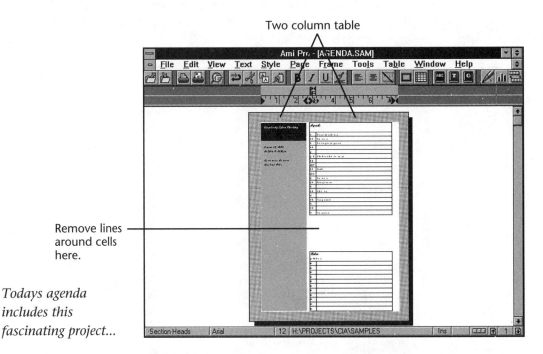

Remove lines
around cells
here.

*Todays agenda
includes this
fascinating project...*

Delete the Notes column, and adjust the width of the newly named Agenda column (formerly Miss "Appointments") to .32. Next, copy the correct times from lower cells and paste them over the 7:00 am start time (unless your meeting starts at 7:00!). Delete the contents of the other cells whose times you won't need, and change their line style to remove the underline with the Table Lines & Color command. That gives you a nice white space between the Agenda and the Notes sections. (I changed the word "Contents" to "Notes" to create a notes section at the bottom of the page.)

Project Schedules

Nothing's more embarrassing than being late. Especially if you're late with a big project that your boss was counting on. Well, worry no more! Open a new document with the _CALMON style sheet, select the month and year when your project begins, and then enter the project information on the appropriate days.

If your project extends over several months, repeat these steps for each month. If you want a breakdown by week instead of by month, use the _CALWK style sheet instead—or why not use both, and have a monthly overall project schedule, and a weekly detailed schedule?

To make it easier on yourself, add lines you create with the drawing tools to show the length of different project segments. For example, I had three days to do the outline for a new book, so I placed a red line from February 7th to the 9th. I copied this line and changed its color for other project segments, and placed these additional lines where I needed them. Finally, I selected all the project days and used the **Table Lines & Colors** command to change their colors, so I could see the entire project at a glance.

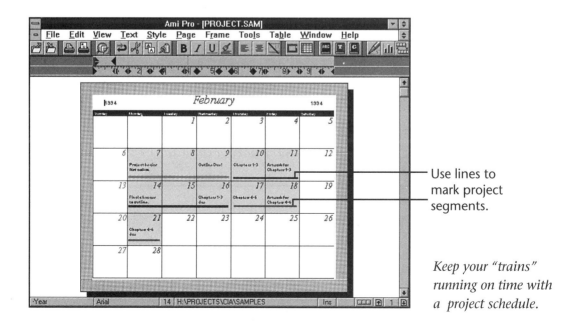

Use lines to mark project segments.

Keep your "trains" running on time with a project schedule.

Overhead Transparencies

Although Ami Pro comes with a nice selection of overhead transparency designs, there's no reason you can't venture out on your own. It's easy to import a picture and place a text frame over it. Or why not create your own shapes (as I have done) and use them instead?

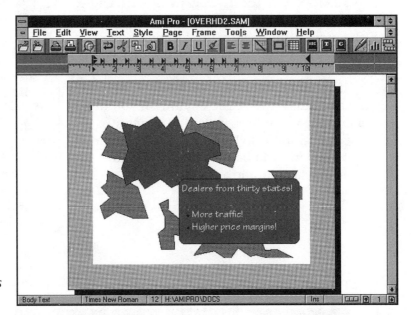

Making transparancies is not over your head.

By creating your own shape, you can easily change it from one transparency to the next, and create a simple theme for your presentation. Make your text frame the same *color* as the large graphic object in the center of your overhead, and it will seem that the text is written right on top of the graphic.

Also, if you use dark background colors, set your text color to white to make it show up better.

Adding Emphasis to Charts

If you read Chapter 22 (and I know that you did), you're well aware that Ami Pro can chart the heck out of any table. What you may not have figured out is that you modify your chart with the drawing tools.

Simply create the chart, select its frame, and then click on the **Drawing** button on the Default SmartIcon set. Click on a chart object (such as a legend, a bar, or a column) and move it or change its color or size, just like any other drawing object.

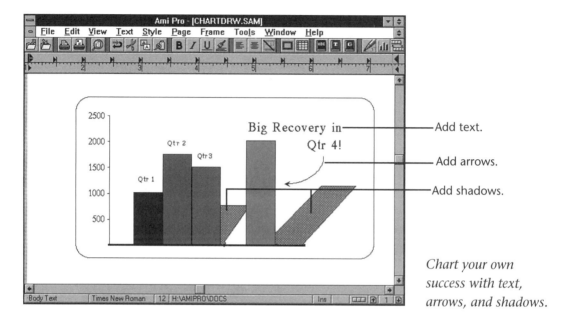

Chart your own success with text, arrows, and shadows.

 Add a shadow by copying part of the chart, selecting it, and clicking on the **Rotate** icon.

 Cut apart a legend by clicking on the **Group/Ungroup** button and dragging pieces to where you want them.

Add arrows by changing the line settings. If you use the Arc tool to draw them, you can bend them to point at exactly the item you want to emphasize.

Cassette, CD, or VCR Labels

If you've ever typed (or hand written) those tiny cassette labels for your cassettes, you know they are a pain. Well, no longer. Avery (those label people) sells labels in just about every size and description—including those sized for cassettes. (I wouldn't be surprised if they also sold labels for VCR tapes and CDs.) Anyway, find the right set of labels for your printer, and you'll be able to print them out using Ami Pro.

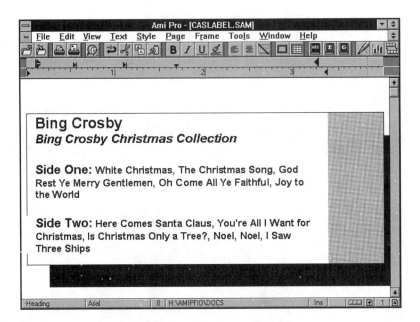

*"I'm dreaming of
a wide label..."*

Just follow the directions in Chapter 19 and create a little data merge file for some cassettes (or VCR tapes, or CDs). You might want to include these fields for cassettes: ARTIST, RECORD NAME, SIDE ONE SONGS, and SIDE TWO SONGS. For CDs, use these fields: ARTIST, RECORD NAME, SONG NUMBER, SONG. For organizing your VCR library, consider these field names: VCR NUMBER, SHOW, and COUNTER NUMBER.

Enter the data and continue the merge. Select _LABEL.STY as your style sheet, and select a label type or enter custom dimensions (for a refresher on labels, see Chapter 19).

Common Problems and How to Get Rid of Them

There's nothing so frustrating as having things go wrong. Believe me, I know. So here's a list you might find helpful when things don't go right (like when you get some cryptic error message and there's no one around to help). If you don't find an answer to your problem here, go get something really fattening to eat, whimper occasionally, and wait for a PC guru to come by and rescue you. Or try re-reading the chapter that covers the task you're working on. In either case, save what you can—and don't try anything desperate (such as turning off the computer) unless specifically told to do so by someone on whom you can place the blame.

Trouble with the Mouse

When I double-click, nothing happens. Try double-clicking a little faster. The clicks have to be close enough together to count as two in a row. If you often have trouble double-clicking, you can adjust the speed of your double-clicks with the Control Panel (have a PC guru help you). As an alternative to double-clicking, in some cases you can click once to select something, and then press **Enter** to open it, instead of double-clicking.

I selected the wrong thing. Just click on something else or press **Esc**.

Drag and drop copying and moving doesn't seem to work. Just select the text, place the mouse pointer over the middle of it, wait a second, click, and then drag. If you want to copy text, press **Ctrl** *before* you click. If it still doesn't work, drag and drop may be disabled. Open the Tools menu and select User Setup. Make sure that Disable drag & drop is *not* selected, and then click **OK**.

I'm having trouble selecting text. To select text, just click on the first letter you want to select, hold the mouse button down, and drag to the end of the text. If you can't seem to select text at all, it may be protected. To unprotect it (if you're sure you should), select the text with the keyboard by pressing and holding **Shift** and using the arrow keys. Then open the Edit menu, select Mark Text, and select Protected Text.

Trouble with Text

I tried to copy formatting with Fast Format, but it didn't work. When you copy formatting, you copy either the text enhancements (such as bold, italic, etc.) or the paragraph's style (its font, text enhancements, alignment, spacing, etc—basically whatever appears in the Modify Style dialog box when you select that style). If you copy a paragraph style that uses Arial font onto a paragraph that contains Times New Roman font, the font will change only if the paragraph's original style used Times New Roman font, and you didn't change it manually.

For example, the default Body Text style uses Times New Roman font. Suppose you changed some of the text to Paradise, and then copied the Title paragraph style onto that same text. The Title paragraph style uses Arial font, so you might expect that the text would change to Arial. Only the text still in the original Times New Roman font would change, because it's set to the paragraph style's default. By overriding the style to apply Paradise, the font stays in effect even when you copy another style onto a paragraph. Just remember that when you copy a style, you copy whatever appears in the Modify Style box, and you can override *only* what appears in the Modify Style box of the paragraph to which you are copying.

The same thing also works in reverse—kind of. Suppose you italicized a paragraph that was assigned the Title style (which is normally bold, centered, and Arial). Then you copy the text enhancements from this paragraph to a paragraph using the Body Style (which is Times New Roman, left-justified). The result would be a paragraph with Arial font, left-justified, bold, and italic. In other words, the text enhancements would change, but not the style (the left-justification) of the paragraph to which you copied the text enhancements. Just remember that when you copy text enhancements, you're basically copying *only* the font, point size, and text attributes, and *not* the style of the paragraph.

My text just disappeared. If you select text and then press **Enter**, **Backspace**, or **Delete**, the text will be deleted. If you select text and start typing, the selected text is replaced. Click on the **Undo** button on the Default SmartIcon set to see if you can get your text back. If the text you are typing replaces the current text, and that text is not selected, you are in Typeover mode. Press **Insert** to return to Insert mode, and your text will be inserted (but it will not replace existing text).

I can't select a particular paragraph style for my text. If the style you want to select appears in red, it is not available. At least one paragraph in your document is using that style, but it was copied from another document (which used a different style sheet than the current one), or the style it's using has been deleted. Just create a new style in this document, which contains the same characteristics as the old style.

When I press Enter at the end of a paragraph, a blank line is inserted. The paragraph style you are typing in includes a blank line after it. If you don't want a blank line to follow the paragraphs with that style, you can modify the style's settings with the **Style Modify Style** command. Select **S**pacing, select the line spacing option you want, and click **OK**. If you want to affect this paragraph only, press **Ctrl+Enter** instead of **Enter**. That will insert a soft return (meaning: this paragraph is not done yet, so don't insert the extra line). You can also use this trick when typing numbered or bulleted lists, where you don't want to insert a bullet or a new number just yet.

Trouble with the Ruler

If the ruler is not displayed, open the View menu and select Show Ruler.

To activate the ruler so you can change its settings, just click on it.

I inserted a tab, but my text is not aligning to it. First, be sure that you select the text whose tabs you want to adjust. Then delete any extra tabs that are in the way by dragging them off the ruler, or just click Clear Tabs to erase all the tabs before you set any tabs at all. (When you click Clear Tabs, everything will clump together temporarily. Ignore it and set some tabs on the ruler, and everything will sort itself out.) Also, make sure you are using the right kind of tab: left, right, numeric, or center. Click on the tab type you want, and *then* click on the ruler to set the tab. If you've set the wrong kind of tab, delete it and start over.

I'm having trouble creating a hanging indent. First, be sure that you have enough text in your paragraph to see the hanging indent (you should have at least two lines of text). Then press **Alt** and drag the bottom blue triangle to the right (There are two blue triangles on the left-hand side of the upper ruler; the triangle you want is the one on the bottom.)

I'm having trouble setting my margins. Be sure to drag the black triangle at the bottom of the ruler to change the margins. To change the indent for a selected paragraph (and change the distance between that paragraph and the margin), drag the set of blue triangles at the top of the ruler. To change the first-line indent of a paragraph, drag the top blue triangle only.

I've really messed this up, and I just want to start over. To return a paragraph to its default settings, select it and press **Ctrl+N**. WARNING: This may change other settings, and not just indents. To remove all the tabs and return a paragraph to normal tab settings, open the **Page** menu, select **Ruler**, and then select **Remove**.

Trouble with a New Document

I can't figure out what this style sheet is for. In the New dialog box, select **Preview**. This will display a sample of the style sheet with fake text, so you can see what a document that uses that style sheet will look like. Check out your "Style Sheet Guide" (which comes with Ami Pro) for more samples.

I tried to open a new document, and my other document disappeared. Unless you selected Close current file when you opened your new document, your old document is still there; just open the **Window** menu and you should see it listed. Click on its name to move to the old document.

Trouble with an Old Document

I can't open this document. If the document was saved with a password, you're going to have to enter the exact password to open it. You must also match the case of the letters you type: a password of "SECRET" is *not* the same as "secret" or "Secret." So be careful to type the upper- and lowercase letters exactly as you did when you entered the password originally.

I can't find my document. Oops! Try selecting **P**review, which will display the document's contents before you open it. If that doesn't work, try looking in a different directory or drive. If the file you're looking for is one on which you've worked recently, try looking at the bottom of the **F**ile menu where recently used files are listed.

Trouble Saving a Document

Ami Pro won't let me save my document. Try entering a different file name, and make sure you use no more than eight characters (no spaces). If there isn't enough room on the disk to save the document, change to a different disk drive or delete some files on the drive (this is pretty tricky, so get help if you can). If you try to save a document over top of an existing document, you'll get a message asking you if you're sure. Click on **Y**es or press **Y** to overwrite the existing document. If you opened two copies of the same document, one of them is marked "Read-Only," and Ami Pro won't let you save changes to it. Just close it and save your changes to the other document window.

Ami Pro always tries to save my files to the wrong directory. By default, Ami Pro saves files to the \AMIPRO\DOCS directory. Just change directories in the Save As dialog box before you click **O**K, or change it permanently through Tools User Setup. Click on **P**aths, and under **D**ocument, enter the directory where you want to store your files. If you click on **U**se working directory, Ami Pro will always use the last directory you referenced as the current directory for saving and opening files.

I tried to save my document, but I didn't get the dialog box. After saving your document one time, you won't see the dialog box again when saving that document; Ami Pro simply uses the original name and directory to save the document over and over, replacing it each time with the new copy. To save a previously saved document under a different name or in a different directory, use the File Save As command.

I saved my document, but it's still on my screen. That is how Ami Pro works—it saves your document on the disk and leaves the document open unless you also tell it to close the document. If you are through with a document, close it by double-clicking on the **Control-menu box**, or by opening the File menu and selecting Close. If you've changed the document since it was saved last, you'll get the Save dialog box.

Trouble Printing a Document

I tried to cancel the print job, but I don't think it worked. When Ami Pro prints something (or tries to), it gathers it up and then turns the stuff over to a Windows program called Print Manager, which prints the document. If you cancel the print job (or turn off your printer), Print Manager is not always aware of what is going on, and it tries to continue to print the canceled print job the next time you attempt to print anything. If you ever interrupt the print process, reset your printer by turning it off and then on again. Then close Print Manager by pressing **Ctrl+Esc**, selecting it from the list, and clicking on End Task. If you see something called AmiPrint listed, select it also and click on End Task. That way, there won't be any "ghost print jobs" floating around waiting to print.

Part of my document didn't print. If you're using a laser printer, and you've set your margins to less than .5", you have some text trying to print in the "no-print zone." Set your margins to at least .5" and try again. If that doesn't solve the problem, click on the **Print** button on the Default SmartIcon set. Click on All and Both, and then click **OK**. Be sure your printer has plenty of paper, and is set to On-Line. If necessary, clear the printer's memory by turning it off and then on again. Then select the Print command again. (See the previous warning about cancelling a print job correctly.)

My entire document didn't print. First, make sure you have something to print. Open your document and verify that the text you want to print is located in the white area (the page) and not in the margins (the blue or gray area). Now, be sure that your printer is on, and on-line. Check the paper supply. If everything checks out, press **Ctrl+Esc** and check out Print Manager. If you see your document is marked "Paused," click on **Resume**.

My document printed okay, but there were some extra blank pages at the end. You may have pressed **Enter** too many times, and inserted a blank page by accident. Go to the end of the document and press **Backspace** to delete the extra blank lines. If this doesn't work, you may have placed an empty frame on the last page of the document. Click on it to select it, and then delete it. If you can't see it because it doesn't have any borders, press **Ctrl+End**, press **Ctrl+G**, select Next item, select **Frame** from the list, and then press **Enter** to locate the hidden frame.

My pictures didn't print. If they are displayed on-screen, click on the **Print** button on the Default SmartIcon set. Click on Options, and be sure that Without **pictures** is *not* selected. Click **OK** twice to start printing.

If you're really having trouble printing, return quickly to Chapter 10 for more tips and how-to's.

Trouble with Outlining

I can't see my entire outline. Click on the number 9 on the Outline bar. To see text and headings, click on the asterisk. To hide lower levels of the outline, click on a higher number.

I want this subheading to be a heading, but I want it to stay where it's currently located within the document. Headings occupy different levels within the outline hierarchy. For example, the heading "Trouble with Outlining" might include a subheading called "Using the Outline Bar." These two headings are at differing outline levels. Another heading, "Trouble With Printing," might be set at the same level of importance as the heading, "Trouble With Outlining." To change a heading's level (importance within an outline), click on the right or left arrows on the Outline bar.

I was trying to move a section up, but it just moved the text and not the heading. You may have used the up or down buttons on the Outline bar. Click **Undo**, and then click on the plus or minus in front of the section you want to move. Drag the section where you want it (you'll see a horizontal line to help you), and release the mouse button. To move a heading but *not* the subordinate text, click on the up or down buttons on the Outline bar. If you want to move part of a section (but not all of its subheadings and text), select what you want to move, click on it, and then drag and drop it into place.

I want to delete this section. To delete a section (headings and all), contract it by double-clicking on its minus sign. When all you see is the heading (and not the subordinate text), select it and press **Delete**.

I want to print just my outline, not my entire document. Click on the number 9 to contract the outline to headings only, and then click on the **Print** button on the Default SmartIcon set.

Trouble with Tables

If your tables do not have lines around each cell on-screen, open the View menu and select View Preferences. Select Table gridlines and click **OK**.

If your tables do not have lines around each cell when printed, open the Table menu and select Lines & colors. Under Line position, click on All, and then click **OK**.

I tried to enter the department number 003120 into a cell, but it displays only 3120. Ami Pro truncates zeroes which precede any number. To tell Ami Pro to treat the number as if it were text (so that it won't cut off those zeroes), enter a space after the number, as in "003120 ."

I tried to insert a row, but it appeared after the current row. If you click on the **Insert Row** button on the Tables SmartIcon set, it will insert the new row below the current row. To insert a row above the current row, open the Table menu, select Insert Column/Row, click on **Rows** and **Before**, and click **OK**. The same thing goes for columns: if you click on the **Insert Column** button on the Tables SmartIcon set, it will insert the column to the right of the current column. To insert a column to the left, use the Table Insert Column/Row command.

I selected the entire table and pressed Delete, but the table is still there. To delete a table, click on it and open the Table menu. Select Delete Entire Table.

I tried to insert a column, but it didn't work. You cannot insert a column if there is no room for it on the current page. Adjust the size of existing columns first, and then add your new column.

I have a column of department numbers, and a column of dollar amounts that I want displayed with a dollar sign. If you change the Table format style to Currency (in the Modify Style dialog box), all numbers will be displayed with dollar signs. Instead, enter the dollar amounts with a dollar sign. Ami Pro will think the cells contain text (because of the $), so you'll have to select the cells and right-align the dollar amounts. Because Ami Pro thinks these cells contain text, you won't be able to perform any calculations on them. Another solution is to change the Table format style by opening the Style menu, selecting Modify Style, clicking on Table format, selecting **Currency**, and clicking **OK**. Since all numbers will then be displayed with a dollar sign, reenter the department numbers with a space after each one so Ami Pro will treat them as text.

I want one number column to use dollar signs, and another to use just commas. This one's a bit tricky. First, change the Table format style by opening the Style menu and selecting Modify Style, clicking on Table format, and selecting **Currency**. You may also want to change the number of decimal places. But before you click **OK**, click on Save As and enter the style name **Dollar**. Then click **OK**, select the cells you want formatted with a dollar sign, and apply the Dollar style to them. You can use this same trick if you want one column to display two decimal places, and another one to display no decimal places.

I tried to adjust the height of a row, but it won't let me. Click on the **Modify Table Layout** button on the Tables SmartIcon set. Deselect the option Automatic, click **OK**, and then try to adjust the height again.

I want to add a title to my table. Move to the first cell in the table and insert a row above it by opening the Table menu, selecting Insert Column/Row, clicking on Rows and Before, and clicking **OK**. Then select the entire row, and click the **Connect Cells** button on the Tables SmartIcon set. Enter your title, and center it if you like by pressing **Ctrl+E**. If your table extends beyond a single page, add a header instead by moving to the title row, opening the Table menu and selecting Headings. The title row will now be displayed as the first row of the table on every page in which the table appears.

I entered a formula, but it didn't do anything. Before you enter a formula, you must click the **Edit Formula** button on the Tables SmartIcon set, or open the Table menu and select Edit Formula. Then type the formula and press **Enter**.

I entered a formula, and now it's displaying REF. Check the cells referenced in the formula. One of them contains text or some other garbage that Ami Pro can't figure out. Also, make sure you don't reference the current cell in the formula. For example, if you enter a formula in cell C3, make sure it doesn't reference C3, as in the range A3:D3 or A3..D3.

Trouble with Merging

Ami Pro doesn't like the field name I chose. A field name cannot begin with a number or consist of only numbers. Try a different field name.

I inserted my field names into the merge document, but something's wrong. You can't just type the fields you want into the document as in <First_Name>. You must insert them via the Insert Merge Field dialog box. Open the File menu and select Merge. Select Create or edit a merge document. Select your document from the list, delete the fields you typed in, and then insert them from the Insert Merge Field dialog box (select a field and click on **Insert**).

When I merged the document with my merge data file, the first and the last names ran together. When you inserted the first and last name fields into your document, you forgot to insert a space. Return to your merge document and insert the space. Then merge the data again.

I added all my fields, but the little index card doesn't display them all. Look for a down arrow at the bottom of the card. Click it to display the hidden fields in this record.

I want to sort my data before I merge so my letters will be in alphabetical order. Open the File menu and select Merge. Select Select, create, or edit a data file. Select your data file and click **Edit**. Click on **Sort** and select the sort field from the list (for example, Last Name). Click **OK**, and the data will be sorted. Click on **Close** and then Yes to save the changes. Continue with the merge.

I need to update the data in the merge data file. Open the File menu and select **Merge**. Select Select, create, or edit a **d**ata file. Select your data file and click **E**dit. Click on a tab to edit its record, or use the left and right arrows to page through the records until you find the one you want. When you're done, click on **Close** and then Yes to save the changes.

Trouble with Frames

My pictures aren't displayed. Open the **V**iew menu and select View **P**refer-ences. Select **P**ictures and click **O**K.

I tried to create a frame, but it didn't work. Be sure you're in Layout mode before you try to create a frame, or nothing will happen.

I'm trying to move this frame, but it won't move. Click on the **Modify Frame Layout** button on the Graphics SmartIcon set, select **T**ype under Frame, and make sure that the option **W**here placed is selected. Then click in the middle of the frame and, while holding down the left mouse button, drag it into place.

I can't select the right frame. If one frame is covering up the frame you're trying to get to, press **Ctrl** as you click on the top frame.

I want to resize this frame. Click on the frame to display the black handles first. Then click on a corner handle and drag. To make the frame wider or thinner, click on a side handle and drag. To make the frame taller or shorter, click on the bottom or top handle and drag.

I moved this frame into place, and all the text around it went ga ga. If you want to place the frame real close to the text but you don't want the text to move, click on the **Modify Frame Layout** button on the Graphics SmartIcon set and select **T**ype under Frame. Then select No wrap around and click **O**K. You can even make the frame itself transparent, so all the text underneath it is displayed (this allows you to place a picture within the frame really close to text). Just select Transparent on the Type screen of the Modify Frame Layout dialog box.

I don't want the frame to show, just the picture. Click on the **Modify Frame Layout** button on the Graphics SmartIcon set, and select **Lines & shadows** under Frame. Set Shadow to None, and deselect all the options under Lines. Click **OK**.

Trouble with Charting

I clicked on the Charting button, and Ami Pro says that I don't have any data. What do I do? If you have a table or columns of data for your chart, select **Cancel**, select the data, click on the **Copy** button, and then click on the **Charting** button. If you don't have any chart data in your document, click **OK** and enter the chart data (remember to insert a tab or a space between columns of data).

I tried to create a chart, but it didn't turn out the way I thought it would. Double-click on the chart. Click on Flip data and click **OK**. If that doesn't help, double-click on the chart again and try a different chart type, such as a Pie or a Line chart. Click on **Data** and verify that it's entered correctly: similar data should be in the same column with a column heading, or in the same row with a row heading.

My chart doesn't have anything to identify what everything stands for. Double-click on the chart and try adding a legend. If that doesn't help, click on **Data** and add row or column headings (if necessary, cut and paste data to make room for column headings). If you need to show a space in a heading, as in "1st Qtr," type it with an underscore, as in "1st_Qtr." Click **OK**. If your chart looks better, click **OK** again.

I'm having trouble changing the colors of my chart. Double-click on the chart and select a color set. Drag the colors you want to use to the left-hand side of the color set. Click **OK**.

Trouble with Drawing

I selected the frame I want and clicked the Drawing button, but nothing happened. You cannot use Drawing on a frame that contains text. Delete the text and insert it with the Drawing buttons, or use another frame.

I'm having trouble selecting one of the objects. Be sure to click on the **Selection** tool before you try to select something. If you still can't select an object and it's partially covered by another object, press **Ctrl** as you click on the top object.

I just changed the line and fill colors, and a part of my drawing became that color. Whatever you have selected when you change the line and/or fill colors will change to match your selections. If you want to change the line and/or fill colors for a new object, be sure nothing in your drawing is currently selected. Just click inside the frame, but not on an object.

Trouble, Period.

I just messed up my document. Help! Try to undo the change by clicking the **Undo** button on the Default SmartIcon set. If that doesn't work, you can undo everything you've done since you last saved this document by opening the File menu and selecting **Revert to Saved**.

I tried to select a command or click on a button, but nothing happened. If the command on the menu is grayed, you can't select it now, no matter what you do. Although the SmartIcons do not appear gray when they can't be selected (actually, that would be a great idea to any of you programmers out there!), their corresponding menu commands do. Sometimes all you have to do is one little thing to make that command available. For example, to select the Copy command, select a word first. To use most of the commands on the Frame or Table menu, you must click on a frame or table first. To use some commands, you must switch to Layout mode first. The trick is knowing what comes first, the chicken or the command.

I tried to spell check my document, but I'm still finding mistakes. First, make sure that Spell Check checked everything by placing your insertion point at the beginning of the document and trying again. If you started Spell Check while the insertion point was in a header, for example, it never checked the main body text. Be sure that Include other text streams is selected when you start Spell Check. It's also a good idea to run Grammar Checker to catch errors in grammar, not spelling. And be careful about clicking either **Skip** or **Skip All** when you're checking the spelling in a document, so you don't skip over misspelled words.

I can't find a word I know is there. First, make sure you spelled the word correctly in the Find & Replace dialog box. If you're looking for part of a word, click on Options and be sure that **Whole word only** is *not* selected. You may want to select **Beginning of document** while you're there to be sure that you check the entire document. If you see that **Find backwards** is selected, you're looking for the word from the insertion point to the beginning of the document, which may not be what you want.

Trouble with Tribbles

Do not feed! Beam excess tribbles onto the nearest Klingon warship; then relax with a nice glass of Saurian brandy.

Glossary

Speak Like a Geek: The Complete Archive

The computer world is like an exclusive club, complete with its own language. If you want to be accepted, you need to learn the lingo (the secret handshake will come later). The following mini-glossary will help you get started.

accelerator keys (1) The one thing you don't want to be pressing when you see a cop. (2) Sometimes called shortcut keys, these are used to activate a command without opening the menu. Usually a function key or a key combination (such as Ctrl+S), accelerator keys are displayed next to the menu command. To use an accelerator key, hold down the first key while you press the second key.

active document The document you are currently working in. The active document contains the insertion point, and if more than one document window is being displayed on-screen, the active document's title bar appears darker than the other title bars.

alignment (1) What your car is out of if it drifts to the left when you're eating a burger and make a grab for that last fry. (2) Controls where the text in a paragraph is placed between the left and right margins. For example, you might have left-aligned or centered paragraphs.

Ami Pro Brought to you by Lotus, Ami Pro is one of the most popular Windows word processing programs, and the reason you bought this book.

application   (1) The placement of shampoo on the head. (2) Also known as a program, a set of instructions that enable a computer to perform a specific task, such as word processing or data management.

ASCII file   A file containing characters that can be used by any program on any computer. Sometimes called a text file or an ASCII text file. (ASCII is pronounced "ASK-key.") For those of you who are curious, ASCII stands for American Standard Code for Information Interchange. And if you want to know more, ask Key, he knows.

axis   One side of a chart. See *x-axis*, *y-axis*, and/or *z-axis*.

background   The box of gray that is placed behind text or a cell in a table in order to emphasize it. Sometimes known as shading or fill.

boilerplate text   (1) Text that's been left on the stove too long. (2) Generic text within a template that is reused by every document created from that template. For example, "Dear Valued Customer" and "Sincerely Yours" qualify as boilerplate text in a form letter.

border   A line placed on any (or all) of the four sides of a block of text, a graphic, a chart, or a table.

bulleted list   Similar to a numbered list. A bulleted list is a series of paragraphs with hanging indents, where the bullet (usually a dot or a check mark) is placed to the left of all the other lines in the paragraph. A bulleted list is often used to display a list of items or to summarize important points.

cascaded windows   Windows arranged so that they overlap, with each window's title bar clearly displayed.

cell   (1) The opposite of "Buy!" (2) The box formed by the intersection of a row and a column in an Ami Pro table. The same term is used when describing the intersection of a row and a column in a spreadsheet. A cell may contain text, a numeric value, or a formula.

chart   Sometimes known as a graph. Graphical representation of columns of related numbers. For example, if one sales figure were larger than another, the column (or bar) representing it on a chart would also be larger. The larger sales figure could also be represented by a larger portion of a pie, or a longer line.

click   After you have moved the mouse pointer over an object or icon, a single press and release of the mouse button.

clip art   A collection of prepackaged artwork, whose individual pieces can be placed within a document.

Clipboard   (1) A wooden or plastic rectangle to which you can affix important notes so you can lose them for a week after the wooden or plastic rectangle accidentally falls behind your filing cabinet. (2) A temporary storage area where Windows holds text and graphics. The Cut and Copy commands put text or graphics on the Clipboard, erasing the Clipboard's previous contents. The Paste command copies Clipboard data to a document.

column   A vertical section of a table. See also *newspaper-style columns*.

command   An order that tells the computer what to do. In command-driven programs, such as DOS, you have to type the actual words of the command to execute it. With menu-driven programs, such as Ami Pro, you select the command from a menu.

computer   (1) A hole on my desk I throw money into. (2) Any machine that accepts input (from a user), processes the input, and produces output in some form.

Control-menu box   A special button located in the upper left corner of a window. It contains a special menu that can be used to move, size, and close a window using the keyboard.

crash   (1) A sound you don't want to hear when you're moving your computer. (2) Failure of a system or program. Usually, you will realize that your system crashed when the display or keyboard locks up. The term crash also refers to a disk crash or head crash, which occurs when the read/write head in the disk drive falls on the disk. This would be like dropping a phonograph needle on a record. A disk crash can destroy any data stored where the read/write head falls on the disk.

cropping   The process of cutting away part of an imported graphic.

cursor   A vertical line that appears to the right of characters as you type. A cursor acts like the tip of your pencil; anything you type appears at the cursor. (See also *insertion point*.)

data   (1) That guy on "Star Trek: The Next Generation." (2) A computer term for information. You enter facts and figures (data) into a computer, which then processes it and displays it in an organized manner. In common usage, data and information are used interchangeably.

database   A type of computer program used for storing, organizing, and retrieving information. Popular database programs include Lotus Approach, dBASE, Paradox, FoxPro, Microsoft Access, and Q&A.

desktop publishing (DTP)   A program that allows you to combine text and graphics on the same page, and manipulate the text and the graphics on-screen. Desktop publishing programs are commonly used to create newsletters, brochures, flyers, résumés, and business cards.

dialog box   (1) Geek name for a telephone. (2) A special window or box that appears when the program requires additional information from you before it can execute a command.

directory   Because large hard disks can store thousands of files, most of us need to store related files in separate directories on the disk so we can find them again. Think of your disk as a filing cabinet, and think of each directory as a drawer in the filing cabinet. By keeping files in separate directories, you can locate and work with related files more easily.

disk   A round, flat, magnetic storage unit. See *floppy disk* and *hard disk*.

disk drive   (1) A street in Silicon Valley. (2) A device that writes and reads data on a magnetic disk. Think of a disk drive as being like a cassette recorder/player. Just as the cassette player can record sounds on a magnetic cassette tape and play back those sounds, a disk drive can record data on a magnetic disk and play back that data.

document   Any work you create using an application program and which you save in a file on disk. Although the term document traditionally refers to work created in a word processing program (such as a letter or a chapter of a book), document is now used rather loosely to include spreadsheets and databases.

document window   A window that frames the controls and information for the document file you're working on. You can have multiple document windows open at one time.

DOS (disk operating system)   DOS, which rhymes with "boss," is an essential program that provides the instructions necessary for the computer's parts (keyboard, disk drive, central processing unit, display screen, printer, and so on) to function as a unit.

DOS prompt   An on-screen prompt that indicates DOS is ready to accept a command. It looks something like C> or C:\>.

double-click   To move the mouse pointer over an object or icon, and press and release the mouse button twice in quick succession.

drag   (1) Losing a winning lottery ticket. (2) To drag the mouse. Move the mouse pointer to the starting position. Then press and hold the left mouse button, and move the mouse pointer to the ending position. With the pointer in the ending position, release the mouse button.

drop cap   A method of text design used to set off the first letter in a paragraph. The letter is enlarged and set into the text of the paragraph, at its upper left-hand corner. Ami Pro calls this letter a dropped capital.

edit   To make changes to existing information within a document. Editing in a word processor usually involves spell-checking, grammar checking, rearranging text, and making formatting changes until the document is considered complete.

embedded object   (1) Any object that sleeps past noon. (2) An object that maintains a connection to the application that created it, so that it can be changed easily as needed. You access that application by simply double-clicking on the object, which is stored within your Ami Pro document.

exit   Technical name for stopping or quitting a program such as Ami Pro.

extension   In DOS, each file you create has a unique name. The name consists of two parts: a file name and an extension. The file name can be as long as eight characters. The extension (which is optional) can be no more than three characters. The extension normally denotes the file type.

face   See *font*.

field   (1) What someone is always out standing in. (2) One part of a data file record. A field contains a single piece of information (for example, a telephone number, ZIP code, or a person's last name). A power field is a code inserted into a document which is updated when the document is opened, such as the Date field.

file   (1) What every prisoner wants to find in a birthday cake. (2) DOS stores information in files. Anything can be placed in a file: a memo, a budget report, or even a graphics image (like a picture of a boat or a computer). Each document you create in Ami Pro is stored in its own file. Every file has a unique file name to identify it.

fill   See *background*.

fixed disk drive   A disk drive containing a non-removable disk, as opposed to floppy drives, in which you can insert and remove disks. See also *disk drive*.

floppy disk drive   A disk drive that uses floppy disks. See also *disk drive*.

floppy disks   Small, portable, plastic storage devices that store magnetic data (the facts and figures you enter and save). To use a floppy disk, it must be inserted into your computer's floppy disk drive (located on the front of the computer).

font   Any set of characters that share the same typeface (style or design). Fonts convey the mood and style of a document. Technically, font describes the combination of the typeface and point size of a character (as in Times Roman 12-point), but in common usage it describes only a character's style or typeface.

footer   (1) The distance my golf ball travels when I tee off. (2) Text that is reprinted at the bottom of each page of a document.

formatting   Changing the look of a character (by making it bold, underlined, and slightly bigger, for example) or a paragraph (by centering the paragraph between the margins, for example, or by adding an automatic indentation for the first line).

frames   (1) What you get at an optical store in only an hour. (2) Small boxes in which you place text or pictures so you can maneuver them easily within your document.

function keys   (1) Those keys that have not yet been gunked up by spilled coffee. (2) The 10 or 12 F keys on the left side of the keyboard, or the 12 F keys at the top of the keyboard. F keys are numbered F1, F2, F3, and so on. These keys are used to change text styles in Ami Pro.

Grammar Checker   A special program within Ami Pro that corrects grammatical errors within a document.

graph   See *chart*.

graphic   A picture imported into Ami Pro to illustrate a point.

graphical user interface (GUI, pronounced "gooey")   (1) Tar on a hot tin roof. (2) A type of program in which you use graphical elements to communicate with the software. These graphical elements are usually pictures, such as icons, which represent commands, files, and (in some cases) other programs. The most popular GUI is Microsoft Windows.

graphics/charting program   A program that converts columns of data into a professional-looking chart.

gridlines   Lines that run horizontally across a chart, making it easier to measure the value of the plot points.

gutter   (1) A leaf, twig, and debris magnet. (2) An unused region of space that runs down the inside edges of facing pages of a document; it's the part of each page that is used when the pages of a book or a magazine are bound together.

handles   (1) Extra fat around your middle. (2) Small black squares that surround a graphic, frame, table, or chart after it is selected.

hanging indent   A special kind of indentation where the first line of a paragraph "hangs" closer to the left margin than the rest of the lines in the paragraph. Typically used for bulleted or numbered lists, so that the bullet or number is closer to the left margin than the associated text.

hard disk   A stationary disk drive that stores many megabytes of data. Because it is fixed in place inside the computer (see *fixed disk drive*), it performs quickly and more efficiently than a floppy disk.

hardware   The physical parts of a computer (such as the monitor, the disk drives, the CPU, and so on). The programs you run are electronic, rather than physical; they're known as software.

header   (1) What you take when you dive off a ten story building face first. (2) Text that is reprinted at the top of each page of a document.

header record   Stores the field names (column headings) for a merge data file.

hyphenation   (1) A small country that was once a part of the U.S.S.R. (2) A feature that allows Ami Pro to break words with a hyphen, and place the remainder on the next line.

hyphenation hot-zone   A region along the right margin. Any word that enters this zone is hyphenated. For example, if the hot-zone is set to 5 characters, and a word is located less than 5 characters from the right margin, it will be hyphenated.

I-beam   (1) Godzilla's secret weapon. (2) Another name for the mouse pointer when it is placed over text.

icon   A graphic image on your screen that represents another object, such as a program or a document.

indent   (1) What happens to your bumper when you back up without looking. (2) The distance from the page margins to the edges of your paragraph.

input   Data that goes into your computer. When you press a key or click a mouse button, you are giving your computer input. Data that your computer gives back to you (by printing it out or displaying it on the monitor) is called output.

Insert mode   The default typing mode for most word processors and text editors. In Insert mode, when you position your cursor and start to type, what you type is inserted at that point, and existing text is pushed to the right. Insert mode is the opposite of Typeover mode.

insertion point   A blinking vertical line used in some word processors to indicate the place where any characters you type will be inserted. An insertion point is the equivalent of a cursor.

jump term   A highlighted word in the Ami Pro Help system that, when selected, "jumps" you to a related section of the Help system.

keyboard   The main input device for most computers.

kilobyte   A unit for measuring quantities of data. A kilobyte (K) equals 1,024 bytes.

landscape orientation   Your document is oriented so that it is wider than it is long, as in 11 by 8 1/2 inches. The opposite of landscape orientation is portrait.

leader   (1) Someone that aliens are always asking to be taken to. (2) Dots or dashes that fill the spaces between tab positions in a columnar list.

legend   (1) What stars often consider themselves, but rarely are. (2) Identifies what each element of a chart represents. For example, the legend for a pie chart explains what each piece of the pie represents.

lines   See *border*.

linked object   An imported object (such as a graphic) that maintains a connection to the program that it was created in. If changes are made to that object, the changes can then be updated (either automatically or through a command) into your document. A linked object is stored separately from your Ami Pro document.

Lotus   (1) A company I wish I had lots of stock in. (2) The company that brought you Ami Pro, Improv, Lotus Approach, Lotus Organizer, Lotus Notes, Freelance Graphics, cc:Mail, and that classic, Lotus 1-2-3.

macro   A recorded set of instructions that can be activated (played back) by pressing a specified key combination. Macros resemble small programs, and are created to automate complicated or frequently performed tasks.

margin   An area running around the left, right, top, and bottom sides of a page that is usually left blank. Text is located between the margins of a page.

Maximize button   An upward-pointing arrow located in the upper right-hand corner of a window; when you click on it, the window fills the screen.

megabyte   (1) A large submarine sandwich. (2) A standard unit used to measure the storage capacity of a disk, and the amount of computer memory. A megabyte is 1,048,576 bytes (1,000 kilobytes). This is roughly equivalent to 500 pages of double-spaced text. Megabyte is commonly abbreviated as M, MB, or Mbyte.

memory   (1) Something I seem to lose quite often lately. (2) Electronic storage area inside the computer, used to store data or program instructions temporarily when the computer is using them. The computer's memory is erased when the power to the computer is turned off.

menu   A list of commands or instructions displayed on the screen. Menus organize commands and make a program easier to use.

menu bar   Located at the top of the Program Window, this displays the names of menus, which contain the commands you'll use to edit documents.

merge data file   A special document file that contains the variable information to be merged later into a main document, producing individualized form letters or mailing labels.

merging   The process of combining variable information stored in a merge data file with a main document to produce a series of form letters or mailing labels.

Minimize button   A downward-pointing arrow located in the upper right-hand corner of a window; when you click on it, the window is reduced to an icon on your screen.

mirror   An option you can use when creating magazine-like reports: when open, the pages of your report "face each other" like the pages in a book or magazine.

monitor   A television-like screen where the computer displays information.

mouse   (1) The last name of a little guy named Mickey. (2) A device that moves an arrow (a pointer) around the screen. When you move the mouse, the pointer on the screen moves in the same direction. Used instead of the keyboard to select and move items (such as text or graphics), execute commands, and perform other tasks. A mouse gets its name because it connects to your computer through a long "tail" or cord.

mouse pad   (1) Where Mickey and his friends hang out. (2) A small square of plastic or foam that the mouse rests on. A mouse pad provides better traction than a desktop, and keeps the mouse away from dust and other goop on your desk.

mouse pointer   (1) Mickey's hand. (2) An arrow or other symbol that moves when the mouse is moved. When the mouse pointer is over text, it changes to an I-beam. When the mouse pointer is over an element of the screen, it usually takes the shape of an arrow.

MS-DOS (Microsoft Disk Operating System)   See *DOS*.

newspaper-style columns   Similar to the style of column found in newspapers. Text in these columns flows between invisible boundaries down one part of the page, and then up to the top of the next column. At the end of the page, text continues at the top of the first column on the next page. Columns can be "interrupted" by graphics (pictures or charts) that illustrate the story being told.

numbered list   Similar to a bulleted list. A numbered list is a series of paragraphs with hanging indents, with the number placed to the left of all other lines in the paragraph. Used in numbering the steps for a procedure.

object   Item that can be manipulated and edited separately from the document as a whole. Common objects include tables, charts, drawings, graphics, and frames. A drawing object is one part of a drawing. For example, a drawing object that is a rectangle could be one part of the more complex drawing of a PC.

output   (1) What you do with a cat right before bedtime. (2) Data (computer information) that your computer gives back to you. Output can be displayed on a computer's monitor, stored on disk, or printed on the printer. Output is the opposite of input, which is the data that you enter into the computer.

page break   A dotted line that Ami Pro inserts at the end of a page. You can force a page break anywhere else within a document by opening the Page menu and selecting **Breaks**.

pane   (1) What I feel when someone touches my shoulder after I've spent all day at the beach. (2) What Ami Pro calls the special boxes that you use when adding headers, footers, footnotes, and annotations. In Normal View, a pane appears in the bottom half of the document window. (Since it's part of a window—rather than being a separate box like a dialog box— it's called a pane.)

paragraph   Any grouping of words that should be treated as a unit. This includes normal paragraphs as well as single-line paragraphs (such as chapter titles, section headings, and captions for charts or other figures). When you press the **Enter** key in Ami Pro, you are marking the end of a paragraph. (Note: some computers call the Enter key Return.)

parallel columns   See *table*.

passive voice   (1) Speaking in a whisper. (2) A type of sentence that states what is done by the subject, rather than what the subject does. For example, compare "the race was won by Mary Ann" (passive voice) to the same phrase in active voice: "Mary Ann won the race."

PC   See *personal computer*.

pica   Typesetter's unit for measuring the width of a character. There are 6 picas to the inch.

pie chart   A type of chart shaped like a circle and divided into pieces, like a pie. Each item that's charted (such as AT&T, MCI, and Sprint) is given a "pie wedge," which represents its portion of the whole amount.

point   (1) Something my mother always told me is not polite. (2) To move the mouse pointer so that it is on top of a chosen object on the screen.

point size   The type size (height) of a particular character. There are 72 points in an inch. Font families usually have only certain point sizes available; if you need larger or smaller letters than your font offers, switch to a different font.

polygon   Any multi-sided object. Polygons include common shapes such as squares, stars, hexagons, and octagons, as well as the exotic ones such as open free-form shapes.

portrait orientation   Your document is oriented so that it is taller than it is wide, as in 8 1/2 by 11 inches. This is the normal orientation of most documents. The opposite of portrait orientation is landscape.

power fields   Special codes that update information in a document as conditions change, such as changing data, page number and figure references, a date field that updates whenever a document is changed, and so on.

printer   Most computers are connected to a printer for creating copies of data. The data that comes out of your computer is called output.

program   (1) Something that tells you who the players in the game are. (2) A set of detailed instructions written in a special "machine language" that the computer understands. Typical programs are word processors, spreadsheets, databases, and games.

program group   A special window within the Program Manager that groups several applications together. In the Lotus Applications program group you'll find two icons: Ami Pro 3.0 and Dialog Editor.

program window   The window that Ami Pro runs in. Close this window, and you close down (exit) Ami Pro. This window frames the tools and the menus for the Ami Pro program.

pull-down menu   A pull-down menu lists the menu selections for a menu command. This type of menu, when activated, is pulled down below the menu bar, the way a window shade can be pulled down from the top of a window frame.

random-access memory (RAM)   What your computer uses to store data and programs temporarily while it uses them. RAM is measured in kilobytes and megabytes. Generally, the more RAM a computer has, the more powerful the programs it can run.

range   (1) What that home, home is on. (2) A rectangular group of adjacent cells in a table. A range is addressed by listing the upper left cell, followed by the lower right cell of the range. For example, the range C2:D3 includes the cells C2, C3, D2, and D3.

readability index   A measure of the educational level needed by a reader if he is to understand the text in a document easily. It is determined by counting the average number of words per sentence, and the average number of characters per word. (A good average is about 17 words per sentence.)

rebooting   The process of restarting a computer that is already on. Press **Ctrl+Alt+Delete** to reboot. Also known as warm booting.

record   (1) A CD's mother. (2) In a data file, this denotes a collection of related information contained in one or more fields, such as an individual's name, address, and phone number. Each record occupies a single row of an Ami Pro merge data file.

Restore button   A special double-headed arrow located in the upper right-hand corner of a window; when you click on it, a window is restored to its previous size.

ruler   Provides an easy method within Ami Pro for setting tab stops, indentations, and margins.

scaling   The process of resizing a graphic so it does not lose its proportions.

scroll   To move displayed text up/down or right/left on a computer screen.

scroll bars   Located along the bottom and right sides of the document window; use these to display other areas of the document.

scroll box   Its position within the entire scroll bar tells you roughly where you are within your document.

selection letters   A single letter of a menu command, such as the *x* in Exit, which activates the command when the menu is open and you press the key for that letter.

shading   See *background*.

SmartIcon set   A bar across the screen that presents the most common Ami Pro commands in an easy-to-access form. For example, clicking on one of the buttons on the Default SmartIcon set saves your document.

software   (1) Ware that's been washed in Downy. (2) Any instructions that tell your computer (the hardware) what to do. There are two types of software: operating system software and application software. Operating system software (such as DOS) gets your computer up and running. Application software allows you to do something useful, such as type a letter or save the whales.

Spell Checker   A special program within Ami Pro that corrects spelling errors in the open document.

spreadsheet   A computer program that organizes mostly numerical information in columns and rows and performs calculations upon that data. If you want to balance a checkbook or analyze last year's budget, use a spreadsheet program. Common spreadsheets include Lotus 1-2-3, Microsoft Excel, and Quattro Pro.

status bar   Located at the bottom of the Ami Pro program window, this displays information about your document.

style   (1) What a person with orange shorts, green shirt, and a striped tie has no sense of. (2) A collection of specifications for formatting paragraphs. A style may include information for the font, size, style, margins, and spacing for a collection of paragraphs. When you apply a style to a paragraph, you format it automatically (according to the style's specifications).

style sheet   Forms the template for a document. A style sheet includes the paragraph styles and page layout for a specific type of document. A style sheet can also include common text (boilerplate text) which is repeated in every version of that type of document. For example, a style sheet for memos might include your name as boilerplate text.

tab   (1) A drink that's just one calorie! (2) A keystroke that moves the cursor ahead to a specified point. Used to align columns of text.

table   (1) A great place for my keys and all those bills I haven't paid. (2) Used to organize large amounts of columnar data. Tables consist of rows (the horizontal axis) and columns (the vertical axis). The intersection of a row and a column is called a cell.

text area   The main part of the document window; this is where you will see the text you type.

text file   A type of file that contains no special formatting (such as bold), but simply letters, numbers, and such. See also *ASCII file*.

text stream   A separate text area within an Ami Pro document. For example, the main document text and the headers and footers are different text streams.

tiled windows   Windows arranged so they divide the screen into equal parts. For example, two tiled windows each occupy one-half of the screen.

Typeover mode   The opposite of Insert mode, as used in word processors and text editors. In Typeover mode when you position your cursor and start to type, what you type replaces existing characters from that point forward.

view mode   A way of looking at a document. Ami Pro comes with several view modes: Layout, Outline, and Draft.

widow/orphan   A widow is the last line of a paragraph that appears alone at the top of the next page. If the first line of the paragraph gets stranded at the bottom of a page, it is called an orphan. Just remember that an orphan is left behind.

windows   (1) Something I don't do. (2) A box that is used to display information in part of the screen.

Windows   A nickname that's often used for Microsoft Windows, a graphical user interface program (see *GUI*).

word processor   A program that lets you enter, edit, format, and print text. A word processor can be used to type letters, reports, and envelopes, and to complete other tasks you used to do on a typewriter.

word wrapping   Keeps text within the margins of a document. As the text you're typing touches the right-hand margin, it's automatically moved to the beginning of the next line. When text is inserted into the middle of a paragraph, the remaining text is moved down within the margins. If text is deleted, the remaining text in the paragraph is moved up.

WYSIWYG   Stands for **W**hat **Y**ou **S**ee **I**s **W**hat **Y**ou **G**et, and it's a type of viewing mode in which all elements of a document (headers, footers, graphics, and the like) are displayed as they will appear when printed.

x-axis   The side of a chart that parallels its width (runs along its horizontal axis).

y-axis   The side of a chart that parallels its height (runs along its vertical axis).

z-axis   The side of a 3-D chart that parallels its depth.

What a waste it is to lose one's mind.

Index

programs, 3, 16, 313
project schedules, 283
Proofing and Tables SmartIcon, View Preferences button, 72
Proofing SmartIcon set, View Preferences button, 128, 167, 237
protected text, 67
pull-down menus, 34, 314

Q-R

question mark, Help, 48
Quick Add command (Table menu), 186
QuickStart Tutorial, 48, 52
quitting
    dialog boxes, 38-39
    Windows, 27

random-access memory (RAM), 314
ranges of cells, 185, 314
readability indexes, 196, 314
rebooting, 314
recipes, organizing, 276
records, 314
    merge data files, 208
    with specific criteria, 212
Rectangle tool (Drawing tools), 263-264
referencing cells, 184
removing character formatting, 124
removing tabs, 145
repeating styles, 153
replacing words, 197
resizing
    frames in documents, 237
    SmartIcons, 42
    windows, 25
Restore button, 24, 314
retrying printing, 111
Revert to Saved command (File menu), 100, 299
reverting documents, 100
right mouse button, 17
right tabs, 142
Rotate dialog box, 267

Rotate icon, 285
rotating objects in drawings, 267
rows in tables, 177, 180
Ruler, 139-140, 165, 314
    Ami Pro window, 32
    deleting, 141
    displaying, 73-74
    indenting paragraphs, 145
    problems, 289
    setting tabs, 143-144
    viewing current, 140-141
Run command (File menu), 273

S

.SAM file extension, 95
Save As command (File menu), 97-98, 292
Save command (File menu), 96
saving
    automatic, 100
    documents, 4, 10, 94-97, 291
    styles to style sheets, 162
scaling graphics, 244, 314
scroll, 314
scroll bars, 32, 315
scroll box, 70, 315
scrolling documents, 59, 70-72
sections of columns, 220
Select Entire Table command (Table menu), 180
Select Row/Column command (Table menu), 180
selecting
    commands, 36
    rows/columns/cells in tables, 180
    text, 4, 60-62, 288
Selection Arrow button (Drawing tools), 263
selection letters, 35, 315
Selection tool, 299
setting tabs with rulers, 143-144
shading
    adding to tables, 181
    text in documents, 238

More Fun Learning from Alpha Books!

If you enjoyed this *Complete Idiot's Guide*
then check out these other books!

**The Complete Idiot's Guide
to PCs**
ISBN: 1-56761-168-0
Softbound, $14.95 USA

**The Complete Idiot's Guide
to DOS**
ISBN: 1-56761-169-9
Softbound, $14.95 USA

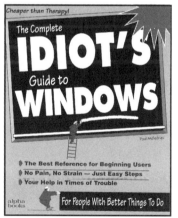

**The Complete Idiot's Guide
to Windows**
ISBN: 1-56761-175-3
Softbound, $14.95 USA

**Look for these books at your favorite computer book retailer,
or call 1-800-428-5331 for more information**

Who cares what you think? WE DO!

We take our customers' opinions very personally. After all, you're the reason we publish these books. If you're not happy, we're doing something wrong.

We'd appreciate it if you would take the time to drop us a note or fax us a fax. A real person—not a computer—reads every letter we get, and makes sure that your comments get relayed to the appropriate people.

Not sure what to say? Here are some details we'd like to know:

- ☛ Who you are (age, occupation, hobbies, etc.)
- ☛ Where you bought the book
- ☛ Why you picked this book instead of a different one
- ☛ What you liked best about the book
- ☛ What could have been done better
- ☛ Your overall opinion of the book
- ☛ What other topics you would purchase a book on

Mail, e-mail, or fax it to:

Faithe Wempen
Product Development Manager
Alpha Books
201 West 103rd Street
Indianapolis, IN 46290

FAX: (317) 581-4669
CIS: 75430,174

SPECIAL OFFER!

Alpha Books needs people like you to give opinions about new and existing books. Product testers receive free books in exchange for providing their opinions about those books. If you would like to be a product tester, please mention it in your letter, and make sure you include your full name, address, and daytime phone.